# Fostering a Civil Workplace

*Fostering a Civil Workplace: Strategies for Personal and Organizational Success* provides research-based solutions to promote a positive work environment. Focusing on internal dynamics, it explores aspects of communication, interpersonal interactions, management techniques, and organizational culture and oversight.

While some work environments are productive and positive, many are not, with employees experiencing incivility, bullying, intimidation, and harassment. Recent developments, such as a shift towards home and hybrid working, can also contribute to this. This book promotes workplace civility in dysfunctional work environments by offering solutions, focusing on playing to personal strengths, which can be utilized by individuals, leaders, and the larger organization. Methods for improvement begin with individual interactions, such as handling a dispute or a difficult co-worker, and extend to online, interdepartmental, and organizational levels, examining ways to improve communication. Suggestions are offered for improving work connections and building empathetic relationships within teams and between departments to foster a civil and productive environment, through sharing, bonding, and encouraging coworkers. A review of positive impacts made possible by effective leadership includes concepts such as trust, authenticity, and adaptability, alongside guidance on navigating conflicts between employees, and an exploration of challenges experienced in middle management. Ideas regarding organizational culture and employer support include promoting active learning, wellness, and training opportunities, with strategies for employee development, and advice on code of conduct policies.

Providing an accessible overview of solutions for workplace incivility to foster a more positive and dynamic workplace for all, this book will appeal to leaders and managers looking to create better workplaces, students of leadership and management, and employees struggling with toxic work situations.

**Jo Henry** is a librarian at Horry-Georgetown Technical College, USA. She holds an MLS from the University of North Carolina Greensboro, USA, and an MPA from Georgia Southern University, USA. In addition to conference and workshop presentations, she has co-authored several books and journal articles in the field of library science. Her interest and research in workplace dysfunction began in 2016.

**Richard Moniz** has over 30 years of experience in library services and holds advanced degrees in history, library science, and higher education administration. He has been the Director of Library Services at Horry-Georgetown Technical College, USA, since 2018 and previously held similar roles at Johnson & Wales University, USA. Dr. Moniz has taught undergraduate and graduate courses at various institutions and published extensively, including authoring and co-authoring several books on management and collaboration in organizations. He has also served on a variety of non-profit boards and held leadership positions for a variety of local, state, and national library associations.

# Fostering a Civil Workplace

## Strategies for Personal and Organizational Success

Jo Henry and Richard Moniz

Routledge
Taylor & Francis Group

NEW YORK AND LONDON

First published 2026
by Routledge
605 Third Avenue, New York, NY 10158

and by Routledge
4 Park Square, Milton Park, Abingdon, Oxon OX14 4RN

*Routledge is an imprint of the Taylor & Francis Group, an informa business*

© 2026 Jo Henry and Richard Moniz

Designed cover image: Getty Images @jean-marc payet

*Library of Congress Cataloging-in-Publication Data*
A catalog record for this title has been requested

ISBN: 9781032966076 (hbk)
ISBN: 9781032962368 (pbk)
ISBN: 9781003590149 (ebk)

DOI: 10.4324/9781003590149

Typeset in Sabon
by Taylor & Francis Books

# Contents

# Tables

# Boxes

# Acknowledgements

We would like to express our appreciation to the Routledge editorial board for their support of this book. We would like to thank our editor, Zoe Thompson-Kemp, for her interest in and support of our idea in its initial stages. The guidance throughout the process of commissioning editor, Hannah Rich, standing in for Zoe Thomson-Kemp while she was on secondment, was invaluable. Thank you, Hannah! Much appreciation also goes to her editorial assistants, Maddie Gray and Shreya Sengupta, for all their administrative support. Additionally, we would like to recognize the copy-editor, Ruth Bourne, Reanna Young, production editor, and the entire production team for navigating the final stages of the book. Lastly, we would like to say thank you to all the other, unseen members of the Routledge team who worked behind the scenes to make this book project a success.

# Preface

Our focus on workplace dysfunction and incivility began in 2016. Like many others who have been in the workforce for any length of time, we have witnessed negative workplace dynamics. We have also addressed such issues from a supervisory perspective through our work in different industries. Over 50 years of combined leadership experience and a discussion of our most challenging moments in those roles led us to the topic of workplace dysfunction. Our book, *The Dysfunctional Library: Challenges and Solutions to Workplace Relationships*, resulted from that discussion. Alongside this publication, we conducted our first study on the topic, "Incivility and Dysfunction in the Library Workplace: Perceptions and Feedback from the Field," which was published in 2018. Subsequently, responses from conference presentations, ecourses, and workshops pushed us in the direction of researching solutions. To that end, our 2020 publication, *Cultivating Civility: Practical Ways to Improve a Dysfunctional Library*, explored ways to improve library work environments.

Since that time, we have continued to engage in the topic. We published a follow-up study in 2022 indicating incivility was on the rise in library work environments. We also conducted an unpublished study of academic workplaces which, like the work of other researchers, found a presence of uncivil behaviors and inadequate methods of communication oftentimes accompanied by a disconnect between high-ranking leaders and frontline employees. Most importantly, over the years we heard from voices of those who had been targets of various levels of such behavior. They conveyed their experiences and of the negative impact toxic work environments had on their lives and careers. These stories drove us to ask, "What more can we do?"

*Fostering a Civil Workplace: Strategies for Personal and Organizational Success* was a response to that question. Prior research and work laid the foundation for areas of need within organizations. Leveraging our skills as librarians, we strove to provide practical, research-based ideas for improving any work environment. It is our hope that this writing will, in some way, bring about positive change for individuals and their broader work environments.

# Chapter 1

# Exploring Uncivil and Toxic Workplaces

Between 1907–1909, Clara Lemlich, head of the Local 25 garment union in New York, led multiple shirtwaist factory workers on strikes to address working conditions (Seifert 2017). Factory owners charged employees for drinking water, electricity used by their sewing machines, and storage locker access for personal items in addition to timing one-minute bathroom breaks, manipulating the time clock, and conducting bodily exit searches (Seifert 2017). More recently, in 2018 approximately 20,000 Google employees walked off the job to protest pay inequities related to race and gender, a lack of consideration of diverse candidates for higher-level positions, forced arbitration, and inadequate responses to sexual harassment reporting (Bhuiyan 2019). Despite a promise to be more supportive, a year later Google employees still reported retaliatory actions for reporting issues of mistreatment (Ghaffary 2019). A 2024 report of the Federal Deposit Insurance Corporation (FDIC), revealed that more than 500 individuals reported experiencing discrimination, bullying, sexual harassment, and an overall disrespectful and toxic culture which included "screaming at people in the hallways" and threats of violence (Kim, Kennedy Park, and Mainoo 2024, 115). These are just a few examples of employees making known their workplace was inadequate, uncivil, or even toxic.

While these instances are only a sampling of stories of workplace issues and protests, they do indicate that challenging work environments have long been a part of labor history and worker struggles continue today. Strikes and walk-outs are still used to bring attention to workplace issues and create leverage for change. While such dramatic protests and reports are often noted and remembered, the questions remain, "What about helping the everyday worker dealing with incivility in the workplace who does not engage in such overt group protests? What about guidance for supervisors who want to lead in more civil ways? How can organizations create a positive, dynamic workplace and promote civility?" It is in answer to these questions that this text will explore ways to foster civility and offer realistic, solution-based options.

DOI: 10.4324/9781003590149-1

Before exploring solutions, it is important to first lay a brief foundation or understanding of common conditions related to dysfunction, incivility, and toxicity which can manifest in the workplace. At the lowest level of deviant behavior, incivility at work is defined as "low intensity antisocial behavior" which involves "rude, insensitive or disrespectful" actions in the workplace (Pearson, Andersson, and Wegner 2001, 1389). This kind of incivility in the workplace manifests in a variety of forms and may include verbal abuse, withholding information, cyberloafing, or a failure to listen. Other forms of workplace dysfunction include more disruptive work behaviors such as passive aggressive actions, various counterproductive work behaviors, and psychological or physical intimidation. Finally, some of the most toxic misconduct in the workplace may involve bullying, cyberbullying, mobbing, sexual assault, or physical violence.

This wide range of deviant behaviors can occur between individuals, within groups, between departments, or be triggered by the larger organization itself. These toxicities have been studied for decades and, while many workplace conditions have improved, incivility and dysfunction not only remain but continue to prevail in many organizations. The 2019 Weber Shandwick study, *Civility in America* found 23% of workers experiencing incivility in the workplace (Weber Shandwick 2019). The 2024 Society for Human Resource Management (SHRM) civility survey found 66% of US workers either experienced or observed workplace incivility (Gonzales 2024). Specific sectors of the labor market experience higher rates as well. A meta-analysis of 60 articles published globally between 1997 and 2019 in the field of nursing indicates 55% of nurses experiencing one or more uncivil work behaviors during their tenure with an organization (Shoorideh, Moosavi, and Balouchi 2021). Incivility in this context was primarily identified as various types of verbal abuse, but it also includes physical abuse, sexual misconduct, and mobbing. In US higher education, multiple studies found faculty being bullied at rates ranging from 26% to 64% in a five to 36-month period (Keashly 2019; Hollis 2015; Hollis 2016). For higher education administrators, 62% have been bullied or witnessed bullying (Hollis 2015). In yet another study, 88% of library workers have experienced incivility (much of it verbal) over their careers and 52% have been bullied by both co-workers and supervisors (Henry, Croxton, and Moniz 2023). From these statistics, there is no doubt that there are persistent issues with incivility in the workplace, and there is a need for reform.

One thing is certain: workplace incivility, dysfunction, and misconduct negatively impacts employee motivation and dedication to the organization in which they work. The 2023 Gallup poll, *State of the Global Workplace: Global Insights*, provides evidence of widespread worker disengagement. More specifically, this report noted that 59% of employees across the globe lack work engagement and another 18% are actively disengaged (Gallup 2023). These disengaged workers cite several areas of the workplace culture that need changing. These include work recognition, approachable management, job autonomy, professional development opportunities, individual respect, clearly defined goals, and opportunities for advancement (Gallup 2023). Incivility is also linked to low energy, decreased resilience, and reduced psychological capital as well as pessimism in the workplace (Kumar, Chandrahasa, and Shashidhar 2023). These are just some of the damaging consequences of workplace incivility.

From the abundance of studies and statistical data, of which a sample has just been shared, there is no doubt workplace incivility is a persistent problem today across a wide variety of industries. It adversely impacts individuals, supervisors, administrators, and larger organizations. With this understanding, what follows is an exploration of the repercussions of such deviant behaviors from lessor to more severe in classification.

## Lesser Workplace Incivilities

Since the late 1990s, researchers have identified varying forms of incivility and have debated the overlap of minor actions with aggressive ones. Much writing has been devoted to this area for the interested reader (see suggested reads at the end of this chapter). While not exclusive, many of the lesser displays of uncivil behavior in the workplace involve ineffective or negative communication. Research has helped identify these behaviors, as well as non-verbal actions, which impact work environments. Such acts include abusive language, belittling, interrupting, neglecting manners, stealing credit for others' work, withholding information, failing to listen, cyberloafing, and aspects of non-verbal communication.

The first of the lesser incivilities is use of abusive language. This involves swearing, yelling, or aggressive verbal communication often between co-workers or between a supervisor and employee. While it is recognized that there is allowance in certain professions for unfiltered language in conversation, this form of abusive language is used with the intent to impart harm or create a state of psychological control. In professional settings where norms do not include abusive language, this type of communication is not acceptable when attempting to maintain a civil and productive organizational environment.

A second form of negative verbal communication which arises in the workplace is when an individual belittles or puts another employee down. Imagine a supervisor commenting, "They are always making mistakes" or a coworker remarking, "They won't be able to do that job." These types of demeaning comments can instantly diminish the quality of a work environment. One research study of such exchanges indicates the instigator sometimes demeans frequently dehumanized groups and lacks understanding of the psychological needs of the individual ("Researchers" 2020). Victims of these types of exchanges can feel devalued and powerless along with perceiving the exchange as unjust (Fernandez, Saguy, and Halperin 2015). Degrading comments not only negatively impact the targeted individual in areas of engagement but may even trigger a desire for retaliation. Additionally, such comments may also be linked to more toxic incivilities, such as bullying or mobbing. It is easy to see how uncivil comments can lead to increasingly challenging workplace problems.

Another of the lesser incivilities in the category of verbal communication is interrupting another worker when they are talking or dismissing their expressed opinions. In sharp contrast to the importance of active listening which will be discussed in chapter three, interruptions are viewed as conversationally impolite. Additionally, when alternate views are not heard and are dismissed through such interruptions, the worker disengages from their work. Moving forward they are less likely to contribute their opinion. This failure to listen coming from a supervisor lowers morale, reduces worker confidence, increases avoidance behaviors, and negatively impacts work output (Saleem et al. 2022).

Non-verbal displays of power in the context of uncivil communications between employees form yet another of lesser workplace incivilities. Dominant characteristics can be conveyed in both standing and seated positions. Individuals who sit upright with one hand on their desk or those standing tall over the desk with both hands planted on top are viewed as more powerful than more constricted poses (Park et al. 2013). Imagine a supervisor leaning over a desk of an employee, hands planted, while delivering a reprimand. That image could be a sign of aggression towards the victim, and if witnessed by others, set an intimidating workplace tone. While other cultures may interpret these differently or even more severely, in Western cultures additional indicators of power include direct eye contact, dominating talking time, and negative facial expressions (Bonaccio et al. 2016). Facial expressions can display anger in specific ways. Some characteristics identified in anger expression are a lower brow ridge, wider nose, thinner lips, and raised upper lip and chin (Sell, Dosmides, and Tooby 2014). When confronted by an individual displaying these mannerisms, a victim may process these as a form of aggression, and similar emotions as exhibited when being on the receiving end of verbal aggression may be triggered. This is termed emotional contagion and it occurs not only in states of anger but with an array of emotions (Herrando and Constantinides 2021). Knowing this, it is easy to see how emotionally charged statements and mannerisms may begin an exchange between two or more employees that can escalate, spread, and become quite disruptive to workplace dynamics.

The absence of basic civilities can also contribute to toxic workplaces. These civilities include greeting coworkers, saying please and thank you, and treating others with kindness. Small gestures can make a difference in fostering positive interactions for workers and those they impact. For example, in the medical field, kindness amongst the staff results in fewer errors and better treatment of patients (Fryburg 2023). Kindness in the workplace leads to resilience and a buffer from stress. The lack of it creates negative and disengaged workers (Fryburg 2023). Conversely, numerous studies have found rudeness results in reduced performance, creativity, recall, and can also increase deviant behaviors (Schilpzand, De Pater, and Erez 2016). While workplaces benefit from thoughtful actions, they are often found lacking within the basic interpersonal dynamics in many work environments.

One of the problems unrelated to communications occurs when others in the workplace take credit for tasks or projects they did not do. This form of incivility is often attributed to a supervisor or higher-ranking employee who sweeps in when a job is complete to capture the accolades and benefits of the completed assignments. This action is tied closely to a betrayal of the unwritten contract (or understood expectations) between employees and the organization. Among these unwritten expectations of the work environment, such as having a safe workspace or appropriate tools to complete assignments, is recognition for what someone has accomplished. While every success may not warrant a grand celebration, it is important to recognize and appropriately acknowledge accomplishments. When supervisors or coworkers hijack ideas from others, the unspoken work contract is breached and a feeling of being wronged prevails. This leads to resentment, frustration, and cynicism in the wronged employee (Abraham 2000).

Withholding information is another type of workplace dysfunction. A conscious refusal to share knowledge or work particulars can come from any area of the organization. Teams may sequester vital information that should be shared with other workers and other departments or areas of an organization. Senior-level administration could fail to share critical information on the direction of the company or decisions on a current or future project. This excludes workers from the communication link and fails to gain feedback, which, if obtained, may lead to improved output. When dealing with a one-on-one situation, withholding information from others is a form of secret sabotage. This action, aligned with other incivilities such as bullying, is often done with the specific intent of harming another individual. The withholding of information could make the individual susceptible to making an error or failing to meet a deadline. As with misinformation, missing information can do just as much harm.

Yet another characteristic of low-level incivility is a failure to listen. On an individual level, when considering the communication cycle of verbal input, receiving and processing, and then responding, a failure to listen creates a breakdown in the exchange. Studies examining the barriers to effective listening in the 1990s helped define the various pitfalls of the listening exchange. These include listener disinterest, thought distractions, external distractions, inattentiveness, and failure to identify important points (box 1.1) (Golen 1990). These issues lead to mistakes, delays, and poor customer service. An example of distracted listening would be an individual checking email while falsely conveying their complete attention when listening to a coworker. Another is the need to repeat requests to supervisors who fail to follow up on conversations or take appropriate actions after an information exchange.

Failure to listen also creates disruption at an organizational level. This wider view includes organizations which fail to listen to employees or solicit necessary feedback. As a result, workgroups display diminished positivity and productivity in their workplace culture. The organization is deprived of necessary feedback from those individuals at lower levels in elements of production, creation, and service on a daily basis. This failure to listen leads to less employee engagement and happiness at work, and, ultimately, may lead to increased turnover as well.

---

**Box 1.1  Golen's Six Listening Barrier Categories**

1  "Laziness": listening avoidance
2  "Closed minded": unwilling to hear others' thoughts
3  "Opinionated": emotional disagreement
4  "Insincerely": no eye contact or emotional understanding
5  "Boredom": impatience, disinterest, distracted
6  "Unattentive": external distractions, unfocused on message

(Golen 1990, 32)

---

Lastly, cyberloafing at work is also deemed dysfunctional and classified as a lower-level incivility. Cyberloafing is when employees do non-work activities on their computer during work time. This could take place in an office setting or through remote work from home. Examples include more minor activities such as online shopping, reviewing social media, reading online news or sports, and handling non-work emails or more serious infringements such as online gambling or visiting adult-only websites (Blanchard and Henle 2008). While an occasional checking of news, sports, or weather may not necessarily negatively impact work, longer or more toxic cyberloafing activities (such as online gambling) can. Impacts to work in these cases include general distraction, less work completed and missed deadlines (Lim and Chen 2012). Cyberloafing also can be an indicator of lower employee commitment to the organization and lower engagement (Lim, Yeik, and Chong 2021).

## Disruptive Work Behaviors

Several forms of disruptive work behaviors can be identified which illustrate how actions can shift upward in severity. The first of these is the passive aggressive type of personality. Dr. Christopher Hopwood, professor of personality psychology at the University of Zurich, defined this type of behavior as being powerless but desiring power which can result in feeling anger which, in turn can cause these individuals to act out through non-compliance (2018). Three features of these individuals are 1) engaging in unproductive or irresponsible behavior, 2) feeling insecure in relation to their individual value, and 3) contemplating their unfair treatment (Hopwood and Wright 2012). Although no longer listed in the current *Diagnostic and Statistical Manual of Mental Disorders* (DSM-5), passive aggressive personalities still can be identified and are found in work settings. Such individuals can slow down work processes and express frustration or anger for their perceived unjust treatment (especially from supervisors). Passive aggressive attitudes may involve aspects of passive resistance to work tasks and displays of argumentativeness or criticism of others (Hopwood and Wright 2012). While these individuals may view themselves as misunderstood, they are often perceived as negative and irritating by co-workers.

Counterproductive work behavior (CWB) is another of these disruptive behaviors that damage work environments. CWB involves "intentional behavior" which goes against the purpose and goal of the organization (Sackett 2002, 5). Anywhere from one-third to three-quarters of workers may either actively or passively engage in acts such as work absences, withdrawal, intentionally causing disruptions, manipulations, production deviance, damaging property, or theft (Marcus and Schuler 2014; Spanouli, Hofmans, and Dalal 2023). These behaviors form a spectrum of deviance based on the intended target (an individual or an organization) and how serious the action (Czarnota-Bojarska 2015). Examples of lessor CWB include calling in sick to skip work, intentionally working slowly, wasting resources, extending breaks, or leaving work early while more serious offenses could include sabotage, property destruction, theft, or even hitting someone at work (Spector, Bauer, and Fox 2010). Individuals may also exhibit counterproductive work behaviors that fluctuate over time. A worker may engage in an appropriate manner one day only to exhibit differing actions the next. Often, triggers for CWB behaviors (box 1.2) include boredom, stress, anger, a perceived unjust work environment, or conflict with supervisors (Spector et al. 2006). The varying deviances of CWB can negatively impact co-workers making it difficult for others to work with them in addition to harming the larger organization.

**Box 1.2 Five Dimensions of CWB**

1   "Abuse" towards coworkers
2   "Production deviance"
3   "Sabotage" of company property
4   "Theft" of co-worker/company property
5   "Withdrawal" and absences from work

(Spector et al. 2006, 446–447)

A final aspect of disruptive work behavior is psychological or physical intimidation. Psychological and physical intimidation fall short of actual physical violence which is among the most toxic of workplace behaviors. Such intimidation includes verbal assaults such as yelling, cursing, threatening, or ridiculing a worker in front of others. Intimidation may also occur through posturing or aggressive gestures such as slamming hands or a fist on a desk, throwing papers at an employee, intruding on one's personal space, or unwelcome touching. As there is some overlap in categories of uncivil behaviors, aspects of intimidation may be tied to bullying or mobbing actions of employees or supervisors. Globally, 16.5% of workers are experiencing psychological violence and harassment at least one time during their work life ("World Risk" 2021). As with many other dysfunctional behaviors, workers may display these behaviors consistently over a long period of time. While falling short of physical violence, this behavior still can harm co-workers and bring toxicity to the working environment.

## Toxic Workplace Misconduct

Toxic incivilities are among the worst expressions of dysfunction in the workplace. They are found in the uppermost range of the low to high spectrum of uncivil actions. The first of these toxic forms of misconduct is bullying. Workplace bullying is most prevalent in the United States, but it is found in other countries as well (box 1.3) (Ciby and Raya 2015). A study of over 1,400 Swiss healthcare workers found 40% of staff considering resigning from their position or changing careers after experiencing a form of workplace violence (Hämmig 2023). The Workplace Bullying Institute's 2021 survey of US workers found 40% of bullied targets exited jobs (either forced or voluntarily), 12% were terminated, and another 15% transferred locations (Namie 2021). That is a 67% turnover of those bullied at work! In a final example, a study of four-year college and university administrators found 35% of bullied targets had either left or planned to leave their institution (White 2018). Bullying not only negatively impacts the organization, but it can leave long-lasting, psychological effects on the individual.

## Box 1.3 Work Bullying Studies: Perceived Exposure by Global Region

(One or more incidents in six months or less)
Scandinavia 2–25%
Europe 3–45%
North America 28–50%
Australia & New Zealand 18%
Asia 21–55%
Africa 35%

(Ciby and Raya 2015, 43)

Bullying in the workplace is an intentional aggressive or negative action towards another employee which occurs with frequency over time (six or more months) (White 2018). It is a one-on-one action and can occur from all three power directions in a work organization—from supervisors, peers, and lower ranking individuals. Previous writing has identified verbal and behavioral techniques which characterize the workplace bully (box 1.4) (Bartlett 2011; Henry, Croxton, and Moniz 2023). Research has found bullies to be aggressive individuals who are often socially challenged and have low self-esteem (Einarsen 2005). Their victims may reflect one of three profiles. The first profile is an individual with a personality disturbance who may deal with depression or anxiety (Duffy and Yamada 2018). Another profile reflects "depression and suspiciousness" (Duffy and Yamada 2018). The third is viewed as a normal personality and is often a competent, well-liked contributor to the workplace (Suskind 2021). Much media attention and writing has been given to the topic of bullying, but it continues to damage work environments.

## Box 1.4 Bullying Techniques

- Belittling in front of others
- Blaming for others' mistakes
- Condescending comments
- Dismissive of ideas
- Disrespectful actions
- Domineering actions
- Gossiping about the individual
- Insulting comments
- Isolating target from group
- Overloading work assignments
- Policing type behavior

- Retaliatory behaviors
- Showing favoritism
- Stealing from co-workers

(Bartlett 2011; Henry, Croxton, and Moniz 2023)

Historically, workplace bullying has been only an in-person occurrence. However, with the increase of remote work it is now also found during online meetings. The 2021 Workplace Bullying Institute survey found 50% of online meeting attendees bullied at least one time during remote work (Namie 2021). A Swedish study of government workers for a virtual workplace found a bullying incident occurring 19% of the prior month of work (Eriksson 2023). Workers have often experienced condescending comments and humiliation online, typically from the online meeting organizer (Eriksson 2023). With the increase of remote work and utilization of online meetings to connect those in separate locations, the environment is in place for continued or even increasing incidents of virtual workplace bullying.

Alongside in-person bullying exists cyberbullying. Cyberbullying has been defined as electronic attacks on individuals which occur anywhere and at any point in time through cell phones, computers, or tablets (Corcoran 2015). This method may employ the use of email or some other social platform. It differs from in-person bullying as it can occur outside of work hours or work locations and victims are often defenseless from attack (Muhonen and Jonsson 2017). Another critical factor in cyberbullying is the potential for anonymity of the perpetrator. While an email sender can be readily identified, attacks on social media can be done anonymously giving a powerful edge to the aggressor. The frequency of workplace cyberbullying has been quite varied in studies—from a low percentage of impacted individuals to over 40% (Kowalski, Toth, and Moran 2018). Regardless, work-related cyberbullying has become a relatively new means of creating toxic incivility.

Another form of toxic behavior is mobbing. While mobbing is sometimes combined with bullying in studies and research, its definition is generally accepted as multiple workers joining forces to target a single individual in the workplace. Heinz Leymann, the first to study this form of deviance, identified 45 techniques and some of the more relevant methods are identified in box 1.5 (Silva et al. 2021). This form of incivility often begins with a trigger incident which escalates. Mobbed victims are targeted when they challenge organizational policies, expose corruption, advocate for change, and/or work outside of the cultural norm (Duffy and Sperry 2014). Often there is something different about a mobbed target. This distinction could be their gender, ethnicity, religion, handicap, or anything that identifies them as different from the rest of the working group. Others in the work group utilize both covert and overt actions with the goal of removing the individual from the workplace (Duffy and Sperry 2014). Like bullying, the actions of the group continue over an extended period of time until the worker leaves or is fired. While not as common as bullying, mobbing still has a presence in modern work environments.

## Box 1.5 Common Mobbing Techniques

- Criticism of work
- Micromanagement of work
- Excessive scrutiny
- Unreasonable work demands
- Assignment of menial tasks
- Questioning of beliefs and decisions
- Isolation from colleagues and information
- Verbal assaults, threats, and ridicule

(Silva et al. 2021)

When physical aggression shifts to assault and violence it enters one of the most severe of workplace toxicities. This violence could involve hitting a co-worker or even perpetrating an act resulting in death. While workplace violence may occur by any number of non-employed actors (such as customers, criminals, or an employee's friend or relative), this writing will focus on worker-to-worker actions and ways organizations can minimize or eliminate such incidents.

Research indicates worker-to-worker physical violence may be triggered by varying experiences. Not surprisingly, these triggers include negative behavioral exchanges, retaliatory behaviors, and aggressive supervisor behaviors (Lyubykh et al. 2022). In 2022, the US Department of Justice released the statistics from their workplace violence research 2015–2019. Incidents of workplace aggression in the United States averaged 105,800 per year of which 25% were worker-to-worker (Harrell et al. 2019). These forms of aggression were most often assault (hitting, kicking, or beating) which occurred 83% of the time ("World Risk" 2021). When taking a global view, the 2021 World Risk Poll was conducted on violence and harassment at work and collected data on such incidents occurring one or more times during an individual's time in the workforce ("World Risk" 2021). The poll found 7.4% of workers experienced physical violence. The report characterized these actions as "hitting, restraining, or spitting," and over half of these targets (56%) experience physical aggression three or more times during their work life

("World Risk" 2021). Similarly, the 2022 International Labour Organization survey found 8.5% of workers experiencing physical violence and harassment (also characterized as hitting, restraining, or spitting) at some point in their work life ("Experiences of Violence" International Labour Organization 2022).

---

**Box 1.6 Physical Violence at Work by Global Region**

(Experienced one or more times during work life)
Africa 12.5%
Americas 9.0%
Arab States 7.2%
Asia and the Pacific 7.9%
Europe and Central Asia 6.5%

("Experiences of Violence" 2022, 16)

---

A final form of workplace toxicity is sexual misconduct. Much attention has been given to sexual transgressions or harassment in the workplace, yet it still exists in today's workplace. Sexual harassment may consist of verbal comments and/or physical actions. Verbal misconduct could include sexual jokes, humiliating comments of a sexual nature, or unwanted requests for sexual favors (Vara-Horna et al. 2023). Physical aspects of this type of misconduct also can be displayed through unwanted physical contact or sexual assault (Vara-Horna et al. 2023). These types of deviant, sexual practices create a hostile working environment and cause harm to both individuals and work organizations.

Sexual misconduct in the workplace is found worldwide. A 2021 global risk poll by Gallup and the Lloyd's Register Foundation explored the prevalence of sexual violence at work. Sexual violence was characterized in most questionnaires as "unwanted sexual touching, comments, pictures, emails, or sexual requests," although this question was softened in some countries due to cultural sensitivities and left off the survey in Saudi Arabia, the United Arab Emirates, and Iraq ("World Risk" 2021, 20). The report found 15.8% of Northern America workers rank highest in experiencing sexual violence followed by Australia and New Zealand with 15.4% and then Central Asia (2.2%) ("World Risk" 2021). The 2022 study by the International Labour Organization reveals a global average of 6.3% of the labor force experiencing sexual harassment or violence (unwanted touching, comments, pictures, emails, or requests of a sexual nature) in the workplace with 11.4% of Americans experiencing this misconduct at least once during their work life ("Experiences in Violence" 2022). In 2018 Pew Research Center found even higher percentages of US workers with 44%

experiencing unwanted sexual advances or harassment in the workplace (Graf 2018). Targets are often from lower socio-economic groups, minorities, bisexual, trans or gender non-conforming women, or females characterized as migrants, disabled, or young in age ("Sexual Harassment" 2024). As these statistics indicate, there is a need for continued discussion on the topic and how organizations can work to mitigate its occurrence.

## Organizational Dysfunction

Of the varying workplace civility issues covered, most deal primarily with interactions between individuals. However, the organizational entity as a whole may also contribute to creation of a toxic environment. This takes place because of dysfunctional norms, poor leadership, or a weak or non-responsive human resources department among other dynamics in the workplace. Under these circumstances, dysfunctional behaviors occur because they are allowed or become the cultural norm of the workplace and are rarely an isolated incident. These types of incivilities can include rankism, nepotism, bias, sexism, and forced arbitration (Henry, Eshleman, and Moniz 2018).

In addition to the specific areas of organizational dysfunction mentioned, aspects of poor communication, or sometimes non-communication, contribute significantly to organizational problems. The impact of poor communication cannot be overemphasized as it is one of the leading problems within the dysfunctional workplace. Along with one-on-one communication issues, breakdowns can occur at all levels of the organization. Communication issues may occur within a department or section of an organization, between two divisions, between remote or physically different worksites, from supervisors to direct reports, or upper management down to lower working levels. As exploration into solutions of work environments continues below, many aspects of these types of communication will be covered.

## Conclusion

The range of experienced workplace dysfunction is quite varied. Lesser expressions of negativity and incivility include poor or harmful verbal and non-verbal communication, the withholding of information, stealing credit, listening breakdowns, and cyberloafing on the job. While incidents taken individually may seem minor, over time and with repetitive use, their impact is significant. In addition to these lesser incivilities, more harmful acts take the form of expressions of passive aggressive personalities, counterproductive work behaviors, and non-violent forms of intimidation. The most toxic on the spectrum of incivilities between workers includes bullying, cyberbullying, mobbing, sexual misconduct, and physical violence.

Lastly, the organization itself plays a role in allowing an uncivil workplace. Organizations which allow employees to engage in forms of rankism, sexism, nepotism, bias, or forced arbitration are not creating a positive climate. This allowance of unprofessional norms or even abuse with uncivil tactics often comes from top company administrators, and sets the stage for poor, intolerable, or even hostile work environments. Organizations which combat these actions and work towards promoting civility in the workplace are those to model. How individuals, leaders, and organizations can shift towards building a civil, positive workplace will unfold in the remaining chapters.

## Suggested Reads

Forni, P.M. *Choosing Civility*. New York: St. Martins Griffin, 2002.
Porath, Christine. *Mastering Civility: A Manifesto for the Workplace*. New York: Grand Central Publishing, 2016.
White, Sheila. *An Introduction to the Psychodynamics of Workplace Bullying*. New York: Routledge, 2013.

## References

Abraham, Rebecca. "Organizational Cynicism: Bases and Consequences." *Genetic, Social, and General Psychology Monographs* 126, no. 3 (2000): 269. Gale Academic OneFile. Accessed December 19, 2023. https://link.gale.com/apps/doc/A64776197/AONE?u=horrygtc&sid=bookmark-AONE&xid=e4ca4c21.

Bartlett, James E. "Workplace Bullying: An Integrative Literature Review." *Advances in Developing Human Resources*, February2011. doi:10.1177/1523422311410651.

Bhuiyan, Johana. "The Google Walkout: What Protesters Demanded and What They Got." *Los Angeles Times*, November 6, 2019. https://www.latimes.com/business/technology/story/2019-11-06/google-walkout-demands.

Blanchard, Anita L. and Christine A. Henle. "Correlates of Different Forms of Cyberloafing: The Role of Norma and External Locus of Control." *Computers in Human Behavior* 24 (2008). doi:10.1016/j.chb.2007.03.008.

Bonaccio, Silvia, Jane O'Reilly, Sharon L. O'Sullivan, and Francois Chiocchio. "Nonverbal Behavior and Communication in the Workplace: A Review and an Agenda for Research." *Journal of Management* 42, no. 5 (2016). doi:10.1177/014920631562114.

Ciby, Mariam Anil and Rampalli Raya. "Workplace Bullying: A Review of the Defining Features, Measurement Methods and Prevalence across Continents." *IIM Kozhikode Society & Management Review* 42, no. 1 (2015): 38–47. doi:10.1177/2277975215587814.

Corcoran, Lucie. "Cyberbullying or Cyber Aggression?: A Review of Existing Definitions of Cyber-Based Peer-to-Peer Aggression." *Societies* 5 (2015): 245–255. doi:10.3390/soc5020245.

Czarnota-Bojarska, Joanna. "Counterproductive Work Behavior and Job Satisfaction: A Surprising Rocky Relationship." *Journal of Management & Organization* 21, no. 4 (2015): 460–470. doi:10.1017/jmo.2015.15.

Duffy, Maureen and Len Sperry. *Overcoming Mobbing: A Recovery Guide for Workplace Aggression and Bullying.* Oxford, UK: Oxford University Press, Incorporated, 2014.

Duffy, Maureen, and David C. Yamada, eds. *Workplace Bullying and Mobbing in the United States* [2 Volumes]. New York, NY: Bloomsbury Publishing USA, 2018.

Einarsen, Stale. "The Nature, Causes and Consequences of Bullying at Work: The Norwegian Experience." *Avenues: Interdisciplinary Perspectives on Work and Health*, 7, no. 3 (2005). doi:10.4000/pistes.3156.

Eriksson, Filippa. "Workplace Incivility in Digital Meetings: An Investigation of the Behavior and How it is Associated With Work Behavior." Master of Science in Psychology, Lunds Universitet, 2023. Accessed January 5, 2025. https://lup.lub.lu.se/student-papers/search/publication/9128955.

Fernandez, Saulo, Tamar Saguy, and Eran Halperin. "The Paradox of Humiliation." *Personality and Social Psychology Bulletin* 41, no.7 (2015). doi:10.1177/0146167215586195.

Fryburg, David A. "Kindness Isn't Just About Being Nice: The Value Proposition of Kindness as Viewed through the Lens of Incivility in the Healthcare Workplace." *Behavioral Sciences* 13, no. 6 (2023): NA. Gale Academic OneFile. Accessed December 19, 2023. https://link.gale.com/apps/doc/A754974392/AONE?u=hor rygtc&sid=bookmark-AONE&xid=48a9fdc6.

Gallup. *State of the Global Workplace 2023 Report.* Gallup, 2023. https://www.ga llup.com/workplace/349484/state-of-the-global-workplace.aspx?thank-you-report-form=1.

Ghaffary, Shirin. "Dozens of Google Employees Say They Were Retaliated Against for Reporting Harassment." *Vox* September 9, 2019. https://www.vox.com/recode/2019/9/9/20853647/google-employee-retaliation-harassment-me-too-exclusive.

Golen, Steven. "A Factor Analysis of Barriers to Listening." *Journal of Business Communication* 27, no. 1 (1990). doi:10.1177/002194369002700103.

Gonzales, Matt. "Workplace Incivility is More Common Than You Think." *Society of Human Resource Management*, March 6, 2024. https://www.shrm.org/top ics-tools/news/inclusion-diversity/workplace-incivility-shrm-research-2024#:~: text=Incivility%20Can%20Have%20Business%20Implications&text=Employees %20who%20believe%20their%20workplace%20is%20uncivil%20(38%20p ercent)%20are,over%20the%20next%2012%20months.

Graf, Nikki. "Sexual Harassment at Work in the Era of #MeToo." Pew Research Center, April 4, 2018. https://www.pewresearch.org/social-trends/2018/04/04/sexua l-harassment-at-work-in-the-era-of-metoo/.

Hämmig, Oliver. "Quitting One's job or Leaving One's Profession: Unexplored Consequences of Workplace Violence and Discrimination Against Health Professionals." *BMC Health Services Research* 23, no. 1 (2023): NA. Gale Academic OneFile. Accessed December 21, 2023. https://link.gale.com/apps/doc/A772898480/AONE?u=horrygtc&sid=bookmark-AONE&xid=d33967b8.

Harrell, Erika, Lynn Langton, Jeremy Petosa, Stephen M. Pegula, Mark Zak, Susan Derk, Dan Hartley, and Audrey Reichard. "Indicators of Workplace Violence, 2019." Bureau of Justice Statistics, Office of Justice Programs, US Department of

Justice; Bureau of Labor Statistics, Office of Safety, Health, and Working Conditions, US Department of Labor; and National Institute for Occupational Safety and Health, Centers for Disease Control and Prevention, US Department of Health and Human Services, 2019. Accessed December 26, 2023. https://bjs.ojp.gov/library/publications/indicators-workplace-violence-2019.

Henry, Jo, Rebecca Croxton, and Richard Moniz. "Incivility and Dysfunction in the Library Workplace: A Five-Year Comparison." *Journal of Library Administration* 63, no. 1 (2023). doi:10.1080/01930826.2022.2146440.

Henry, Jo, Joe Eshleman, and Richard Moniz. *The Dysfunctional Library: Challenges and Solutions to Workplace Relationships*. Chicago, Illinois: ALA Editions, 2018.

Herrando, Carolina and Efthymios Constantinides. "Emotional Contagion: A Brief Overview and Future Directions." *Frontiers in Psychology* 12 (2021). doi:10.3389/fpsyg.2021.712606.

Hollis, Leah. "Bruising the Bottom Line: Cost of Workplace Bullying and the Compromised Access for Underrepresented Community College Employees." In *The Coercive Community College: Bullying and its Costly Impact on the Mission to Serve Underrepresented Populations*. Bingley, UK: Emerald Group Publishing, 2016.

Hollis, Leah P. "Bully University? The Cost of Workplace Bullying and Employee Disengagement in American Higher Education." *SAGE Open*, April2015. doi:10.1177/2158244015589997.

Hopwood, Christopher J. "Interpersonal Dynamics in Personality and Personality Disorders." *European Journal of Personality* 32, no. 5 (2018): 499–524. doi:10.1002/per.2155.

Hopwood, Christopher J. and Aidan G.C. Wright. "A Comparison of Passive Aggressive and Negativistic Personality Disorders," *Journal of Personality Assessment* 94, no. 3 (2012): 296–303. doi:10.1080/00223891.2012.655819.

International Labour Organization. *Experiences of Violence and Harassment at Work: A Global First Survey*, 2022. doi:10.54394/IOAX8567.

Keashly, Loraleigh. "Workplace Bullying, Mobbing and Harassment in Academe: Faculty Experience." In *Special Topics and Particular Occupations, Professions and Sectors*, Premilla D'Cruz, Ernesto Noronha, Loraleigh Keashly, Stacy Tye-Willims, eds. Gateway East, Singapore: Springer, 2019.

Kim, Joon H., Jennifer Kennedy Park, and Abena Mainoo. *Report for the Special Review Committee of the Board of Directors of the Federal Deposit Insurance Corporation*. Cleary Gottlieb Steen & Hamilton, LLP, April 2024. https://www.fdic.gov/sites/default/files/2024-05/cleary-report-to-fdic-src.pdf.

Kowalski, Robin M., Allison Toth, and Megan Moran. "Bullying and Cyberbullying in Adulthood and the Workplace." *The Journal of Social Psychology* 158, no. 1 (2018): 64–81. doi:10.1080/00224545.2017.1302402.

Kumar, Raghavendra Prasanna, Ramesh Chandrahasa, and R. Shashidhar. "Does Workplace Incivility Undermine the Potential of Job Resources? The Role of Psychological Capital." *FIIB Business Review*, 2023. doi:10.1177/23197145221137963.

Lim, Pang Kiam, Koay Kian Yeik, and Wei Ying Chong. "The Effects of Abusive Supervision, Emotional Exhaustion and Organizational Commitment on Cyberloafing: A Moderated-mediation Examination." *Internet Research* 31, no. 2 (2021). doi:10.1108/INTR-03-2020-0165.

Lim, Vivian K.G. and Don J.Q. Chen. "Cyberloafing at the Workplace: Gain or Drain on Work?" *Behaviour and Information Technology* 31, no. 4 (2012). doi:10.1080/01449290903353054.

Lyubykh, Zhanna, Kathryne E. Dupre, Julian Barling, and Nick Turner. "Retaliating Against Abusive Supervision with Aggression and Violence: The Moderating Role of Organizational Intolerance of Aggression." *Work and Stress* 36, no. 2 (2022): 164–182. doi:10.1080/02678373.2021.1969478.

Marcus, Bernd and Heinz Schuler. "Antecedents of Counterproductive Behavior at Work." *Journal of Applied Psychology* 89, no. 4 (2014): 647–660. doi:10.1037/0021-9010.89.4.647.

Muhonen, Tuija and Sandra Jonsson. "The Mediating Roles of Social Support and Social Organisational Climate." *International Journal of Workplace Health Management* 10, no. 5 (2017): 376–390. doi:10.1108/IJWHM-10-2016-0075.

Namie, Gary. "2021 WBI Workplace Bullying Institute Survey." *Workplace Bullying Institute*, 2021. Accessed December 12, 2023. https://workplacebullying.org/wp-content/uploads/2023/06/2021-Full-Report.pdf.

Park, Lora E., Lindsey Streamer, Li Huang, and Adam D. Galinsky. "Stand Tall but Don't Put Your Feet Up: Universal and Culturally-specific Effects of Expansive Postures on Power." *Journal of Experimental Psychology* 49 (2013): 965–971. doi:10.1016/j.jesp.2013.06.001.

Pearson, Christine M., Lynne M.Andersson, and Judith W. Wegner. "When Workers Flout Convention: A Study of Workplace Incivility." *Human Relations* 54, no. 11: 1387–1419. doi.org/10.1177/00187267015411001.

"Researchers from University of California Berkeley Provide Details of New Studies and Findings in the Area of Personality Research (Demeaning: Dehumanizing Others By Minimizing the Importance of Their Psychological Needs)." *Psychology & Psychiatry Journal*, (October 17, 2020): 970. Gale Academic OneFile. Accessed December 17, 2023. https://link.gale.com/apps/doc/A638062977/AONE?u=horrygtc&sid=bookmark-AONE&xid=9ef4340e.

Sackett, Paul. "The Structure of Counterproductive Work Behaviors: Dimensionality and Relationships with Facets of Job Performance." *International Journal of Selection & Assessment* 10, no. 1/2 (March, 2002): 5. doi:10.1111/1468-2389.00189.

Saleem, Farida, Muhammad Imran Malik, Iqra Asif, and Awais Qasim. "Workplace Incivility and Employee Performance: Does Trust in Supervisors Matter? (A Dual Theory Perspective)." *Behavioral Sciences* 12, no. 513 (2022). doi:10.3390/bs12120513.

Schilpzand, Pauline, Irene E. De Pater, and Amir Erez. "Workplace Incivility: A Review of the Literature and Agenda for Future Research." *Journal of Organizational Behavior* 37 (2016): S57–S88. doi:10.1002/job.1976.

Seifert, Christine. *The Factory Girls: A Kaleidoscopic Account of the Triangle Shirtwaist Factory Fire.* Minneapolis, MN: Lerner Publishing Group, 2017.

Sell, Aaron, Leda Dosmides, and John Tooby. "The Human Face Evolved to Enhance Cues of Strength." *Evolution of Human Behavior* 35, no. 5 (2014). doi:10.1016/j.evolhumbehav.2014.05.008.

"Sexual Harassment in the World of Work." International Labour Organization. Accessed January 25, 2024. https://www.ilo.org/wcmsp5/groups/public/—dgreports/—gender/documents/briefingnote/wcms_738115.pdf.

Shoorideh, Foroozan Atashzadeh, Soolmaz Moosavi, and Abbas Balouchi. "Incivility Toward Nurses: A Systematic Review and Meta-analysis." *Journal of Medical Ethics and History of Medicine* 3, no. 14 (November, 2021): 15. doi:10.18502/jmehm.v14i15.7670.

Silva, Rui, Margarida Simões, Ana Paula Monteiro, and António Dias. "Leymann Inventory of Psychological Terror Scale: Development and Validation for Portuguese Accounting Professionals." *Economies* 9, no. 3 (2021): 94. doi:10.3390/economies9030094.

Spanouli, Andromachi, Joeri Hofmans, and Reeshad S. Dalal. "Coping with Daily Boredom: Exploring the Relationships of Job Boredom, Counterproductive Work Behavior, Organizational Citizenship Behavior, and Cognitive Reappraisal." *Motivation & Emotion* 47, no. 5 (October2023): 810–827. doi:10.1007/s11031-023-10017-2.

Spector, Paul E., Jeremy A.Bauer, and Suzy Fox. "Measurement Artifacts in the Assessment of Counterproductive Work Behavior and Organizational Citizenship Behavior: Do We Know What We Think We Know?" *Journal of Applied Psychology* 95, no. 4 (2010): 781–790. doi:10.1037/a0019477.

Spector, Paul E., Suzy Fox, Lisa M.Penney, KariBruursema, AngelineGoh, and Stacey Kessler. "The Dimensionality of Counterproductivity: Are All Counterproductive Behaviors Created Equal?" *Journal of Vocational Behavior* 68, no. 3 (2006): 446–460. doi:10.1016/j.jvb.2005.10.005.

Suskind, Dorothy. "Why Are You Being Bullied at Work?" *Psychology Today* (February, 2021). www.psychologytoday.com/us/blog/bully-wise/202102/why-are-you-being-bullied-at-work.

Vara-Horna, Arístides, Zaida Asencios-Gonzalez, Liliana Quipuzco-Chicata, Alberto Díaz-Rosillo, and Dante Supo-Rojas. "Preventing Workplace Sexual Harassment and Productivity Loss during Crisis Periods: The Protective Role of Equitable Management." *Sustainability* 15, no. 23 (2023): NA. Gale Academic OneFile. Accessed December 24, 2023. https://link.gale.com/apps/doc/A775892599/AONE?u=horrygtc&sid=bookmark-AONE&xid=1f8a7d3e.

Weber Shandwick. *Civility in America*, 2019. https://cms.webershandwick.com/wp-content/uploads/2023/01/CivilityInAmerica2019SolutionsforTomorrow.pdf.

White, Sheila. *An Introduction to the Psychodynamics of Workplace Bullying*. New York, NY: Routledge, 2018.

"World Risk Poll 2021: Safe at Work? Global Experiences of Violence and Harassment." *Lloyds Register Foundation*, 2021. Accessed December 24, 2024. https://wrp.lrfoundation.org.uk/LRF_2021_report_safe-at-work.pdf.

# Chapter 2

# Developing Oneself

A good starting point in the exploration of civility in the workplace begins with understanding one-self. Failure to recognize how words and actions are received can have significant impacts on the work environment as a whole. Such failure can even come from a single individual. One historical example of this comes from the entrepreneur Howard Hughes. Hughes began his career by running the Hughes Tool Company, then pursued work in motion pictures by acquiring RKO Pictures and entered the aviation industry through ownership of Hughes Aircraft Company and later Trans World Airlines ("Howard Robard Hughes" 1998). However, throughout his life and career Hughes' actions displayed a lack of personal insight as his inter-actions with those he worked with were controlling and devoid of empathy. As an example, during the filming of "Jet Pilot" Hughes sent camera crews thousands of miles over several weeks looking for just the right clouds to film (Voeltz, 2016). Such obsession for perfection led to multiple conflicts between Hughes and those under his direction. Hughes also clashed with many of his film's directors, firing three in the production of "Hell's Angels" (Barber 2016). Hughes' interpersonal disagreements were also with those holding leadership positions in his organizations resulting in a break with his business manager of Hughes Tool Company, clashes with TWA board members, and the resignation of the TWA president (Marrett 2016). While noted for many successes, Hughes also illustrates how one individual can negatively impact many work relationships.

Rigorous self-assessment and knowing and building awareness of personal strengths and weaknesses is crucial to becoming a positive contributor to work group dynamics. How does one go about understanding who they are and more specifically, how does that inform interactions in the workplace? Strategies to develop one's work self can mitigate damage from incivility and help one to serve as an example for others for a kinder and more civil workplace. Such strategies can include a number of tools, activities, and professional development opportunities that promote continuous learning, improve empathy, and strengthen emotional intelligence.

DOI: 10.4324/9781003590149-2

## Personality Tools

In the early 1990s, researchers Robert McCrae and Oliver John, building on the work of others, introduced their Five-Factor Model which defined and grouped similar personality traits into categories or "dimensions" (box 2.1) (McCrae and John 1992, 175). Attributes of these dimensions applied to the workplace can impact the workplace climate. For example, an agreeable personality may more easily express empathy where a neurotic one may display anxiety (McCrae and John 1992). Because of this, understanding the various dimensions of one's personality and how they impact the workplace is a good starting point for self-reflection.

### Box 2.1  Dimensions of Personality

- Extraversion
- Agreeableness
- Conscientiousness
- Neuroticism
- Openness

(McCrae and John 1992, 175)

There are numerous tools for self-reflection and Clifton Strengths Finder is one of these. This tool is especially valuable because it has been taken by more than 15 million people worldwide and is remarkably consistent in identifying a person's strengths and weaknesses which tend to be fairly stable over their lifetime (Matson and Robinson 2017). While it highlights these strengths and weaknesses one particularly useful aspect of Clifton Strengths Finder is its ability to identify blind spots even when they are connected to strengths. For example, a person who enjoys gathering data and information might have a tendency to overwhelm others in communications sharing more than the other person can absorb. This can lead to less than productive workplace interactions. Another example would be having a keen sense of focus. This could lead to an individual being perceived as emotionally distant or rude. In addition to consideration of blind spots, leaders in particular can use their strengths identified through this tool to improve the workplace environment. For example, if Clifton Strengths Finder identifies that leader or someone on their team as being especially strong in optimism that leader or team member could be utilized during times in which the organization or department is experiencing a lack of hope or morale (Lopez and Robinson 2009).

Another useful tool similar to Clifton Strengths Finder is the Big Five personality traits test. Like Clifton Strengths Finder, the Big Five personality traits test shows a lot of stability over time indicating that it accurately measures someone's strengths and weaknesses as they can relate to the workplace (Johnson 2005). This test is very useful in identifying traits or tendencies that can impact civility in a variety of ways. For example, according to one study, people high in extraversion, conscientiousness, neuroticism, and openness are more susceptible or likely to report bullying (Bokek-Cohen, Shkoler, and Meiri 2023). If someone was identified as one of these people, it might give them a greater sense of awareness as to why an interaction or situation is particularly distressing. Another study, conversely, notes that, while overall workplace culture is very important in terms of levels of incivility experienced by employees, those individuals who are low in agreeableness or conscientiousness tend to be more likely to bully others (Di Stefano, Scrima, and Parry 2019). This is not to explain away bad behavior but can provide personal insight when interacting with individuals that have certain tendencies.

Yet another test or instrument that can be useful for understanding one's workplace self is the Hogan Assessment. More than 11 million people have used this to better understand themselves. It explores individuals across a number of dimensions such as how one processes their own identity, a person's reputation, personality strengths and weaknesses when working with others, internal values, and cognitive style (Hogan Assessments 2024). One particularly useful aspect of Robert Hogan's work is that it is helpful in identifying what traits or habits are part of one's "dark side" or behaviors that tend to derail one's success. This can be very relevant to issues associated with navigating incivility in the workplace. For example, someone who is assessed as being bold can also come across as overly demanding to others, especially when under stress (Rio 2024). This could easily be interpreted as acting with incivility. While having an executive coach to help with follow-up on this assessment can be helpful, it is not an absolute necessity. If individuals can find someone in the workplace that they trust, this co-worker can help by providing feedback on behavior or perception of behavior. From an incivility perspective this can have benefits on both sides. That is, understanding how an individual in the workplace might be coming across as uncivil or, conversely, how or why they might be perceiving incivility could be better understood and addressed. Generally speaking, tools such as the Hogan Assessment are useful at improving self-awareness which can, in turn, help with managing conflict, understanding others, and developing one's own skills and resilience.

Another tool that can be of use in helping to understand oneself is the DiSC Personal Profile System. DiSC is unique relative to the other assessments mentioned in that the emphasis is on understanding one's role in relation to a team or in collaboration with others. It can help to determine if one's primary focus is on bottom line results, maintaining relationships, cooperation or quality and details ("What is DiSC?"). DiSC claims to be one of the oldest personality profile assessments and has been used by more than 50 million people. Standing for Dominance, Influence, Steadiness, and Conscientiousness this assessment looks to explore how people behave within the context of specific situations. In its most simplistic sense, it tends to separate individuals into those that seek to shape their environment versus those that tend to focus more on adapting to their environment (Puccio and Grivas 2009). Those that seek to shape their environment may be more willing to address incivility head on but could also cause conflict to escalate if they do not approach situations carefully. Conversely, those that seek to adapt to their environment may internalize incivility when witnessed creating stress. While they might seek a systematic solution to problems, they see it would be useful to be aware of the internalization and find a constructive way to handle it.

## Professional Training

Professional development activities that seek to improve individual skills specific to civility are wide and varied. Many focus on developing a practice of mindfulness which will be discussed later in this chapter. Other activities and workshops exist, however, which also seek to address problems and challenges. Many of these focus on practicing responses to specific situations within the workplace. The most effective of these programs are not one-shot trainings but rather programs that are practiced over a longer period of time. Six months is fairly common. The Civility, Respect, and Engagement in the Workplace (CREW) model is just one example. This approach seeks to allow individuals and groups to take an active role in defining what civility means to them and then implementing a plan to develop a culture and support system around this. Interventions and training center around both interrupting incivility when it occurs as well as proactively working to create a positive work environment where civility and mutual respect are prevalent. A central tenet of this approach is to recognize that people narrow their choices and responses under stress and that these can be expanded by creating an environment of psychological safety (Leiter et al. 2011). The idea behind CREW is to allow people to break old patterns, develop new positive relationships and practice new ways of interacting under the guidance of experts. This builds an individual's skill set while simultaneously improving team dynamics. According to one group of authors who studied the process and its positive results:

> CREW uses structured exercises to help participants move out of their comfort zone, such that they are not simply perpetuating their existing behavior patterns. By behaving differently in structured exercises, participants will initiate new patterns of interaction. Facilitators further

that process by structuring the exercises and encouraging participation.

(Leiter et al. 2011, 6)

From an individual perspective there are many takeaways from training such as this. Maintaining boundaries and seeking support from others within the organization when encountering incivility is key. This is probably going to be more difficult for anyone new to an organization. As one builds trust and understands the culture and level of support within the institution or organization a more realistic and informed approach can be taken.

If an individual or organization is looking for training, there are numerous options similar to CREW. Another example is the workplace training provided by the Institute for Civility. Founded in 1997, this institute's training is comprehensive and focuses on the historical challenges faced by marginalized groups when it comes to workplace incivility. According to their website their programs are

designed to address the stresses of incivility directly, equipping individuals with the tools they need to step outside the emotionally and psychologically destructive systems of attack and defense. Participants learn to recontextualize their experience of themselves and others in ways that produce healthier, less stressful, and more productive outcomes

(Institute for Civility)

They provide a wealth of information on their site including a detailed reference list of sources that seek to broadly and deeply define what civility means both in an academic as well as pragmatic sense and a very long list of book titles for further inquiry and understanding. Unlike some of the longer-term training, theirs tends to consist of half-day, all-day, or multi-day retreats. The Institute for Civility also has online or virtual options for training. While not as comprehensive as the six-month or longer programs, they do provide hands-on and practical solutions that include handling stress and dealing with triggers.

While perhaps a bit less engaging than in-person or customized workshops on the topic, training through sources such as LinkedIn Learning can also be valuable. "Teaching Civility in the Workplace" facilitated by Catherine Mattice is one good example. It provides video examples of employees confronting incivility and addressing it in specific ways. It also provides suggestions of ways for individuals to stand up for others in the workplace as well when they notice negative interactions (LinkedIn Learning). Other similar useful role-playing interactions can be viewed through one's local or academic library's streaming video resources as well.

Workplace civility can be improved by increasing the individual empathy of those in that workplace. Formal empathy training programs are also possible. These may include education based, simulation based, or role-playing approaches to increase understanding and methods for social interaction (box 2.2) (Wu et al. 2024). Some evidence indicates that when people are taught to think of empathy as a skill that can be developed as opposed to a fixed trait, they can both increase their empathy and improve their relationships. While leaders play an especially crucial role in combating incivility and promoting kindness and empathy, anyone within the organization can play a role. Evidence exists that empathy can actually be contagious in a very positive way (Zaki 2019). It can also be improved by simply getting to know other co-workers and understand their stories, struggles, and challenges. Opening up about one's own story is one way to do this. It should be noted, however, as issues such as bullying, opening up and sharing are considered, they need to be approached with some degree of caution. Sometimes bullies use people's weaknesses or insecurities for verbal attacks. While it's not necessary for everyone to be friends at work, fostering mutual understanding is essential—especially in today's often divided society.

**Box 2.2 Empathy Training Approaches**

- Personal: emotion regulation, loving-kindness meditation, emotion recognition practice
- Secondary: experience simulated difficulties, experience and reflect on emotion-based stories, movies, or pictures
- Social-oriented: improve social skills, role-play, virtual reality

(Wu et al. 2024)

## Emotional Intelligence

Developing emotional intelligence is something that can really help from an individual perspective in combating workplace incivility and so will be covered in some length here as well as in other parts of this book. Emotional intelligence includes a number of elements such as self-awareness, self-regulation, self-motivation, social awareness, and social skill. By definition the starting point for emotional intelligence centers on the individual or self. Without self-awareness it is really hard, if not impossible, to improve one's own experience and interactions in the workplace. Self-regulation is the next piece as it builds on awareness and acknowledges control of one's own behavior and reactions to workplace situations. Social awareness and social skills related to emotional intelligence focus on kindness and understanding (Harvard DCE Professional & Executive Development 2024). Evidence suggests that some critical elements must exist in order to improve emotional intelligence. These include a desire to improve one's skills as well as an opportunity to both practice those skills and receive feedback on one's progress (Oliver 2020).

One possible tool for developing emotional intelligence is 360 feedback. Its value comes from its ability to gather feedback about one's behaviors and perceptions of oneself from a variety of different perspectives. An instrument is distributed to a person's colleagues, supervisor, direct reports, and other parties as appropriate and this information is then amalgamated into a single picture illustrating strengths, weaknesses, blind spots, and other attributes. This feedback method should be used with caution, however. Its creators intend its use as a development tool as opposed to being used as a more formal, year-end evaluation (Moniz 2010). There are any number of ways that this type of instrument and feedback can be valuable in our context here. For just one example, an individual can get a good sense of how their communication style is perceived by others. If one comes across as harsh or unapproachable this could be something to pay more attention to and work on. Likewise, if someone came across as overly shy and timid the instrument could show a need to be more assertive, especially in the face of incivility or bullying from other team members.

Emotional intelligence is a very important part of maintaining civility in the workplace. Any number of examples could be shared here to illustrate its value with regard to the individual more generally. Increasing self-awareness for someone who has a tendency to become overly defensive when receiving feedback can help them approach feedback with a more open mind. For self-regulation, one could better understand their tendencies under stress. Oftentimes, when under stress, some individuals can lash out or, conversely, shut down. Knowing oneself in this regard one could take a minute to breathe, go for a short walk in nature, or engage in some other brief practice before responding to a difficult situation. With regard to social skills, someone who tends to dominate conversations might work on holding back some and listening more. Conversely, someone who tends to not engage can work on sharing more or speaking up more in meetings and in other contexts. Emotional intelligence, when applied mindfully to conflict resolution, can allow one to step back and explore options in a more positive and proactive way.

## Mindfulness

Somewhat related to emotional intelligence is mindfulness. The authors of this text have written extensively and conducted numerous workshops on this topic. While mindfulness will not be covered in its entirety here, some key concepts are important to understand as an individual seeking to improve workplace civility and interactions. For starters, there are many excellent definitions of mindfulness available. One comes from the book *Fully Present: The Science, Art, and Practice of Mindfulness* by Susan Smalley and Diane Winston. They state, "Mindfulness is the art of observing your physical, emotional, and mental experiences with deliberate, open and curious attention" (Smalley and Winston 2010). Add emphasis to the word deliberate. Mindfulness at its core is purposefully and proactively being in the present moment.

One of the most critical concepts associated with mindfulness is the "beginner's mind." Charles Gordon-Graham provides a clear description of what this means relative to mindful practice,

> Beginner's mind is a mind that is open, fresh, curious, present here and now, natural, free and uncluttered … with beginner's mind comes a sense of wonder … Beginner's mind, being open and curious, promotes empathy; the related quality of compassion— awareness of other's suffering and a wish to help them.
>
> (Moniz et al. 2016)

There are some fairly obvious connections here to individuals and civility. By approaching the self and personal assumptions with an open mind individuals tend to be more open to feedback from others and also open to new ways of understanding our own behavior. This can help in innumerable ways. For just one example, if an individual is having problems or challenges with how they are coming across to others, they can explore new approaches to communicating and interacting. Likewise, a beginner's mind also allows one to extend empathy to others and better understand why they may be behaving in a certain way towards us. Justifying or excusing incivility or bullying should never happen but understanding where it is coming from and how it is perceived can be a great first step towards a solution.

Presence is another important concept which points back to the definition of mindfulness shared above. Many of us are busy multitasking on a regular basis. There are cell phones, smart watches, email messages, and any number of other constant distractions pulling for our attention. One thing that is clear is that it is much more likely that individuals and others will be civil and kind when they are more present in the moment. Aside from work distractions, teachings on mindfulness note that individuals are very frequently caught up in the past or worried about the future. These things are just a part of life but dwelling on the past tends to lead one towards regret and depression, whilst focusing too much on the future creates unnecessary anxiety. While there is a place for considering the past and future, neither of these help us to be more present or civil in the moment. While awareness is a key step, one of the goals of mindful practices such as meditation and yoga is to train oneself to keep attention in this present moment.

The science behind mindfulness is overwhelming. Mountains of research have been conducted showing its benefits, especially in recent years. A review of multiple studies indicates mindful training increases positive attributes, such as empathy, while reducing negative impacts of work stressors (box 2.3) (Johnson, Park, and Chaudhuri 2020). These studies indicate that engaging in even the smallest or quickest of practices, such as a short breathing exercise, can help disrupt negative patterns in our behaviors and thought processes (Wu et al. 2019). This becomes extremely beneficial when looking to interrupt incivility and encourage kindness and positive workplace behaviors.

---

**Box 2.3  Benefits of Mindfulness Training Impacting Civility**

*Outcomes Increased*

- Active listening
- Empathy
- Group cohesion
- Social support
- Team cooperation

*Outcomes Decreased*

- Anxiety
- Emotional exhaustion
- Relationship conflict
- Social undermining
- Stress

(Johnson, Park, and Chaudhuri 2020, 347)

---

## Nature

As has already been alluded to in this chapter, protecting and caring for oneself is important. One last suggestion will be shared here in this regard. Spending time in nature seems to be a remedy for many when feeling down. Is there a scientific basis for this? It turns out there is. A recent study of military veterans who were engaged in a white-water rafting experienced a boost in mood and well-being. The study's conclusion states,

For John Muir, the outdoors were a source of both restoration and awe. In the current study, we captured both these properties of nature experience, showing for the first time that awe mediates the effect of nature experience on well-being. These findings suggest that awe may be one active ingredient in the remedy that is time spent outdoors.

(Anderson, Monroy, and Keltner 2018, 1201)

Yet another recent study which explored exposure to a variety of outdoor environments

confirmed the hypothesized increase of feelings of restoration, vitality, and positive mood in green environments and their decrease in a built urban setting. In addition, feelings of creativity were higher in green environments. The findings of the study also confirmed that experiential restoration can take place after a short period of nature exposure.

(Tyrväinen et al. 2014, 8)

It should be noted that this study, while finding a positive effect, acknowledged the difficulty in definitively measuring something as obscure as exposure to nature. That said, there is additional promising research in this regard. One last example will do. According to another documented experimental study, just spending a minimum amount of time in nature on a regular basis can potentially reduce cortisol levels. In this study which lasted 8 weeks subjects were asked to spend at least 10 minutes in nature at least three times a week. Their cortisol levels were then measured against a control group. Those who averaged 20–30 minutes saw the greatest gains in reduced stress (Hunter, Gillespie, and Chen 2019). Some employees in the workplace spend the majority of their day indoors. These few sampled studies should point out the value, however, of getting outside, when possible, whether during a break or on one's non-work schedule. This can help give one time to recharge, reframe, and proactively approach workplace civility.

## Conclusion

Understanding oneself is foundational to fostering civility and kindness in the modern workplace. Tools such as Clifton Strengths Finder, the Big Five personality traits, the Hogan Assessment, and DiSC Personal Profile System can offer valuable insights into strengths, weaknesses, and potential blind spots that someone may have. Developing emotional intelligence and engaging in mindfulness practices can enhance one's ability to manage stress, navigate conflicts, and build meaningful, empathetic relationships. Professional training and structured interventions can also play a significant role in promoting a culture of respect and psychological safety in one's workplace and beyond. Sometimes just stepping away and spending time in nature, when possible, can also be a remedy. Ultimately, continuous self-reflection and intentional efforts to improve both individual awareness and, in turn, team dynamics are essential for creating a kinder, more civil workplace.

## Suggested Reads

Buckingham, Marcus and Donald O. Clifton. *Now, Discover Your Strengths.* New York: Free Press, 2001.

Eurich, Tasha. *Insight: Why We're Not as Self-Aware as We Think, and How Seeing Ourselves Clearly Helps Us Succeed at Work and in Life.* New York: Crown Business, 2017.

Smith, Julie. *Why Has Nobody Told Me This Before?* New York: Harper-One, 2022.

## References

Anderson, Craig L., Maria Monroy, and Dacher Keltner. "Awe in Nature Heals: Evidence from Military Veterans, at-Risk Youth, and College Students." *Emotion* 18, no. 8 (December2018): 1201.

Barber, Nicholas. "Was This Billionaire Recluse Truly Mad?" BBC. December 6, 2016. Accessed February 27, 2025. https://www.bbc.com/culture/article/20161205-was-howard-hughes-really-insane.

Bokek-Cohen, Ya-arit, Or Shkoler, and Eitan Meiri. "The Unique Practices of Workplace Bullying in Academe: An Exploratory Study." *Current Psychology* 42, no. 23 (2023): 19466–19485. doi:10.1007/s12144-022-03090-2.

Di Stefano, Giovanni, Fabrizio Scrima, and Emma Parry. "The Effect of Organizational Culture on Deviant Behaviors in the Workplace." *International Journal of Human Resource Management* 30, no. 17 (2019): 2482–2503. doi:10.1080/09585192.2017.1326393.

Harvard DCE Professional & Executive Development. "How to Improve Your Emotional Intelligence." Harvard Division of Continuing Education. Last updated January 9, 2024. https://professional.dce.harvard.edu/blog/how-to-improve-your-emotional-intelligence/.

Hogan Assessments. "Our Assessments Measure Reputation, Not Identity." Accessed December 5, 2024. https://www.hoganassessments.com/assessments/.

"Howard Robard Hughes." In *Encyclopedia of World Biography Online*. Detroit, MI: Gale, 1998. Gale in Context: Biography.

Hunter, MaryCarol R., Brenda W. Gillespie, and Sophie Yu-Pu Chen. "Urban Nature Experiences Reduce Stress in the Context of Daily Life Based on Salivary Biomarkers" *Frontiers in Psychology* 10 (2019). doi:10.3389/fpsyg.2019.00722.

Institute for Civility. "Civility Training." Accessed December 6, 2024. https://www.instituteforcivility.org/training-and-programs/civility-training/.

Johnson, Karen R., Sunyoung Park, and Sanghamitra Chaudhuri. "Mindfulness Training in the Workplace: Exploring its Scope and Outcomes." *European Journal of Training and Development* 44, no. 4/5 (2020): 341–354. doi:10.1108/EJTD-09-2019-0156.

Johnson, Malcolm ed. "Personality Stability and Change During Adulthood and Old Age." In *The Cambridge Handbook of Age and Ageing*, 1st ed. Cambridge, UK: Cambridge University Press, 2005. https://search.credoreference.com/articles/Qm 9va0FydGljbGU6MjM5NjEzNQ==?aid=96519.

Leiter, Michael, Heather K. Spence Laschinger, Arla Day, and Debra Gilin Oore. "The Impact of Civility Interventions on Employee Social Behavior, Stress, Distress, and Attitudes." *Journal of Applied Psychology* 96, no. 6 (2011): 1258–1274. doi:10.1037/a0024442.

LinkedIn Learning. "Teaching Civility in the Workplace: Be an Upstander for Others." Accessed December 6, 2024. https://www.linkedin.com/learning/teaching-civili ty-in-the-workplace/be-an-upstander-for-others?resume=false&u=232052538.

Lopez, Shane and Jennifer Robison. "Why Hope Matters Now." *Gallup Management Journal Online* 1 (2009). https://news.gallup.com/businessjournal/121211/ Why-Hope-Matters.aspx.

Marrett, George J. *Howard: Aviator*. Annapolis, MD: Naval Institute Press, 2016.

Matson, Tom and Jennifer Robison. "The Rewarding Work of Turning Talents Into Strengths." *Gallup Business Journal* 1 (2017). https://news.gallup.com/busi nessjournal/202526/hard-work-turning-talents-strengths.aspx.

McCrae, Robert R. and Oliver P. John. "An Introduction to the Five-Factor Model and Its Applications." *Journal of Personality* 60, no. 2 (1992): 175–215. doi:10.1111/j.1467–6494.1992.tb00970.x.

Moniz, Richard. *Practical and Effective Management of Libraries: Integrating Case Studies, General Management Theory and Self-understanding*. Cambridge, MA: Elsevier Science & Technology, 2010.

Moniz, Richard, Joe Eshleman, Jo Henry, Howard L. Slutzky, and Lisa Moniz. *The Mindful Librarian: Connecting the Practice of Mindfulness to Librarianship*. Witney, Oxfordshire, UK: Chandos Publishing, 2016, p. 7.

Oliver, Tiffany. "The Importance of Subordinate Emotional Intelligence Development in the Workplace." *The International Trade Journal* 34, no. 1 (2020): 162–172.

Puccio, Gerard and Chris Grivas. "Examining the Relationship between Personality Traits and Creativity Styles" *Creativity & Innovation Management* 18, no. 4 (2009): 247–255. doi:10.1111/j.1467–8691.2009.00535.x.

Rio, Ave. "Shining Light on the Dark Side." *Chief Learning Officer* 17, no. 7 (2018): 48–56. https://issuu.com/chief-learning-officer/docs/co0918.

Smalley, Suan and Diana Winston. *Fully Present: The Science, Art, and Practice of Mindfulness*. Boston, MA: Da Capo Lifelong Books, 2010.

Tyrväinen, Liisa, Ann Ojala, Kalevi Korpela, Timo Lanki, Yuko Tsunetsugu, and Takahide Kagawa. "The Influence of Urban Green Environments on Stress Relief Measures: A Field Experiment." *Journal of Environmental Psychology* 38, (June 2014): 1–9. doi:10.1016/j.jenvp.2013.12.005.

Voeltz, Richard Andrew. "Howard Hughes and the Cold War Aviation Film Jet Pilot (1957)." *CINEJ Cinema Journal* 5, no. 2 (2016): 28–52. doi:doi:10.5195/ cinej.2016.133.

"What is DiSC?" John Wiley & Sons, Inc. Accessed December 6, 2024. https://www. discprofile.com/what-is-disc?gad_source=1&gclid=Cj0KCQiA88a5BhDPAR

IsAFj595hQ7n2z0sv5lUbXm2EY-avulcmsVMfamT7FJGB5VeRS5pAg8q2FsowaAp thEALw_wcB.

Wu, Ran, Lin-Lin Liu, Hong Zhu, Wen-Jun Su, Shi-Yang Zhong, Xing-Hua Liu, and Chun-Lei Jiang. "Brief Mindfulness Meditation Improves Emotion Processing." *Frontiers in Neuroscience* 13 (2019). doi:10.3389/fnins.2019.01074.

Wu, Xiao, Su-Chen Yau, Xue-Jing Lu, Yu-Qing Zhou, Ya-Zhuo King, and Li Hu. "Categories of Training to Improve Empathy: A Systematic Review and Meta-analysis." *Psychological Bulletin* 150, no. 10 (2024): 1237–1260. doi:10.1037/bul0000453.

Zaki, Jamil. "Making Empathy Central to Your Company Culture." *Harvard Business Review*, May 30, 2019. https://hbr.org/2019/05/making-empathy-central-to-your-company-culture.

# Chapter 3

# Elevating In-person Communication

Communication issues are among the leading causes of workplace dysfunction. Among these, challenges regarding in-person verbal exchanges are particularly common. Many such exchanges took place during the early COVID-19 years where concerns about safety prompted much debate. One such incident which received attention occurred at Trader Joe's. When manager David Fuller reduced store safety measures in May 2021, eight-year employee Jill Groeschel raised concerns (Chan et al. 2024). As the animosity grew, Fuller began giving Groeschel negative performance reviews which ultimately led to her suspension and firing (Chan et al. 2024). This was followed by litigation which at the time of this writing was not yet settled. However, this incident provides just one example of how in-person exchanges can escalate to much larger issues and conflict in the workplace.

Understanding communication, both verbal and non-verbal aspects, is a beginning to improving the process. It encompasses mastering listening skills and understanding cultural implications in communication. More importantly, methods for dealing with uncivil exchanges and navigating aggressive verbal attacks from co-workers are tools everyone in the workplace can use. Exploration of methods to handle the many variations of the communication exchange, feedback loop, and hostile interactions is a good starting point in the attempt to promote civil exchanges in the workplace.

## Communication Exchange

Exploring specific insights into verbal communication lays a foundation for finding ways to improve this process. What exactly is involved in this form of communication? To answer this question a brief review of a basic communication model from 1948, the Shannon-Weaver Model, is a good place to begin. This model's description of the structure of communication provides the essentials of an exchange, and it starts with a specific message that is conveyed or transmitted to another person through the spoken word. These words, along with gestures, are channelled towards a listener in a

DOI: 10.4324/9781003590149-3

one-way transmission. It is at this transmission stage that theorists Claude Shannon and Warren Weaver expanded the Shannon-Weaver Model to include what they termed noise (Foulger 2004). Shannon and Weaver define noise as something that could distract from or block the initial information package in transit potentially altering a clear understanding by the listener. When the message is received, the final part of the communication process is the mental processing and interpretation of the message. While these early communication theories only focused on this one-way, linear communication process, they do lay out the process and point out two possible ways verbal communication can be derailed—by distractions and misinterpretations. Distractions, such as noise, glancing at a computer screen, responding to a phone text, or picking up on other surrounding conversations, may result in the listener hearing only part of the message or missing the real intent. Other misunderstandings could be attributed to listeners simply not correctly comprehending the message. Tips for addressing these mistakes in understanding are explored further in this chapter.

Building on Shannon-Weaver and other theorists, a more complex look at verbal communication came in 1970 through theorist Dean C. Barnlund. Barnlund who posited that the information exchange was much more dynamic than the one-way process described by Shannon-Weaver. Barnlund theorized that interpersonal communication occurs simultaneously with cues from the physical environment, the self, and non-verbal behaviors (Watson and Hill 2015). All of these elements play a role in message interpretation and listener response. This model acknowledges that verbal communication is complex and involves individuals correctly processing a number of elements, in addition to words, to accurately interpret the intended communication. Imagine a meeting of several employees working on a new project. What kind of communication dynamics occur? Where is the meeting taking place? What emotions and tone are displayed by participants? The scenario may involve individuals sharing different perspectives and providing immediate feedback to ideas. The group may be seated and following some formal meeting norms or gathered in a more casual way with a shared screen or design. What ideas do all the players bring to the meeting? As can be imagined, understanding the verbal communication process is complex but necessary as it lays the foundation for exploring a variety of ways to improve the process.

## Improved Listening

As these communication models infer, hearing the verbal message (or spoken words) is a critical part of the process. The use of listening skills is important in all areas of the work environment from imparting information, giving feedback, or expressing emotions. Listening is also important in establishing positive interpersonal dynamics between co-workers. Research shows that when the listener has withdrawn, shut down, or dismissed the message, the speaker perceives being unheard (Kriz, Kluger, and Lyddy 2021). This could lead to a frustrating and unproductive verbal exchange or even result in the individuals reducing worker interactions. Conversely, conversations can have a positive impact when listening is active and engaged. Supervisors skilled in areas of listening have increased worker engagement. Research has found that workers reporting to these types of supervisors have more enthusiasm, energy, optimism, and focus, and they are also more proactive and healthier (Jonsdottir and Kristinsson 2020). Listening is a critical part of the verbal exchange and improving these skills is one way to foster a positive work environment.

A method for improving listening is to apply active listening skills. Active listening involves a focused and responsive listener who is involved in the process as the information exchange is occurring. The first aspect of active listening is acknowledging the message is being received. This can be accomplished by restating or summarizing what has been said, which gives the speaker confirmation the message was received and understood. A listener could say, "I understand that you want to …" or "The approach you want to take is …" to confirm they have correctly heard the intended message. Another aspect of active listening is to respond to the non-verbal clues that are being conveyed such as a speaker being unsure, concerned, puzzled, or some other emotion. This could be as simple as verbal acknowledgement that a specific emotion is being observed. For example, "You look frustrated over this problem" is a response that acknowledges that emotion. Conveying an understanding of the speaker's message as well as emotions is important and fosters a back-and-forth verbal exchange between individuals until the intended message is clearly understood (Knippen and Green 1994). Once the initial message is complete, the listener may pause before asking follow-up questions, clarifying statements, or acknowledging emotion behind the message before offering their opinion, counter statement, or other response (box 3.1) (Henry, Eshleman, and Moniz 2020). This completes the first part of the exchange—from speaker to listener and back to speaker—which is usually followed by additional verbal exchanges until the conversation is complete.

## Box 3.1  Active Listening Tips

- Ask clarifying questions
- Reflect speaker's feelings
- Repeat/Rephrase concepts
- Signal interest while listening
- Utilize pausing in reflection

(Henry, Eshleman, and Moniz 2020)

While active listening involves being focused on hearing the message and understanding emotion, it also encompasses other aspects of body language. Being positioned correctly in front of the speaker is important not only to increase engagement but also to let the speaker know the receiver is focused on what they are saying. The listener should always face the speaker and be attentive by leaning forward with arms in an open position at a desk or uncrossed if standing (Goleman 2020). Listeners can also include a head nod or short comment to let the speaker know there is real engagement in the information exchange. Research shows listeners who make eye contact with the speaker 70% of the time while glancing to the side every four to five seconds to avoid staring are perceived as engaged in the information exchange (Goleman 2020). These basic tips in a listener's body language can be learned and when applied can considerably improve interactions.

While active listening is a listen–acknowledge process, it does not end there. It often requires follow up in some way, especially in an environment where the information exchanged is complex. Follow up with a related and real action after the completed conversation is the most common way that an employee validates their message was actually heard. For example, if an employee conveys a problem with a work process and the listener responds by improving or correcting the issue, the worker perceives they have been heard. While this exchange may appear simple, these follow-up responses to information not only resolve individual issues but lay the foundation of trust for future exchanges. Another aspect of follow up after a conversation is "conversational growth" or where the listener builds and expands on what the speaker has said (Kriz, Kluger, and Lyddy 2021). This may require additional questions and multiple exchanges between individuals to accomplish a goal or resolve an issue. Follow up is critical for fostering a positive and productive work environment. When it is missing, not only do issues go unresolved, but individuals may be less likely to bring problems forward as they perceive their concerns as being unheard. Follow up and focused exchanges are important elements to maintaining vibrant work communications.

Along with active listening, empathetic listening can make a positive difference in verbal exchanges as well. While empathetic listening is often mentioned along with active listening, it is slightly different. The concept of empathetic listening was first utilized by psychologist Carl R. Rogers in the 1940s who developed client-centered therapies (Rosner 2008). This approach involves recognizing, understanding, and acknowledging the feelings being experienced by the other individual in a non-judgmental way. This may include perceiving impatience with a task, anger in disagreement, trepidation with a new assignment, or hurt from coworker gossip. The listener must be able to put themselves in the place of the speaker and truly recognize how it feels to be them. Often, just empathetic listening itself and acknowledging the emotion is all that the individual needs. Work situations could involve the need to vent frustrations or for supervisors to listen to an experience not directly work-related that is emotionally impacting their employee. Other times, recognition of feelings can lead to opportunities for continued discussions or even resolutions of issues. Pausing to reflect on how the other person feels, understanding the emotion, and putting oneself in their place before responding is all a part of empathetic listening.

Blocking or minimizing distractions also improves the communication exchange. As mentioned, the ping of a cell phone or arrival of a new email on the computer screen can become distractions. Others include eating while listening, performing a secondary task, or customer or work-related noises. Studies have shown that both external distractions, as well as interrupting conversations, contribute to a decrease of task accuracy in the workplace (Clapp, Rubens, and Gazzaley 2010). To avoid this, consider the timing and topic of conversations. Everyone understands it is important to have a private office or location for meeting one-on-one with staff or for a staff meeting intended for sharing information, but what about more casual information exchanges? Supervisors should offer corrections or advice to an employee in a quiet setting rather than a noisy workroom or front-facing workspace where customers or co-workers can overhear. Co-workers should work out a disagreement in a private space or meeting room free from distractions. To maintain focus and minimize distractions during conversations in an office setting, it is advisable to turn off the computer screen and refrain from multitasking. Considering the surroundings and limiting distractions during important conversations will make them better.

A final tip for improving conversations involves withholding judgment. Refraining from forming an opinion, taking a position, or judging content before the speaker has completely conveyed their message is also important. This can be challenging for many. Often listeners tend towards formulating a response while someone is still speaking. Their mind anticipates what is going to be said, whirls into possible responses immediately, and in doing so disengages from real listening. Part of this is due to the listener's ability to process up to 250 words per minute (or more) while speech averages 150 words per minute (Murphy et al., 2022; Steinemann and Larson 1973). Other times listeners interrupt the speaker without waiting for them to finish their delivery. This type of response could take the form of prematurely attacking, criticizing, or dismissing the message. Professor and author Judi Brownell's book, *Listening: Attitudes, Principles, and Skills* offers practical tips and guidance for improving listening habits such as mentally summarizing aspects of the message or relating information to prior experiences (2017). In-person verbal communication is a process that cannot be rushed. Patience should rule. For those who struggle with this part of the process, minimize impatience by taking a deep breath, blocking mental distractions, and keeping the mind focused on the conversation. Doing this adds to an effective communication exchange.

While the concepts of verbal communication appear to be a simple process of speaking and listening, they become quite important when much of workplace dysfunction lies in poor communication. Applying concepts to improve the exchange will make a difference. Thinking about singular information exchanges in the workplace, typically they are tied to larger ideas or layers of information. These work communications involve much back and forth and feedback loops resulting in real actions. Whether formal or informal, informative or directive, improving listening skills will help.

## Box 3.2 Tips for Improved Listening

- Acknowledge the speaker is being heard
- Actively listen, distraction free
- Be patient, avoid interrupting the speaker
- Face the speaker with open body language
- Note non-verbal cues and facial expressions
- Recognize emotions behind the words
- Refrain from judgment or formulating responses too soon

## Non-Verbal Communication

Another area of consideration in the communication dialogue is non-verbal clues. As mentioned, understanding the non-verbal communications part of the information exchange along with the spoken word is important. Research in the area of non-verbal communication is extensive. Entire books are dedicated to this topic. It can encompass a number of aspects including movement, expressions, gestures, voice qualities, and eye contact as well as other elements. What aspects of non-verbal clues impact verbal communication exchanges in the workplace?

An overview of literature and research on non-verbal communication by Silvia Bonaccio, Professor of Workplace Psychology in the Telfer School of Management at the University of Ottawa, and her research group summarizes five areas of impact in the organization, three of which directly impact the verbal communication exchange (Bonaccio et al. 2016). The study's first category is a display of personal attributes or expressions of "personality, intentions, and attitude" (Bonaccio et al. 2016). For example, an employee's frown when asking for help may not necessarily be interpreted as a negative response if this expression simply reflects their normal facial expression. Power and hierarchy impact the next aspects of the study which involved direct eye contact, lower vocal pitch, and dominating verbal exchanges. These characteristics could appear in an exchange where a supervisor, or even a co-worker, is trying to dominate and control the conversation. Aggressive verbal exchanges may also include anger. A facial expression of this emotion may be displayed with furrowed brows, tight lips, and widely open eyes (Keltner et al., 2019). Another category in Bonaccio's research includes non-verbal emotional expressions which provides clues to what the speaker is feeling and plays a role in empathetic listening (Bonaccio 2016). Understanding these clues through non-verbal expressions adds to the listener's message interpretation. While the remaining two areas of the research impact the social and relational aspects of organizational life, they are not as directly tied to the verbal communication exchange process. Personality expressions, signals of power, and identifying emotions are three areas to build awareness of in better understanding non-verbal communication.

Training will improve the identification of expression and emotion in people. Along with readily available books, workplace training options are also a possibility. One example used in the workplace is provided by Skillsoft. They offer an online course which explores the recognition of non-verbal behaviors, facial expressions, body movements, and tone of voice (*Making Impact* 2020). Simply focusing on improving emotional perception of facial expressions can positively impact interactions. Nineteen emotions of the face have been identified, and these expressions can convey not only what the individual is feeling but help define the context surrounding the information being presented (Table 3.1) (Keltner and Cordaro, 2017; Keltner et al. 2019). Non-verbal expressions can provide insight into what the speaker may be asking the listener to do or what action they themselves plan to take (Keltner et al. 2019). One example of successfully increasing emotional perception comes from Germany. A web-based Emotional Intelligence Training program (WEIT) showed improvement in emotional perception in participants directly after training (Koppe, Held, and Schutz 2019). This program utilized four, one-hour modules of audio and video files along with interactive questions and quizzes delivered over four days and then a four-week online practice. Another successful training comes from Spain. Medical students used E-motion Training which was a group-facilitated training using online tutorials and games to improve recognition

*Table 3.1* 19 Emotions of the Face

| Amusement | Contentment | Disgust | Interest | Shame |
| --- | --- | --- | --- | --- |
| Anger | Coyness | Embarrassed | Pain | Surprise |
| Boredom | Desire (food) | Fear | Pride | Sympathy |
| Confusion | Desire (sex) | Happiness | Sadness | |

(Keltner and Cordaro 2017, 70)

of facial expressions. After a 45-minute training class, emotion recognition increased and empathetic abilities necessary for patient interactions were much improved, especially in students who were lacking in this area before training (Vázquez-Campo et al. 2019).

Beyond such traditional training methods, future learning may entail the use of AI. One example comes from an augmented reality training in the field of nursing in caring for dementia patients which showed positive change with nurses in areas of communication including non-verbal aspects. Humanitude AR Training System (HEARTS) focuses on improving face-to-face interactions, talking, and touch (Nakazawa et al. 2023). With virtual feedback the HEARTS artificial intelligence trains individuals to maintain eye contact longer, adjust tone and word choice, and correct touch patterns. While not directly related to the work environment, the future use of AI and robotics for improving non-verbal communication is found with social robot applications associated with autism therapy. Here KASPAR, a humanoid robot created by the Adaptive System Research Group at the University of Hertfordshire, was used to improve eye contact and understand facial expressions among other applications (Bouhali et al. 2023). These examples which illustrate training in the area of non-verbal communication can range from the traditional to the utilization of artificial intelligence.

The implementation of various training methods can improve emotion perception and non-verbal interactions in the workplace. The focus of other studies, such as emotion recognition training, may lead to new applications. Research in this area reflects reduced social aggression, improved student learning, or elevated empathy (Li, Li, and Kou 2023; Bouhlal et al. 2020). While new methods evolve, the understanding and identifying of various non-verbal expressions improves the verbal communication exchange and resulting interactions in the work environment.

## Cultural Influences

In addition to improved listening and emotion recognition, awareness of cultural influences on communication can also play an important role in work interactions. Cultural impacts play a growing role in the workplace as organizations become more culturally and demographically diverse. It is not unusual in today's interconnected world to work with individuals that have different upbringings, belief systems, or even countries of origin. Shared beliefs that impact communications come from three culture frameworks across the globe—dignity, honor, and face (box 3.3) (Maitner et al. 2022). As workplaces become increasingly diverse, often these cultural influences impact verbal communications and employee actions. A general understanding of these cultural differences and how they may influence how a coworker responds is important to maintaining positive work rapport.

**Box 3.3 Cultures by Country**

*Dignity*: Australia, Canada, Denmark, Finland, France, Germany, Netherlands, Norway, Switzerland, United Kingdom, United States, other North-Western European countries
*Honor*: Argentina, Brazil, Chile, India, Israel, Jordan, Mexico, Morocco, Pakistan, Peru, Poland, Portugal, Qatar, Russia, Spain, United Arab Emirates
*Face*: China, Indonesia, Japan, Korea, Malaysia, Singapore, and Vietnam

(Maitner et al. 2022)

Dignity cultures place an emphasis on personal achievement, sharing information, and group harmony. Those from dignity cultures are guided by their own internal standards. While application of rules is important, what these individuals say or do may differ depending on their internal guidelines (Leung and Cohen 2011). This can evolve into back-and-forth exchange between individuals as both have a sense of being right. Additionally, direct conflict resolution with cooperative negotiation is the preferred method for resolving disputes.

Individuals from honor cultures have a reputation to maintain. This is developed with positive actions that are acknowledged by the group. Along with this is the belief family and friends should be defended. However, the honor culture is double-edged, and the individual may be involved in negative exchanges to defend their reputation. Small slights may result in retaliation (Novin and Oyserman 2021). Applied to the workplace, this cultural belief with regard to defense could shift a minor verbal exchange into a heated argument. There is also potential for criticism of work triggering a strong worker response. Awareness of this cultural influence could help both coworkers and supervisors navigate these types of exchanges.

With face cultures self-worth is determined by what others think, and group harmony is important to maintenance of respectful interactions. When face cultures put an emphasis on group harmony this may result in group shaming, punishing, or ostracizing a group member who is disruptive (Frey et al. 2021). Face cultures also value individual humility and consider this to be important to the harmony of the group. A person's rank in the work hierarchy should also be respected. Typically, conflict is avoided as harmony is always the desired condition. However, an expectation of self-restraint and refraining from criticism is also a part of face cultures. This could potentially clash with other workers who tend to correct behavior or verbalize their critiques of other's work. If conflict does occur, resolution often tends to be more competitive (Leung and Cohen 2011).

There can also be other cultural influences with non-verbal aspects of communication. Research into facial expressions and culture has concluded that there are six universal emotions that are understood and expressed with all cultures—anger, disgust, fear, happiness, sadness, and surprise (Matsumoto and Hwang 2013). However, the degree to which these emotions are expressed through facial expressions differs. While there are exceptions, generally dignity cultures are the most expressive followed by honor and face. Researchers David Matsumoto, Seung Hee Yoo, and Johnny Fontaine (2008) found the highest four geographic cultures with facial expressions to be Zimbabwe, Canada, United States, and Australia with the lowest four ranking countries Russia, Bangladesh, Indonesia, and Hong Kong (Matsumoto, Yoo, and Fontaine 2008). In addition to facial expressions, there are other non-verbal indicators which vary with culture. Those cultures with higher facial expression tend to gesture more often, have a relaxed posture, and use direct eye contact (Matsumoto and Hwang 2013). Conversely, more reserved cultures may use fewer motions and may not look at a speaker directly. These cultures also touch less and may speak softer and slower than their expressive counterparts.

Understanding there may be cultural influences in the non-verbal aspects of an information exchange could explain misinterpretations. For example, a speaker might be offended by the lack of maintained eye contact but then recognize this was a normal behavior from an individual from a face culture. Raised voices in an exchange between individuals of a dignity culture may disturb someone from a less expressive culture as this volume of verbal exchange is outside the norm of expected behavior. However, if there is awareness of cultural differences, this exchange would be identified as normal aspects of communication. As with verbal communication, non-verbal cultural influences listed are generalizations as many individuals have adopted the culture of the region or country where they live and work.

## Navigating Disagreements

Part of navigating work conversations includes navigating disagreements. To some degree disagreements are a part of all work environments. These disputes are typically rooted in either relationship issues or work-related tasks. Relationship conflicts may be centered around personal viewpoints, opinions, values, or styles while work-related task conflicts deal more with processes, guidelines, or viewpoints of work events or procedures (De Dreu and Weingart 2003). If handled well, these types of conflicts can be managed and result in lower levels of incivility rather than escalating into more hostile or bullying interactions. Methods for handling these types of conversations include honest evaluation of information conveyed, disengaging from unproductive conversation patterns, and de-escalating emotions through counter arguments or questions.

An extension of active listening is to correctly determine the core of what a speaker is conveying, and this is vital when navigating disagreements. As mentioned, part of active listening is interpreting what the speaker says. However, it is important to correctly understand the meaning behind the words. As a conversation unfolds, asking questions to oneself can help. Is the information factual? Informative? Persuasive? What are the core facts or the main point of the conversation? How do you know this is right? Clarifying any points that are unclear can help the listener determine the core of the conversation in order to respond correctly. This type of honest evaluation of the message will negate any misunderstandings or inappropriate responses which may trigger a defensive or emotional reaction from the speaker.

Conversations may also result from a conflict with one's internal value system. These core values are often strongly defended and can lead to negative verbal exchanges. Katie Shonk, editor of Harvard's *Negotiation Briefings* newsletter and author, offers suggestions when responding to these types of value conflicts (Shonk 2023). Shonk suggests seeking out and highlighting an efficient solution which has advantages for both parties. Compromise can also be found when each party concedes one aspect of their own value system. Finally, Shonk offers that the most effective strategy in resolving value conflict is to identify and recognize positive qualities of the other individual. Similarly, Paul Santagata, Head of Industry at Google, suggests keeping the perspective of collaborator, not competitor, in mind (Delizonna 2017). He suggests a simple reminder that the other person in many ways is "just like me" (Delizonna 2017). Exploring commonalities and objectives rather than engaging in less thoughtful emotional disputes helps move past perceived violations of core beliefs.

Another way to handle disagreements is to recognize unwanted repetitive patterns (URP). In 1979, communication theorists Vernon E. Cronen, W. Barnett Pearce, and Lonna M. Snavely studied and identified undesired communication patterns or URPs (since referred to unwanted repetitive patterns) (Cronen, Pearce, and Snavely 1979). These are conversation patterns where two parties exchange words in a back-and-forth pattern without progressing towards resolution or a positive ending. Often these conversations occur more than once with similar statements and exchanges from each of the parties. The individuals can feel trapped in this conversation to nowhere and fail to focus on the key points of the message (Sostrin 2009). Recognizing the URP pattern is the first step to ending it. Next, one party disengaging from the looping pattern puts an end to it. Finally, altering the message to refocus the conversation or choosing a new conversational direction would bring the two individuals back to a discussion that is productive, not combative (Sostrin 2009).

A final way to navigate through difficult discussions is by de-escalating emotions. One method is asking follow-up questions of a speaker. This method does play a role in active listening. A secondary benefit is the reduction of emotion even if both parties disagree. A study by Francis S. Chen et. al. found that when listeners ask follow-up questions to learn more about the topic or viewpoint they are perceived positively as open minded, even though opinions may differ (Chen, Minson, and Tormala 2010). Additionally, both parties in the exchange will hold a favorable view of future exchanges and debates. Other research also indicates that when individuals ask questions it creates a positive effect in the speaker (Huang et al. 2017). In addition to probing questions, the opportunity to counterargue also can mitigate emotions. Individuals who have a chance to express their views can reduce the negative effect of the information (Zhao et al. 2020). Another study points to the importance of being receptive to information. If opposing opinions or viewpoints are heard and acknowledged with receptive language, the positive benefits include cooperation, reduced conflict, and openness to future interactions (box 3.4) (Yeomans et al. 2020, 132). Lastly, there is value in disengaging from an escalating conversation to give each party time to cool off from emotions and revisit the discussion at another time. When emotions run high and workers find themselves in the middle of a heated exchange, applying one or more of these emotion de-escalation methods can assist.

## Box 3.4 Receptive Language

- "Acknowledgement" of understanding
- "Positive emotional words"
- "Reasoning" statements
- Use of "I" statements
- Word "hedging" to soften facts

(Yeomans et al. 2020, 135, 140)

## Navigating the Passive Aggressive

People who become passive aggressive if conflict arises can also create uncivil verbal exchanges. The impact of passive aggressive individuals in the workplace was discussed in chapter one. As it relates to communication, characteristics of this type of worker may include "feelings of inadequacy and the need for acknowledgement" in addition to perceiving authority figures with contempt (Hopwood and Wright 2012). In Dr. Martin Kantor's book, *Passive-Aggression: Understanding the Sufferer, Helping the Victim*, individuals with passive-aggressive personalities (box 3.5) can be come defensive if they are blamed or corrected, and instead of using outright anger (because they wish to maintain the persona of being nice) may deny or argue their actions. Kantor also notes these exchanges lead the passive aggressive person to blame others or make excuses for their own actions. As a result, their behaviors in the workplace will reflect these feelings and trigger uncivil exchanges.

Given these dynamics of polite hostility, navigating these exchanges can be challenging but possible. One response that diminishes passive aggressive expressions is to express empathy, avoid direct confrontation, and utilize a softer approach to interactions (Kantor 2017). Another method is asking the aggressor how they would feel if on the receiving end of actions. Kantor offers other ideas including being suggestive, not demanding, letting minor issues run their course, avoiding giving advice, utilizing humor, and encouraging mutual respect in the workplace. Working with a passive aggressive person is possible, but it requires recognizing the characteristics and intentionally utilizing some of these neutralizing methods of interaction.

---

**Box 3.5 Types of Passive-Aggressives**

*Narcissistic Passive-Aggressive*: Goodness for others equates to goodness for self and individuals who are different are defective

*Obsessive-Compulsive Passive-Aggressive*: Less than total support equates to no support

*Depressive Passive-Aggressive*: Attacks others for criticisms perceived of their own self

(Kantor 2017, 96, 211–212)

---

## Navigating Hostile Interactions

One of the more challenging aspects of work conversations is handling negative interactions. Unlike disagreements, these interplays may involve rude comments, uncivil responses, or angry retorts which may be stand-alone events or occur with regularity. Even more challenging is for a worker to navigate bullying or mobbing situations. Sometimes these incidents involve personality issues, a clash of belief systems, or a difference in regional or organizational norms. While there is no easy solution to handling any of these types of exchanges, understanding what is available can be valuable to those under assault. With varying results, research indicates individuals choose to navigate these exchanges by either not engaging, minimizing the severity, directly confronting the instigator, or formally reporting the issue.

Avoiding the instigator's hostility is the response method most often chosen by victims of such incivility. Wanting to escape the stress and negativity associated with this demeanor as well as avoid stress over the idea of confronting the instigator, individuals often choose this passive option (Hershcovis, Cameron, and Bozeman 2018). Avoidance methods could come in the form of evading the perpetrator entirely, tuning out verbal attacks, internalizing emotions, or deflecting instigator outbursts with humor (West and Beck 2019). The target may also minimize the incident, get managerial assistance, or solicit help and emotional support from their social network (Lane 2017). While these are popular options, they are also the most ineffective response with these hostile interactions. However, one benefit of disengaging from negative exchanges is potentially limiting the spread of negative opinions or viewpoints. Otherwise, doing nothing does not improve the victim's situation.

A more assertive approach is another option available. This may come as an immediate reaction from some workers or after avoidance has failed leaving no other option. Taking action against a perpetrator gives the target the opportunity to express their side rather than internalizing their victimization. One way to do this is with the DESC technique. DESC is an acronym which means describe, express, suggest, and consequence (*Tool* 2023). The target first describes the uncivil incident and expresses how it made them feel. The use of "I" statements is the best approach for this part of the conversation. This is followed by suggestions for change, improvements, or reconciliation between the two parties. Finally, the positive results or consequences of following a suggestion or finding a mutually agreeable way to move forward are presented. This approach avoids blaming the perpetrator and should be delivered in a civil but firm tone.

Another approach to an assertive response is a seven-step method with the acronym ASERTIV. ASERTIV equates to attention, situation, emotion, reaction, test, involvement, and valorization (Pipas and Jaradat 2010). First, gain the attention of the perpetrator in a way that encourages them to listen rather than immediately become defensive. Then, describe the situation or incident that is of concern and explain the emotion felt as well as the resulting reaction. Test the perpetrators' concern by asking their opinion or for input or what could be changed. In response, this leads to involvement by both parties and a shift towards resolution. Finally, thanking the individual and expressing the value of a positive relationship with them is the ASERTIV last step.

Unfortunately, there is a downside to taking assertive action against an uncivil coworker. First, others in the workplace who observe or hear of the incident may deem the action outside the acceptable workplace behavioral norms, and, as a result, the victim may actually be ostracized by their peers (Cortina and Magley 2003). Another dynamic to consider comes with rank. Assertive communication aimed at an abusive supervisor could result in the worker facing disciplinary actions, receiving a formal write-up, or being issued negative performance evaluations. Finally, studies indicate retaliation and escalation of the negative interactions between individuals could result once a perpetrator is confronted (Hershcovis, Cameron, and Bozeman 2018). Often, speaking up starts a path towards dismissal or the employee leaving the organization. For those choosing the assertive option, awareness of the possible outcomes should be weighed along with the organization's support (or lack of support) for workplace incivility.

Officially reporting an uncivil incident or repeated occurrences is another option for targeted individuals. This is typically the least utilized option behind avoidance and confrontation. Only 10% of respondents to the *Civility in America 2019* survey filed a formal complaint (Weber Shandwick 2019). Some individuals may not report out of fear of perpetrator retaliation, or they feel the level of incivility is not high enough for a formal complaint (Hershcovis, Cameron, and Bozeman 2018). Additionally, the organizational response to such incidents is another reason for non-reporting. *The 2021 Workplace Bullying Survey* found a positive organizational response 37% of the time and action taken in only 24% of the cases (Namie 2021). More often, the study indicates organizations defend, deny, rationalize, or even encourage workplace bullying, and it is the bullied targets, not perpetrators, who either quit, transfer, or are terminated 67% of the time. Those organizations who ignore aspects of social relationships of their workers and embrace an unfeeling, competitive climate are ripe for incivility and bullying (Cortina, Hershcovis, and Clancy 2022). Human resource departments, and even some unions, tend to take the side of the organization in reported cases setting the precedent that discourages incivility reporting moving forward. All of these factors combined result in both limited reporting and negative responses to those who do report incidents. Before officially reporting such negative events, workers should evaluate their organization's stance and the possible outcomes of such action.

## Conclusion

Improving in-person communication begins with the understanding of the verbal communication cycle. Impacting this are a variety of elements which may alter the intended message. Among those are external or self-allowed distractions along with the receiver's interpretation of the message which may distort the verbal communication. Enhancing this exchange includes an understanding of how to improve listening and utilizing follow-up questions. Identifying non-verbal attributes of both listener and speaker adds to message feedback and engagement of both parties. Understanding cultural influences that may play a role in misunderstandings during conversations is also helpful. Finally, resolution can be found by utilizing methods for navigating difficult to hostile verbal exchanges from navigating conversation patterns to methods for recognizing and de-escalating emotion to more assertive responses. Understanding both the elements of the conversational exchange as well as the options for responding to uncivil communications can shift negative encounters at work towards positive interactions.

## Suggested Reads

Cava, Robert. *Interpersonal Communication at Work: How to Communicate with Customers, Bosses, Colleagues and Subordinates*. Queensland, Australia: Cava Consulting, 2019.

Sorenson, Michael. *I Hear You*. Saratago Springs, UT: Autumn Creek Press, 2017.

Younger, Heather R. *The Art of Active Listening: How People at Work Feel Heard, Valued, and Understood*. Oakland, CA: Berrett-Koeler Publishers Inc., 2023.

## References

Bonaccio, Silvia, Jane O'Reilly, Sharon L. O'Sullivan, and Francois Chiocchio. "Nonverbal Behavior and Communication in the Workplace: A Review and an Agenda for Research." *Journal of Management* 42, no. 5 (2016): 1044–1074. doi:10.1177/0149206315621146.

Bouhlal, Meriem, Kawtar Aarika, Rachida Ait Abdelouahid, Sanna Elfilali, and El Habib Benlahmar. "Emotions Recognition as Innovative Tool for Improving Students' Performance and Learning Approaches." *Procedia Computer Science* 175 (2020): 597–602. doi:10.1016/j.procs.2020.07.086.

Bouhali, Rayane, Haniah Al-Tabaa, Sarah Abdelfattah, Manar Atiyeh, Seyed Esmaeili, and Hanan Al-Tabbakh. "Otisma: An Integrated Application and Humanoid Robot as an Educational Tool for Children with Autism." *Journal of Medical Engineering & Technology* 47, no. 1 (2023), 44–53. doi:10.1080/03091902.2022.2097327.

Brownell, Judi. *Listening: Attitudes, Principles, and Skills*. Milton: Taylor & Francis Group, 2017. ProQuest eBook Central. Accessed December 30, 2023. https://ebookcentral.proquest.com/lib/hgtc/reader.action?docID=5056461&ppg=115.

Chan, Grace, Allison Burquist, Hannah Dodge, and Madison Tanner. "Trader Joe's Unlawfully Fired Employees After Employee Raised Concerns About COVID-19 Policies." *Private Education Matters*, September2024: 11–12. https://issuu.com/lcwlegal/docs/pem_september_2024.

Chen, Frances S., Julia A. Minson, and Zakary L. Tormala. "Tell Me More: The Effects of Expressed Interest on Receptiveness During Dialog." *Journal of Experimental Social Psychology* 46 (2010): 850–853. doi:10.1016/j.jesp.2010.04.012.

Clapp, Wesley C., Michael T.Rubens, and Adam Gazzaley. "Mechanisms of Working Memory Disruption by External Interference." *Cerebral Cortex* 20, no. 4 (April2010): 859–872. doi:10.1093/cercor/bhp150.

Cortina, Lilia M., M. Sandy Hershcovis, and Kathryn B. H. Clancy. "The Embodiment of Insult: A Theory of Biobehavioral Response to Workplace Incivility." *Journal of Management* 48, no. 3 (2022). doi:10.1177/0149206321989798.

Cortina, Lillia M. and Vicki J. Magley, "Raising Voice, Risking Retaliation: Events Following Interpersonal Mistreatment in the Workplace." *Journal of Occupational Health Psychology* 8, no. 4 (2003): 247–265. doi:10.1037/1076-8998.8.4.247.

Cronen, Vernon E., W. Barnett Pearce, and Lonna M. Snavely. "A Theory of Rule-Structure and Types of Episodes and a Study of Perceived Enmeshment in Undesired Repetitive Patterns ('URPS')." *Annals of the International Communication Association* 3, no. 1 (1979). doi:10.1080/23808985.1979.11923763.

De Dreu, Carsten K. W. and Laurie R. Weingart. "Task Versus Relationship Conflict, Team Performance, and Team Member Satisfaction: A Meta-Analysis." *Journal of Applied Psychology* 88 no. 4 (2003): 741–749. doi:10.1037/0021-9010.88.4.741.

Delizonna, Laura. "High-Performing Teams Need Psychological Safety. Here's How to Create It." *Harvard Business Review*. August 24, 2017. https://hbr.org/2017/08/high-performing-teams-need-psychological-safety-heres-how-to-create-it.

Foulger, David. "Models of Communication Process." February 25, 2004. Accessed January 15, 2024. https://davis.foulger.info/research/unifiedModelOfCommunication.htm.

Frey, Karen S., Adaurennaya C. Onyewuenyi, Shelley Hymel, Randip Gill, and Cynthia R. Pearson. "Honor, Face, and Dignity Norm Endorsement Among Diverse North American Adolescents: Development of a Social Norms Survey." *International Journal of Behavioral Development* 45, no. 3 (2021): 256–268. doi:10.1177/01650254209496.

Goleman, Benedict. *Dark Psychology 6 Books in 1*. Brentford, UK: Carpe Diem 3.0 Ltd., 2020.

Henry, Jo, Joe Eshleman, and Richard Moniz. *Cultivating Civility: Practical Ways to Improve a Dysfunctional Library*. Chicago, IL: ALA Editions, 2020.

Hershcovis, M. Sandy, Ann Frances Cameron, and Jennifer Bozeman. "The Effects of Confrontation and Avoidance Coping in Response to Workplace Incivility." *Journal of Occupational Health Psychology* 23, no. 2 (2018): 163–174. doi:10.1037/ocp0000078.

Hopwood, Christopher J. and Aidan C. J. Wright. "A Comparison of Passive Aggressive and Negativistic Personality Disorders." *Journal of Personality Assessment* 94, no. 3 (2012): 296–303. doi:10.1080/00223891.2012.655819.

Huang, Karen, Michael Yeomans, Alison Wood Brooks, Julia Minson, and Francesca Gino. "It Doesn't Hurt to Ask: Question-Asking Increases Liking." *Journal of Personality and Social Psychology* 113, no. 3 (September2017): 430–452. https://psycnet.apa.org/doi/10.1037/pspi0000097.

Jonsdottir, Inga Jona and Kari Kristinsson. "Supervisors' Active-Empathetic Listening as an Important Antecedent of Work Engagement." *International Journal of Environmental Research and Public Health* 17, no. 21 (2020). doi:10.3390/ijerph17217976.

Kantor, Martin. *Passive-Aggression: Understanding the Sufferer, Helping the Victim*, 2nd edition. Santa Barbara, California: Praeger, 2017.

Keltner, David and Daniel T. Cordaro. "Understanding Multimodal Emotional Expressions: Recent Advances in Basic Emotion Theory." In *The Science of*

*Facial Expression*, J.-M. Fernández-Dols and J. A. Russell, eds.. Oxford, UK: Oxford University Press, 2017.

Keltner, Dacher, Disa Sauter, Jessica Tracy, and Alan Cowen. "Emotional Expression: Advances in Basic Emotion Theory." *Journal of Nonverbal Behavior* 43, no. 2 (2019):133–160. doi:10.1007/s10919-019-00293-3.

Knippen, Jay T. and Thad B. Green. "How the Manager Can Use Active Listening." *Public Personnel Management*, Summer (1994): 357–359. Gale Academic OneFile. Accessed December 30, 2023. https://link.gale.com/apps/doc/A15592851/AONE?u=horrygtc&sid=bookmark-AONE&xid=b5b25c71.

Koppe, Christina, Marco Jurgen Held, and Astrid Schutz. "Improving Emotion Perception and Emotion Regulation Through a Web-Based Emotional Intelligence Training (WEIT) Program for Future Leaders." *International Journal of Emotional Education* 11, no. 2 (2019): 17–32. Accessed January 11, 2024. https://files.eric.ed.gov/fulltext/EJ1236233.pdf.

Kriz, Tiffany D., Avraham N. Kluger, and Christopher J. Lyddy. "Feeling Heard: Experiences of Listening (or Not) at Work." *Frontiers in Psychology*, 12 (2021): 659087. doi:10.3389/fpsyg.2021.659087.

Lane, Shelley D. *Understanding Everyday Incivility: Why Are They So Rude?* New York: Roman & Littlefield, 2017.

Leung, Angela Ka-yee and Dov Cohen. "Within- and Between-Culture Variation: Individual Differences and the Cultural Logics of Honor, Face, and Dignity Cultures." *Journal of Personality and Social Psychology* 100, no. 3 (2011): 507–526. doi:10.1037/a0022151.

Li, Fangmin, Xue Li, and Hui Kou. "Emotional Recognition Training Enhances Attention to Emotional Stimuli Among Male Juvenile Delinquents." *Psychology Research and Behavior Management* 16(2023): 575–586. doi:10.2147/PRBM.S403512.

Maitner, Angela T., Jamie DeCoster, Per A. Andersson, Kimmo Eriksson, Sara Sherbaji, Roger Giner-Sorolla, Diane M. Mackie, Mark Aveyard, Heather M. Claypool, Richard J. Crisp, Vladimir Gritskov, Kristina Habjan, Andree Hartanto, Toko Kiyonari, Anna O. Kuzminska, Zoi Manesi, Catherine Molho, Anudhi Munasinghe, Leonard S. Peperkoorn, Victor Shiramizu, Rachel Smallman, Natalia Soboleva, Adam W. Stivers, Amy Summerville, Baopei Wu, and Junhui Wu. "Perceptions of Emotional Functionality: Similarities and Differences Among Dignity, Face, and Honor Cultures." *Journal of Cross-Cultural Psychology* 53, no. 3–4 (2022): 263–288. doi:10.1177/00220221211065108.

*Making Impact with Non-Verbal Communication*. Skillsoft. April 23, 2020. https://skillsoft.digitalbadges.skillsoft.com/30aeee96-ed3c-42a8-a7b7-5ec77468099c#acc.4iuGpExP.

Matsumoto, David and Hyi Sung Hwang. "Cultural Influences on Nonverbal Behavior." In *Nonverbal Communication: Science and Applications*, D. Matsumoto, M. G. Frank, and H. S. Hwang, eds. Thousand Oaks, CA: Sage Publications, Inc., 2013. doi:10.4135/9781452244037.n5.

Matsumoto, David, Seung Hee Yoo, and Johnny Fontaine. "Mapping Expressive Differences Around the World: The Relationship Between Emotional Display Rules and Individualism Verses Collectivism." *Journal of Cross-Cultural Psychology* 39, no. 1 (2008). doi:10.1177/002202210731185.

Murphy, Dillon H., Kara M.Hoover, Karina Agadzhanyan, Jesse C. Kuehn, and Alan D.Castel. "Learning in Double Time: The Effect of Lecture Video Speed on Immediate and Delayed Comprehension." *Applied Cognitive Psychology* 36, no. 1 (2022): 69–82. doi:10.1002/acp.3899.

Nakazawa, Atsushi, Miyuki Iwamoto, Ryo Kurazume, Masato Nunoi, Masaki Kobayashi, and Miwako Honda. "Augmented Reality-Based Affective Training for Improving Care Communication Skill and Empathy." *PLoS ONE* 18, no. 7 (2023): e0288175. Gale Academic OneFile. Accessed January 7, 2024. https://link.gale.com/apps/doc/A756683249/AONE?u=horrygtc&sid=bookmark-AONE&xid=98af234c.

Namie, Gary. *2021 WBI US Workplace Bullying Survey*. Workplace Bullying Institute (2021). Accessed January 21, 2024. https://workplacebullying.org/wp-content/uploads/2023/06/2021-Full-Report.pdf.

Novin, Sheida and Daphna Oyserman. "Honor as Cultural Mindset: Activated Honor Mindset Affects Subsequent Judgment and Attention in Mindset-Congruent Ways." *Frontiers of Psychology* 7 (2021): 1921. doi:10.3389/fpsyg.2016.01921.

Pipas, Maria Daniela and Mohammad Jaradat. "Assertive Communication Skills." *Annales Universitatis Apulensis Series Oeconomica* 12, no. 2 (2010). doi:10.29302/oeconomica.2010.12.2.17.

Rosner, Rachael I. "Rogers, Carl Ransom." In *Complete Dictionary of Scientific Biography*, 274–280, vol. 24v. Detroit, MI: Charles Scribner's Sons, 2008. Gale eBooks. Accessed December 30, 2023. https://link.gale.com/apps/doc/CX2830906054/GVRL?u=horrygtc&sid=bookmark-GVRL&xid=57e17a84.

Shonk, Katie. "Conflict Management Styles: Pitfalls and Best Practices." Harvard Law School Daily Blog. August 17, 2023. https://www.pon.harvard.edu/daily/conflict-resolution/conflict-management-styles-pitfalls-and-best-practices/.

Sostrin, Jesse. "Get Rid of Your URPs." *Breaking Barriers* [blog], November 23, 2009. https://jessesostrin.blogspot.com/.

Steinemann, John H. and Orvin A. Larson. "Investigation of Rate-Controlled Speech for Training Applications." Navy Personnel Research and Development Center. October1973. https://apps.dtic.mil/sti/tr/pdf/AD0769689.pdf.

*Tool: DESC*. Agency for Healthcare Research and Quality. Last updated July 2023. https://www.ahrq.gov/teamstepps-program/curriculum/mutual/tools/desc.html.

Vázquez-Campo, Miriam, Leticia Vidal, Angela Juana Torres, Raimundo Mateos, Jose Manuel Olivares, Isabel García-Lado, and Alejandro Alberto García-Caballero. "Facial Emotion Perception Training for Medical Students." *Creative Education* 10, no. 8 (2019). doi:10.4236/ce.2019.108128.

Watson, James and Anne Hill. "Barnlund's Transactional Models of Communication, 1970." In *Dictionary of Media and Communication Studies*, Bloomsbury, 2015. Accessed January 15, 2024. https://search.credoreference.com/articles/Qm9va0FydGGljbGU6Mzk0OTA2MQ==?aid=96519.

Weber Shandwick. *Civility in America*, 2019. https://cms.webershandwick.com/wp-content/uploads/2023/01/CivilityInAmerica2019SolutionsforTomorrow.pdf.

West, Richard and Christina S. Beck, eds. *The Routledge Handbook of Communication and Bullying*. New York: Routledge, 2019.

Yeomans, Michael, Julia Minson, Hanne Collins, Frances Chen, and Francesca Gino. "Conversational Receptiveness: Improving Engagement with Opposing

Views." *Organizational Behavior and Human Decision Processes* 160 (2020): 131–148. doi:10.1016/j.obhdp.2020.03.011.

Zhao, Xuan, Taya R. Cohen, Charles A. Dorison, Juliana Schroeder, Michael Yeomans, Xuan Zhao, Heather M. Caruso, Julia Alexandra Minson, and Jane Risen. "The Art and Science of Disagreeing: How to Create More Effective Conversations About Opposing Views." *Proceedings*, 2020. doi:10.5465/AMBPP.2020.15153symposium.

# Chapter 4

# Promoting Cyber Civility

Communicating and connecting remotely with other workers has become standard practice in the work environment and accomplished through a variety of formats from email to social media to video conferencing. Email communication rose from its early governmental use in the 1960s to widespread messaging, including its use in most workplaces, in the following two decades (Kleinrock 2010). Social media brought another method of sharing online information to the workplace. With the creation of LISTSERVs in 1986, companies began connecting individuals and sharing specific information (Burns 2017). As platforms grew in the 2000s, organizations embraced a variety of software messaging programs. Along with this, individuals established personal accounts and created their own online presence including work-related LinkedIn, X (formerly Twitter), and tumbleblogs (Burns 2017). Modern video conferencing evolved from the first video call system in 1964, the AT&T Picturephone, to video phones of the 1980s before the first camera and computer monitor were combined to observe a break room coffee pot at the University of Cambridge (Kesby 2012; Spaulding 2021). After connecting this feed to the world wide web, the staff gave birth to the video conferencing services used in workplaces today (Uenuma 2020). Along with these evolving forms of cyber communication, the future of work and technology may include the use of virtual reality, augmented reality, and other AI-based tools. Regardless of method, virtual communications are now firmly rooted in the workplace.

Along with this evolution of technology, the means of conducting rude and uncivil work behaviors has pushed past the boundaries of in-person occurrences into the cyber world. General cyber incivility had grown from 9% in 2011 to 25% in 2016 according to the Civility in America studies by Weber Shandwick (*Civility in America* 2017). Online interactions also increased with the expansion of remote work, broadening opportunities for cyber incivility. From only 9.5% of employees working at least one day from home in 2010, the numbers grew to 17.9% working primarily at home in 2021 (Mateyka, Rapino, and Landivar 2012; "The Number of People" 2022). Pew Research also found a high number of workers in remote

DOI: 10.4324/9781003590149-4

settings with 35% working from home and another 41% working some days from home in a 2023 survey. This increase in virtual connectivity allows for uncivil actions through online methods—emails, direct messaging, social media, or web meetings.

Examples of cyber incivility are often in the news. One such incident occurred in 2021 at Netflix. Three senior executives were fired for sharing negative comments about leadership on Slack, an internal messaging software (Sonnemaker and Reuter 2021). According to Netflix co-CEO Ted Sarandos, the managers made "critical, personal comments … over several months" about their supervisors which led to their dismissal (Smith 2021). Another example comes from Amazon which utilized artificial intelligence (AI) to manage workers. Amazon algorithms and tracking systems monitored work output, firing those who fell short, and its text-to-speech software reporting system was used to sabotage workers (Mulugeta 2022). These examples illustrate news-worthy cyber incivility from large companies. Yet, disparaging and negative online behavior can occur at any level and any size organization.

The specific definition of cyber incivility has varied through the years. It was identified in 2000 by Christine M. Pearson, Lynne M. Andersson, and Christine L. Porath who highlighted its potential for enabling quick, asynchronous means of mistreating or undermining colleagues (Pearson, Andersson, and Porath 2000). In 2009, researchers Vivan K. G. Lim and Thompson S. H. Teo defined cyber incivility as "communicative behavior exhibited in computer-mediated interactions that violate workplace norms of mutual respect" (Lim and Teo 2009). Most researchers who have since conducted studies on cyber incivility include aspects of repetition (or existence online over time), intent to do harm, and aggressive messaging in their definitions. Characteristics of such messaging may convey disapproval, hostility, blame, or disregard (Torres, Morman, and Mistry 2024). Other defined elements have included anonymity, victim perception, norm violation, and power imbalance relating to technical knowledge (Vanderbosch and Van Cleemput 2009). As mentioned in chapter one, cyberbullying is a specific method of cyber incivility where one individual is targeted (Table 4.1). It too is characterised by anonymity and aggressive messaging

Table 4.1  Direct and indirect methods of cyberbullying

| Direct Cyberbullying | Indirect Cyberbullying |
| --- | --- |
| Sharing an infected file | Sharing entrusted information |
| Internet used for a verbal threat | Posting or messaging from a false identity |
| Internet used for a non-verbal threat | Gossiping about others |
| Excluding someone from online communication | Engaging in defamatory online posts |

(Vanderbosch and Van Cleemput 2009, 1352)

with the potential of delivery from a wide range of electronic forms. Combining the main aspects from this research, cyber incivility can be defined as an intent to impart harm through electronic means and may include elements of repetition, anonymity, and power imbalance. It is with increased understanding of these processes, along with methods for improving online communications, that this form of behavior can be minimized.

## Behavioral Dynamics

Behavioral dynamics of the workplace influence both in-person and online interactions. The impact of a co-worker's actions and words, whether delivered in-person or electronically, can alter behavior. The study of such group influence began with theorists in social learning who have been researching how individuals' behaviors are affected by their environment since the 1950s. One theorist in particular, Albert Bandura, conducted experiments concerned with the effects of negative behaviors. Bandura's Bobo doll experiment in 1961, where children imitated adult aggression after witnessing abuse of an inflatable clown, demonstrated the influence of learned, negative behaviors (Peters, Killcoyne, and Zumbusch 2015). He labeled this relationship between an individual, behavior, and their environment as "reciprocal determinism" (Longe 2016). Hostile or aggressive behavior can result in more of the same. For work environments this means deviant behavior, including in online meetings or electronic communications, can set the tone that these negative actions are acceptable.

To shift away from rude, disrespectful, or hostile actions to those that are more civil, the role of organizational norms becomes important. Norms in an organization are those unwritten rules of behavior which determine what behavior is acceptable. Social norms of the work environment help define how employees behave. To what degree is civility or incivility allowed in the workplace? These norms can be divided into subjective, injunctive, or descriptive. Subjective normative behaviors are rooted in the beliefs formed from actions of others who are "perceived as being important to us" and the degree of "value" given to behaving similarly ("Social Cognitive Models 2008). How do managers and leaders behave? How do mentors or long-time employees act? How will behaving similarly be beneficial? Next, injunctive norms involve the "value judgment ... [of] proper and improper behavior" as defined by others (Longe 2016). What do co-workers think of rude behaviors? How are norm violations handled by the working group? Lastly, descriptive norms are defined by what "the majority of people do" and they often define conformity to the social norms of the organization (Longe 2016). Do the employees treat each other with respect? Are they courteous? Do they share ideas and information? These types of norms define attitudes, respect, and behaviors amongst workers.

Organizational norms extend to online communications in the workplace. Are email exchanges civil or does the organization allow disrespectful or even bullying language without consequence? Often organizations use other types of software for internal communications which can become a means for negative communications. This was illustrated by the incident at Netflix with negative, internal communications through Slack. Social media, both company-based and individual accounts, have become another host for uncivil communication exchanges. Additionally, online meetings can turn toxic with verbal exchanges. Specific methods for improving in these areas will be reviewed in this chapter.

Another aspect of behavioral dynamics which impacts online communications is deindividuation. The concept of deindividuation was first recognized by Gustave le Bon in 1895 and was defined as a loss of "normal constraints" when being in a crowd (Gackenbach 2006). Since that time, other researchers have expanded the definition of deindividuation. Steven Prentice Dunn and Ronald W. Rogers suggested the influence of reduced accountability (from being one of the group) along with a decrease in private self-awareness of their personal thoughts, attitudes, and values. Through the years, numerous researchers have tied aggression to deindividuation which brings this concept into the dynamics of workplace civility discussion (Vilanova et al. 2017). Generally, deindividuation is the loss of one's sense of individuality and behaviors can result which are not grounded in their set of internal values or standards. As a result, impulsive and often negative actions may occur.

Those studying the influence of online dynamics have found several factors that lead to deindividuation. One perspective is that the lack of social cues with electronic communications may lead to an emotional disconnect from the real person on the receiving end of messages. This may result in messages that are perceived as negative, harsh, or offensive. Other researchers take the position that the lower public self-awareness or lack of concern for how others perceive the communication may contribute to deindividuation (Gackenbach 2006). Consider someone thoughtlessly posting or responding to a social media post which may harm the intended victim. The lack of social self-awareness makes this easier to do when compared to saying something directly to the individual. A third factor is asynchronous messaging where negative communications can be sent without immediately dealing with a response (Gackenbach 2006). All of these factors could lead to a disregard of others and aggressive online communications.

Combating the impacts of deindividuation online can occur in several ways. First, simply understanding the concept and how it manifests can increase awareness and lead to a re-evaluation of methods of online communications. Second, individuals then can step back from their online communications and evaluate messages and posts for their impact and empathy. For example, pausing before sending to reread an email from the perspective of the receiver or creating an email draft and returning to its semantics after a period of time for a fresh perspective. Along with this comes the recognition of emotional polarization or positive identification with their perceived group and negative perceptions of other groups (Fischer and Lelkes 2023). More positive emotions are associated with work groups or departments an individual is a part of or closely associated with as opposed to those that are unfamiliar. As an example, consider divisions within an organization where one group may be in favor of a new idea or concept, but another division opposed. This difference in opinion has the potential to lead to negative online communications from a member of one faction to the other. Third, raising one's conscious attention, and in turn self-awareness, reconnects individuals with their internal, moral standards and mitigates negative online interactions (Greenber and Musham 1981). (Methods for improving oneself were discussed in chapter two.) A final way to minimize deindividuation is for supervisors and organizations to hold individuals accountable for their electronic communications. This involves curbing such actions with "reproach and punishment" (Dill and Darwall 2014). The department or division and organization as a whole must define, both in writing and through organizational norms, the expectations of civil communications. Overall, understanding that deindividuation may lead to negative online interactions but can be mitigated through self-improvement, increased self-awareness, and organizational standards, leads to improved online interactions.

Disinhibition is another aspect of behavioral dynamics that can lead to negative, online behaviors. *The American Heritage Dictionary of Medicine* defines this concept as "unrestrained behavior resulting from a lessening or loss of inhibitions or disregard of cultural constraints" (Editors 2015). Online, this may involve conveying uncivil or toxic messaging through electronic means or during online meetings because of a lack of self-control. As cyber related disinhibition has also been linked to loneliness, work from home settings can contribute to a disconnect between the real self and one's online presence (Mueller-Coyne, Voss, and Turner 2022). This in turn can lead to negative forms of disinhibition displayed through online work communications.

Again, a further means of minimizing the possibility of initiating or contributing to this aspect of behavioral dynamics comes from understanding its causes. Psychologist John Suler has identified six causes for online disinhibition. The first cause is the perception that their online persona is not their real self because of the ability to comment in some online formats without one's true identity being revealed (Suler 2004). As a result, an individual sender may put forth a communication or comment that is hostile but validate it by believing their online presence is fictitious. While much research points to the impact of such anonymity, other studies have shown it does not necessarily have to be a factor for flaming or hostile messaging to result (Lapidot-Lefler and Barak 2012). A second contributor to disinhibition is the invisibility of the receiver of an online message. There is no eye contact nor immediate feedback of facial expressions or emotions felt by those on the other end of communications. This may embolden someone to be more aggressive in messaging and is often found in social media posts. The third contributor to disinhibition involves asynchronous messaging. Because there is no real-time exchange of ideas which may shape thoughts, Suler writes that the messages are interpreted "using one's own voice" in their head creating a mental dialog (Suler 2004, 323). Fourth, individuals experience what Suler terms dissociative imagination. This involves the belief their online persona is not real but make-believe lacking "demands and responsibilities of the real world" (Suler 2004, 323). Conversely, the fifth cause involves the merging of online personas of self and others in the mind to become an "intrapsychic world" where written exchanges can extend into imagined interactions (Suler 2004, 323). Because this takes place in the mind, individuals feel safe in thinking of exchanges which otherwise may be unethical or harmful. Lastly, Suler points out the influence of power equalization and personality as contributors to online disinhibition. The online environment can eliminate the power structures found in organizations, equalize the opportunity in exchanges, and reduce inhibitions. (Suler 2004).

Another way to counter disinhibition is increased self-control. Organizations that engage in netiquette training is one way to help in this area. Areas of self-control should focus on proper online communication methods, identification and recognition of improper communication, and increasing purposeful intent to communicate properly (Voggeser, Singh, and Göritz 2018). Additionally, both perceiving and processing internal and external cues alerts individuals to inappropriate online communicative behavior which, in turn, leads to modifying negative actions (Voggeser, Singh, and Göritz 2018). Social cues online might include emoticons or text emphasis (bold, italics, or capitalization), language, message length, or conveyed reactions (Voggeser, Singh, and Göritz 2018). (Additional netiquette tips are found in the email section to follow.) Understanding the emotion, impact, and cognitive process behind messaging helps define appropriate from inappropriate responses. This, along with netiquette training, can diminish online disinhibition through improving self-control.

One last aspect of behavioral dynamics involves emotional contagion. While the topic of emotional contagion is widely researched and somewhat complex, for simplicity this text will focus on its definition and application to online communication impacting work environments. Emotional contagion is defined as a type of behavior where individuals exposed to other's emotions display similar emotions (Wróbel et al. 2021). Emotional contagion impacts work in organizations by influencing employees' moods and emotions either in-person or virtually. Additionally, these positive or negative emotions may "influence attitudinal, cognitive, and behavioral outcomes" such as increased cooperation and effort (Barsade, Coutifaris, and Pillemer 2018, 137). Studies also indicate that emotional contagion occurs more often when the initial emotion comes from a trusted friend, associate, or other individual and can be a conscious or unconscious response (Barsade, Coutifaris, and Pillemer 2018). When applied to online communication, this involves a reflection of emotions expressed online by another individual. Negative emotions may lead to negative word choice in correspondence. However, emotional contagion works both ways. Displaying positive emotions and selecting positive phrasing or words will have a beneficial impact on those in the workplace. Understanding emotional contagion and making conscious, positive choices in communications can improve the work environment.

## Email Communications

The first email was officially sent by Ray Tomlinson in 1971, and by the end of the decade and into the 1980s, the use of email exploded with the creation of the IBM personal computer and Apple Macintosh (Kleinrock 2010). Companies and employees quickly embraced the new technology and means of communication. Along with this explosion of email for work communication, a new environment was available to host incivility or even cyberbullying tactics.

Email issues initially arose from varying degrees of formality, limited oversight of messaging, interpretation of information received, and differences in reading speeds and comprehension (Ruth 2008). As with other forms of online incivility, recent studies point to issues with deindividuation, disinhibition, and message perception. With email the sender can disconnect from the human emotions of the receiver, and this may lead to an escalation of negative exchanges through a virtual back and forth (Ruth 2008). Emails may lack emotional cues, and as a result be perceived as neutral or negative in tone leading to a communication breakdown (Bryon 2008). In more toxic instances such as cyberbullying, elements of frequency (of malicious emails) and a power imbalance (such as a supervisor to subordinate) are contributors to email issues.

To minimize email issues, managing email perception through netiquette is a helpful approach. A common form of incivility or dysfunction in organizations can be found when an employee's emails or messages are simply ignored. Thus, merely responding in a timely fashion to email messages is important. Additionally, the use of netiquette in employee emails has a positive impact in messaging. Information delivered this way is more likely to be understood and creates a positive impression of the sender. Emails with a negative message, if crafted correctly, are more likely to be correctly interpreted (Bartl 2017). Netiquette rules for email include having a clear subject line, personalized salutation, concise and clear body of content, and appropriate closing signature (Bartl 2017, 36). While at times informal email exchanges may take place in organizations, it is still good practice to maintain a professional tone. Maintain a focused message and refrain from derogatory comments or targeted language crafted in second person ("you") (Zhong et al. 2022). At the receiving end, timely responses should be the norm.

Larger organizations can also play a role in minimizing uncivil email correspondence in the workplace. First, leadership can provide guidance for expectations of formal, outfacing email communications as well as internal correspondence (Ruth 2008). This can be done in the form of written guidelines or even formal training. Part of the organization's guidelines may include defining what constitutes a formal email as compared to an informal response between employees. They can also set up a method for reporting emails that break the boundaries of civility to a human resources department or other mediation group (Ruth 2008). Finally, certainty of detection will reduce email cyberbullying (Choi 2018). Organizations can utilize text analysis software to identify instances of toxic language with natural language processing and emotion detection within staff emails to minimize its occurrence.

There are yet other methods for employees to minimize uncivil emails. One way is to reduce multitasking while handling emails. A recent study found that when this occurs, workers experience an increase in stress, display negative emotions, and are more likely to express antisocial behaviors (Blank et al. 2020). Another method is to reduce proactive email checking and set boundaries for email responses (box 4.1) (Ruth 2008). Reading emails when they arrive leads to impulsive responses and cyberbullying tendencies (Zang et al. 2021). Third, improving emotional control when reacting to messages is also important. Being aware of emotional triggers and refraining from immediate responses is important. Lastly, limiting responses to email from mobile devices also reduces incivility as responses from these devices have been shown to have higher degrees of cyberbullying (Zang et al. 2021).

## Box 4.1 Email Management Tips

- Consider alternative methods for group communications
- Create pre-set standard responses for common questions/issues
- Prioritize emails for immediate verses lengthy responses
- Set specific blocked times for email responses

(Ruth 2008, 129)

## Video Conferencing

Improper workplace behavior also takes place during online meetings. As chapter one presented, rude behavior and even cyberbullying can take place in this cyber format. Many forms of such conduct are similar to in-person behavior such as interrupting the speaker, offensive or condescending remarks, inappropriate language, arguing or yelling, or conveying threats. Other actions, while present during in-person exchanges, can be applied more easily online. These include displaying negative facial expressions, questioning judgment, or turning cameras off to hide or multitask. Also, participation has the potential to be controlled by the online meeting leader who may ignore raised online hands or even mute participants.

Improving online meetings directly starts with the meeting leader. As the individual with the most control, online decorum begins here. Meetings should have an agenda and be kept short, perhaps 15–30 minutes, to be most effective. Both the agenda and ground rules for the online meeting should be shared at the beginning of the session. Along with this, starting and stopping on time is important online just as it is in-person. While light multitasking may not impact an individual's engagement, working on complex issues does disengage the online participant. Multitasking not only leads to less engagement, but it can also be perceived by others as impolite or disrespectful (Karl, Peluchette, and Aghakhani 2022). To limit the urge to multi-task, online meetings should also require active involvement or contributions from attendees (Cao et al. 2021). Those in control of online work meetings should be respectful and allow participants to voice opinions, share information through both chat and verbal (microphone on) options. No one participant should be allowed to dominate the online meeting or conversation. Proper leadership of online meetings can promote respectful behavior among participants.

Participants also play a role in productive online meetings. First, they should join on time, mute microphones, turn cameras on, and limit distractions (box 4.2) (Karl, Peluchette, and Aghakhani 2022). An online meeting is already limited due to the format with mere headshot visibility, no real eye contact or cues from body language, or other interpersonal dynamics which may occur in-person. However, showing one's face online signals respect for the meeting, leader, and participants, increases engagement, and limits multitasking (Cao et al. 2021). Finally, participants should practice self-control, refraining from demeaning, short, negative comments, or rude behaviors when they do communicate during a video conferencing session.

### Box 4.2 Online Meeting Participant Guidelines

- Join from a distraction-free area
- Join the meeting on time

- Keep the camera on
- Limit eating and drinking
- Mute microphones until speaking

(Karl, Peluchette, and Aghakhani 2022)

## Social Media

Discussions and debates about social media and civility are commonplace in today's online environment. Opinionated, biased, or hateful posting online stirs emotions and has led to social media companies applying algorithms to review posts and methods of messaging. However, for this writing, the question becomes focused on the workplace. How can social media contribute to the positive aspects of an organization's internal operation? How can those tasked with handling social media accounts best manage civility in online interactions? What guidelines can employees follow to limit negative work-related posts? Answers to these questions may provide some guidance when managing work-related social media issues as it applies to the topic of civility.

Social media has become a communication tool for organizations in a variety of ways. They employ it both externally (such as Facebook or X) and internally (such as Slack, Teams, or Yammer). Leveraging social media in this way allows for sharing of information and increased collaboration among workers which in turn increases engagement and job dedication (Zhao et al. 2021). That sharing and connecting can also extend to business relationships both inside or outside of the organization (Langer 2014). Consider an external partner who connected with someone in the organization through LinkedIn which in turn led to new business or another positive impact on the organization. To encourage polite and civil exchanges through these mediums, organizations can provide both guidelines and training to clarify expectations in this area. Thomson Reuters's social media guidelines provide such an example. These include adhering to their business code of conduct, refraining from false posts, being respectful, avoiding hostile or offensive statements, and maintaining business confidentiality among others ("Social Media" 2012). By way of example, Best Buy also includes in their policies language that discriminatory content regarding age, gender, race, nationality, or disability will not be allowed ("Best Buy" n.d.). In addition to guidelines, as with other forms of online communication, organizational oversight and a clear method for reporting and following up on issues should also be in place.

Those who manage social media for organizations are also challenged to maintain civil discourse, especially if part of the position involves handling responses and posts from those outside the organization. Studies indicate when there is a sensitive or passionate topic, comments are likely to turn negative, rapid, and aggressive in nature (Antoci et al. 2019). Company social media requires active oversight and moderation. This includes informing and educating those posting on the organization's social media site of guidelines for civil exchanges and consequences if not adhered to. Such social media policy infringements should always be addressed, and a written log of online issues and responses be kept. For some organizations, software (such as Hootsuite, Buffer, or Sendible), overseen by customer service representatives, can be used to handle social media complaints and offer automated responses and reporting of issues. For example, software used by Domino's Pizza offers ticketed reference numbers and a support link or direct message options to resolve complaints (Concannon 2023). Whether monitored by individuals directly or through software oversight, immediate responses to negative posts limit escalation and shift the issue in a more positive direction.

Along with internal guidelines, employees often are challenged to balance their personal and professional social media interactions as often these intersect. Organizations can provide guidance such as having employees include a tag line informing readers posts are their personal opinions on a work-related subject. Confidentiality of customer and company information also prohibits in most organizations sharing certain information on private social media accounts. Intel offers three simple guidelines for employees and personal social media: promote involvement with Intel (#IamIntel), share positive aspects of Intel's products, and use good judgment and professionalism ("Intel Social Media" n.d.). While these are examples of standard guidelines, each entity may differ. For example, in the United States, federal workers are prohibited from posting or sharing information about a political candidate or group under the Hatch Act ("Think Before 2021"). Another illustration is when educational institutions restrict contact between teachers and students or discourage potentially controversial posting and group affiliations on personal social media accounts ("Educators' Rights" 2023). Guidelines provided by organizations which apply to employees' personal social media usage will limit offensive posts and promote a more positive presence in that virtual world.

## Conclusion

With the establishment of online work communications, maintaining cyber civility has become another organizational challenge. Opportunities for deindividuation and disinhibition resulting from online interactions are now found in the workplace. To combat such behavioral deviations, improvements in understanding dysfunctional, online processes, increasing self-awareness, and establishing organizational norms lay the foundation for positive behaviors. Organizations also can lead the way by establishing netiquette guidelines and methods for reporting uncivil communications. Video conferencing can lead to negative communications but this can be avoided with proper leadership, co-worker respect, civil discourse, and online meeting guidelines. Along with these challenges, social media interactions are improved with organizational codes of conduct, oversight, and guidance for employees balancing private and work social media posts. Through awareness, training, and organizational support, cyber incivility, while never completely eliminated, can be greatly reduced in the workplace.

## Suggested Reads

Britton, Jennifer. *Effective Virtual Conversations: Engaging Digital Dialogue for Better Learning, Relationships and Results*. Newmarker, Ontario: Potentials Realized Media, 2017.

Dhawan, Erica. *Digital Body Language: How to Build Trust & Connection, No Matter the Distance*. New York: St. Martin's Press, 2021.

Reed, Karin M. and Joseph A. Allen. *Suddenly Virtual: Making Remote Meetings Work*. Hoboken, NJ: John Wiley & Sons, Inc., 2021.

## References

Albery, I.P. and M. Munafò, "Social Cognitive Models." In *Key Concepts in Health Psychology*, Ian P. Albery and Marcus Munafò, 1st edition, 2008. Sage UK. https://search.credoreference.com/articles/Qm9va0FydGljbGU6Mjc2MTYwNg==?aid=96519.

Antoci, Angelo, Laura Bonelli, Fabio Paglieri, Tommaso Reggiani, and Fabio Sabatini. "Civility and Trust in Social Media." *University of Wisconsin-La Crosse Journal of Economic Behavior & Organization*, 160 (2019): 83–99. doi:10.1016/j.jebo.2019.02.026.

Barsade, Sigal G., Constantinos G.V. Coutifaris, and Julianna Pillemer. "Emotional Contagion in Organizational Life." *Research in Organizational Behavior* 38 (2018): 137–151. doi:10.1016/j.riob.2018.11.005.

Bartl, Ramon, 2017. "Impact of Netiquette on Email Communication," *Journal of Applied Leadership and Management 5* (2017): 35–61. Accessed January 23, 2025. https://ideas.repec.org/a/zbw/hkjalm/175334.html.

"Best Buy Social Media Policy." Best Buy. (n.d.) Accessed September 23, 2024. https://corporate.bestbuy.com/wp-content/uploads/downloads/SOCIAL-MEDIA-POLICY2010.pdf.

Blank, Christopher, Shaila Zaman, Amanveer Wesley, Panagiotis Tsiamyrtzis, Dennis R. Da Cunha Silva, Ricardo Gutierrez-Osuna, Gloria Mark, and Ioannis Pavlidis. "Emotional Footprints of Email Interruptions." Proceedings of the 2020CHI Conference on Human Factors in Computing Systems: 1–12. doi.org/10.1145/3313831.337682.

Bryon, Kristin. "Carrying Too Heavy a Load? The Communication and Miscommunication of Emotion by Email." *Academy of Management Review* 33, no. 2 (2008): 309–327. doi:10.5465/amr.2008.31193163.

Burns, Kelli S. *Social Media: A Reference Handbook*. Santa Barbara, CA: ABC-CLIO, 2017.

Cao, Hancheng, Chia-Jung Lee, Shamsi Iqbal, Mary Czerwinski, Priscilla Wong, Sean Rintel, Brent Hecht, Jaime Teevan, and Longqi Yang. "Large Scale Analysis of Multitasking Behavior During Remote Meetings." Proceedings of the 2021CHI Conference on Human Factors in Computing Systems, article no. 448: 1–13. doi:10.1145/3411764.3445243.

Choi, Youngkeun. "A Study on the Prevention of Cyberbullying in the Workplace." *International Journal of Technoethics* 9, no. 1 (2018). doi:10.4018/IJT.2018010102.

"Civility in America VII: The State of Civility."*Weber Shandwick*. 13 June 2017. Accessed September 4, 2024. https://webershandwick.com/uploads/news/files/Civility_in_America_the_State_of_Civility.pdf.

Concannon, Lance. "10 Social Media Customer Service Examples to Learn From." Meltwater. November 20, 2023. https://www.meltwater.com/en/blog/social-media-customer-service-examples.

Dill, Brendan and Stephen Darwall. "Moral Psychology as Accountability." In *Moral Psychology and Human Agency: Philosophical Essays on the Science of Ethics*. Justin D'Arms, and Daniel Jacobson, eds. Oxford, UK: Oxford University Press, 2014.

Editors of the American Heritage Dictionaries, ed. "Disinhibition." In *The American Heritage Dictionary of Medicine*, 2nd edition. Boston MA: Houghton Mifflin, 2015. https://search.credoreference.com/articles/Qm9va0FydGljbGU6MzkxNzQxNQ==?aid=96519.

"Educators' Rights on Social Media." National Education Association. April 4, 2023. https://www.nea.org/resource-library/educators-rights-social-media.

Fischer, Sean and Yphtach Lelkes. "Emotion, Affective Polarization, and Online Communication." In *Emotions in the Digital World: Exploring Affective Experience and Expression in Online Interactions*, Robin L. Nabi and Jessica Gall Myrick, eds. Oxford, UK: Oxford University Press, 2023.

Gackenbach, Jayne ed. *Psychology and the Internet: Intrapersonal, Interpersonal, and Transpersonal Implications*. San Diego: Elsevier Science & Technology, 2006. Accessed September 5, 2024. ProQuest Ebook Central.

Greenber, Jerald and Catherine Musham. "Avoiding and Seeking Self-Focused Attention." *Journal of Research in Personality* 15, no. 2 (1981): 191–200. doi:10.1016/0092-6566(81)90018-0.

"Intel Social Media Guidelines." Intel Corporation. (n.d.) Accessed September 23, 2024. https://www.intel.com/content/www/us/en/legal/intel-social-media-guidelines.html.

Karl, Katherine A., Joy V. Peluchette, and Navid Aghakhani. "Virtual Work Meetings During the COVID-19 Pandemic: The Good, Bad, and Ugly." *Small Group Research* 53, no. 3 (2022): 1–23. doi:10.1177/10464964211015286.

Kesby, Rebecca. "How the World's First Webcam Made a Coffee Pot Famous", BBC News, November 22, 2012. https://www.bbc.com/news/technology-20439301.

Kleinrock, Leonard. "An Early History of the Internet." *IEEE Communications Magazine* 48, no. 8 (August2010): 26–36. doi:10.1109/MCOM.2010.5534584.

Langer, Emily. "What's Trending? Social Media and its Effects on Organizational Communication." *Journal of Undergraduate Research* XVII (2014). Accessed

January 25, 2025. https://www.uwlax.edu/globalassets/offices-services/urc/jur-online/pdf/2014/langer.emily.cst.pdf.

Lapidot-Lefler, Noam and Azy Barak. "Effects of Anonymity, Invisibility, and Lack of Eye-Contact on Toxic Online Disinhibition." *Computers in Human Behavior* 28 (2012): 434–443. doi:10.1016/j.chb.2011.10.014.

Lim, Vivien K.G. and Thompson S.H. Teo. "Mind Your E-manners: Impact of Cyber Incivility on Employees' Work Attitude and Behavior." *Information & Management* 46 (2009): 419. doi:10.1016/j.im.2009.06.006.

Longe, Jacqueline L. ed. "Social Learning Theory." In *Gale Encyclopedia of Psychology*, 3rd edition, 2016. Gale. https://search.credoreference.com/articles/Qm9va0FydGljbGU6NDc3MTgxMw==?aid=96519.

Mateyka, Peter J., Melanie A. Rapino, and Liana Christin Landivar. "Home-Based Workers in the United States: 2010." *US Department of Commerce*. October2012. https://www.census.gov/library/publications/2012/demo/p70-132.html.

Mueller-Coyne, Jessica, Claire Voss, and Katherine Turner. "The Impact of Loneliness on the Six Dimensions of Online Disinhibition." *Computers in Human Behavior Reports* 5 (2022); 100169. doi:10.1016/j.chbr.2022.100169.

Mulugeta, Helen Esayas. "Human Rights Issues at Amazon Corporation." *Management Science and Business Decisions* 2, no. 2 (2022): 19–31. doi.org/10.52812/msbd.50.

Pearson, Christine M., Lynne M. Andersson, and Christine L. Porath. "Assessing and Attacking Workplace Incivility." *Organizational Dynamics* 29, no. 2 (2000): 123–137. doi:10.1016/S0090-2616(00)00019-X.

Peters, Elisa, Hope Lourie Killcoyne, and Amelie Von Zumbusch, eds. *Psychology*. Chicago, IL: Rosen Publishing Group, 2015. Accessed September 5, 2024. ProQuest Ebook Central.

Ruth, Alison. "Don't Talk to Me About Email! Technology's Potential Contribution to Bullying." *International Journal of Organisational Behavior* 13, no. 2 (2008): 122–131. https://api.semanticscholar.org/CorpusID:150863522.

Smith, Lydia. "Netflix Slack Chat Firing of Staff and the Risk of Office Gossip." *yahoo!finance*. July 29, 2021. https://uk.finance.yahoo.com/news/netflixs-slack-chat-firing-of-staff-and-the-risk-of-office-chatting-050159469.html.

"Social Media Guidelines." Thomson Reuters. Updated November2012. http://blog.legalsolutions.thomsonreuters.com/wp-content/uploads/2012/09/TR-social-media-guidelines-November-2012-version.pdf.

Sonnemaker, Tyler and Dominick Reuter. "Netflix co-CEO Says 3 Execs Were Fired for Repeated Making 'Critical, Personal Comments' About Their Peers in a Public Slack Channel." *Business Insider*. July 29, 2021. https://www.businessinsider.com/netflix-fires-marketing-executives-who-complained-about-company-leadership-slack-2021-7.

Spaulding, Hannah. "Reach Out and Watch Someone: Televisuality, Gender, and the Short Life of the Picturephone." *JCMS: Journal of Cinema & Media Studies* 60, no. 5 (2021): 150–173. doi:10.1353/cj.2021.0059..

Suler, John. "The Online Disinhibition Effect." *Cyber Psychology & Behavior* 7, no. 3 (2004). doi:10.1089/1094931041291295.

"The Number of People Primarily Working From Home Tripled Between 2019 and 2021." United States Census Bureau. September 15, 2022. https://www.census.

gov/newsroom/press-releases/2022/people-working-from-home.html#:~:text= SEPT.,by%20the%20U.S.%20Census%20Bureau.

"Think Before You Post. Ethics Guidance on Personal Social Media Use." US Department of the Interior. Last updated September 23, 2021. https://www.doi. gov/ethics/think-you-post-ethics-guidance-personal-social-media-use.

Torres, Edwin N., Brianna Morman, and Trishna G. Mistry. "Incivility Meets Remote Work: A Typology of Cyber Incivility Behaviors." *International Journal of Hospitality Management* 118 (2024): 103689. doi.org/10.1016/j.ijhm.2024.103689.

Uenuma, Francine. "Video Chat is Helping Us Stay Connected in Lockdown. But the Tech Was Once a 'Spectacular Flop'." *Time.* May 11, 2020. https://time.com/ 5834516/video-chat-zoom-history/.

Vanderbosch, Heidi and Katrien Van Cleemput. "Cyberbullying Among Youngsters: Profiles of Bullies and Victims." *New Media & Society* 11, no. 8 (2009): 1349–1371. doi:10.1177/1461444809341263.

Vilanova, Felipe, Francielle Machado Beria, Ângelo Brandelli Costa, Silvia Helena Koller, and Justin Hackett. "Deindividuation: From Le Bon to the Social Identity Model of Deindividuation Effects." *Cogent Psychology* 4, no. 1 (2017). doi:10.1080/23311908.2017.1308104.

Voggeser, Birgit J., Ranjit K.Singh, and Anja S.Göritz. "Self-control in Online Discussions: Disinhibited Online Behavior as a Failure to Recognize Social Cues." *Frontiers in Psychology*, January 11, 2018, 2372. doi:10.3389/fpsyg.2017.02372.

Wróbel, Monika, Magda Piórkowska, Maja Rzeczkowska, Adrianna Troszczyńska, Aleksandra Tołopiło, and Michał Olszanowski. "The 'Big Two' and Socially Induced Emotions: Agency and Communion Jointly Influence Emotional Contagion and Emotional Mimicry." *Motivation & Emotion* 45, no. 5 (2021): 683–704. doi:10.1007/s11031-021-09897-z.

Zang, Sixuan, Dorothy Leidner, Xin Cao, and Ning Liu. "Workplace Cyberbullying: A Criminological and Routine Activity Perspective." *Journal of Information Technology* 37, no. 1 (2021): 51–79. doi:10.1177/026839622110278.

Zhao, Junzhe, Tengfei Guo, Sudong Shang, and Minghui Wang. "Work along Both Lines: The Positive Impact of Work-Based Social Media Use on Job Performance." *International Journal of Environmental Research and Public Health*, 18, no. 21 (2021): 11578. doi:10.3390/ijerph182111578.

Zhong, Jinping, Jing Qiu, Min Sun, Xiuan Jin, Junyi Zhang, Yidong Guo, Xinxin Qiu, Yujie Xu, Jingxiu Huang, and Yunxiang Zheng. "To Be Ethical and Responsible Digital Citizens or Not: A Linguistic Analysis of Cyberbullying on Social Media." *Frontiers in Psychology* 13 ( April 28, 2022). doi:10.3389/fpsyg.2022.861823.

# Chapter 5

# Improving Worker Interactions

While aspects of improving workplace communication with coworkers were laid out in chapter three from the perspective of an individual, there are other interactions of the working group which also influence civility. This typically involves individuals who are in close contact, perhaps interacting daily in the work environment. A historical example of interactions gone awry comes from the feud of two paleontologists, Othniel Charles Marsh and Edward Drinker Cope, who pursued the unearthing and identification of dinosaurs in the American West in the late 1800s (Huntington 1998). Although they began as friends and worked together, a trigger event changed their relationship. Marsh brought public attention to a bone identification error Cope had made in a scientific paper, and it was taken as a personal affront. After that point, their working relationship turned hostile and became known as the "Bone Wars" (Huntington 1998). Both displayed a lack of civility and shared combative communications that were recorded through letters and news articles. Cope said of Marsh in the 1890 New York Herald his work was "the most remarkable collection of errors and ignorance of anatomy and literature on the subject ever displayed" and accused him of plagiarism and immorality (Huntington 1998, 14). Marsh countered by writing he had "… doubts as to [Cope's] sanity" (Huntington 1998, 14). The divisiveness led to uncivil worker interactions by those employed by each man resulting in property destruction, sabotage, spying, and subterfuge (Rosamund 2023). This historical recounting brings attention to the fact work-related incivility has long existed. If the context was altered, this feud could easily be a modern-day occurrence. What could have prevented this type of toxicity? What may have changed the interpersonal dynamics of Cope, Marsh, and their employees? This chapter covers three areas which help answer those questions as it explores solutions rooted in peer interactions, worker emotions, and relational communication.

DOI: 10.4324/9781003590149-5

## Peer Interactions

Peer interactions in the workplace were studied in 1978 by Gerald R. Salancik and Jeffrey Pfeffer, and their work became the foundation of the social informational process theory. This theory advanced the idea that an individual's work attitude and personal views of their job are influenced by social work dynamics including overt employee statements, coworker opinions about work, and observation of other's work interactions (Salancik and Pfeffer 1978). The working peer group can influence the attitudes, emotions, and levels of polite, respectful interactions of others in their group. Utilizing bystander interruptions, moral elevation, and social support are some ways civility within these work groups can be improved.

Bystander interruptions in the workplace involve the actions of co-workers to mitigate an act of incivility or disruptive behavior. It is someone speaking up when they see an improper interaction. Use of interventions by bystanders has expanded to include other aspects of worker interactions such as impolite or hostile verbal communications which would apply when talking about worker interactions. Individuals who step forward and say something to a colleague perceived as uncivil are often emotionally triggered by what is occurring in the workplace and feel that not speaking up goes against their own moral code (Porath and Erez 2009). Typically, these interventions are in line with the already established norms of the organization, including the social norms of the peer work group (Moisuc and Brauert 2019). If, for example, an organization promotes and expects cooperation and sharing among employees, refusing to provide necessary information to a colleague would be in violation of norms and a case for bystander intervention. In support of such interventions, a multi-year study on bias in the workplace indicated such actions mitigated and reduced this antisocial behavior (Shea et al. 2023). Other research of multinational organizations also supports the use of bystander intervention. Actions of both group members and group leaders to publicly admonish actions of a bullying employee reduced its occurrence (Harvey, Treadway, and Heames 2007). Such interruptions by peers can occur in other ways as well, such as interceding when a colleague is interrupted when speaking or making disparaging comments towards another worker. Co-workers can offer support to a target, redirect a conversation, or even talk to the instigator about their behavior in private. As an example, Michigan State University promotes such strategies through their Prevention, Outreach, and Education Department (box 5.1) (2021). Additionally, to facilitate such actions, organizations can offer more formal bystander intervention training to define actionable behaviors and follow up after incidents. However applied, intervention by bystanders has been shown to be an effective tool in minimizing disrespectful and unprofessional interactions.

## Box 5.1 Michigan State University Bystander Strategies

*Delegate*: Ask for assistance with intervention
*Distract*: Take action to start a different conversation
*Direct*: Ask questions of target or perpetrator drawing attention to emotional impact

(MSU Prevention, Outreach and Education Department 2021)

While some individuals may speak directly to co-workers when they witness rude or improper behavior, others prefer to report rather than confront the offender. This takes the form of whistleblowing, and its accepted definition is "disclosure by organizational members ... of illegal, immoral or illegitimate practices ... to persons or organizations that may be able to effect action" (Near and Miceli 1985). While this type of reporting can involve external bodies, reporting to internal channels, typically speaking with a supervisor is the first step (Anvari et al. 2019). This type of intervention was first used to address sexual harassment and can still be applied in this area to address both verbal and physical conduct (Jennings et al. 2024). However, whistleblowing can also report hostile or toxic work behaviors as well as acts that undermine the larger organizational operation. Because whistleblowers are breaking from their work group to report an issue rather than remaining silent, they risk retaliation if the organization fails to protect them. Often whistleblowers find themselves as a target for attack by fellow workers or a supervisor, even when anti-retaliation provisions are in place (Heese and Perez-Cavazos 2021). However, a meta-study of whistleblower research points to positive impacts from whistleblower protections, a responsive and ethical organizational culture, and perceived organizational justice (Scherbarth and Behringer 2021). Such organizational support provides the framework which makes whistleblowing one method for promoting a more civil and positive workplace.

Another way to improve workgroup civility is through moral elevation. Moral elevation is defined as the positive feelings experienced when "unexpected acts of human goodness, kindness, and compassion" are witnessed (Haidt 2000). Imagine witnessing a co-worker step up to help another employee to complete a task they were struggling with or a team member filling in on a presentation when a co-worker was sick. What was the impact of those actions on the work group? Ideally, the employee showed appreciation for the gesture and others who witnessed it were also positively impacted by the act. Just as incivility in the workplace, if unchecked, leads to more incivility, positive interventions can have such an uplifting effect on other group members. Research shows that moral elevation results in prosocial group behaviors, and this response is even greater with individuals within the group who have a strong moral identity (Aquino and McFerran 2011). Moral elevation can invoke optimism, inspiration, respect, and openness in others (Pohling and Diessne 2016). Along with co-workers, leaders can promote this positive impact among their employees by displaying self-sacrifice, being moral role models, and displaying fair and equal treatment of workers (Vianello, Galliani, and Haidt 2010). Along with ethical norms and policies, organizations may embrace an award system for excellence or use storytelling to highlight moral or kind behavior (Passon 2019). Through these kinds of positive, moral acts in the workplace, civility is promoted and the demeanor of all employees lifted.

As moral elevation indicated, a third way peers contribute positively to the workplace is through social support. The social interactions of co-workers can influence behavior both negatively and positively. While recognizing unchecked dysfunctional behaviors may lead others to similar actions, the opposite is also true—good deeds lead to more good deeds. One method of positive co-worker impact occurs through micro-interventions or positive interjections during worktime (box 5.2) (Schweitzer et al. 2023). Workgroup belongingness, support, and assistance also play a role in this and lead to increased engagement, job performance, and job satisfaction. According to the job demands–resources (JD–R) theory, this type of peer support is a personal resource for workers and promotes positive work engagement while buffering the strain of job demands (Bakker and Demerouti 2017). Along with this, performing acts of support by co-workers can lead to a desire to reciprocate the action. This reciprocal exchange in the workplace adds to the continuation of positive and supportive interactions and increases trust among employees ("Social Exchange Theory" 2008). If an employee helps another understand a concept or offers positive reinforcement, the impacted individual is more inclined to return the favor. This type of reciprocal social support works best when the work group is cohesive and has close relationships. Because of this, being a part of the group is an important factor impacting positive work conditions, and to further that bond group leaders should promote team building activities, emphasize shared goals, and encourage group projects. (More specifics on creating effective teams are available in chapter seven.) Overall, when employees are more outwardly supportive of each other it will expand the positive dynamics of the group.

### Box 5.2 Positive Micro-Interventions

- Compliment co-workers
- Display happiness for co-worker achievements
- Gesture of appreciation for co-worker

- Post a joke for staff to read
- Share a funny video

(Schweitzer et al. 2023)

## Worker Emotions

In addition to peer interactions, it is well understood that emotions have a large impact on the interactions of a working group. Already reviewed are aspects of identifying, navigating, and expressing emotions. However, as it relates to improving worker interactions, two additional areas are worth examining—communication anxiety and anger mitigation. Communication anxiety may inhibit communication with others in the work group. Anger is another emotion which, if not checked, can lead to emotional contagion or "the transfer of emotions between people" (Kelly, Iannone, and McCarty 2016, 182). Studies show that a negative emotion such as anger is even more likely to lead to emotional contagion than positive ones (Kelly, Iannone, and McCarty 2016). Exploration of these concepts and ways to mitigate their impact may contribute to improved interpersonal communication.

Communication anxiety or communication apprehension associated with oral or written exchanges can impact workplace interactions. Communication researcher and professor James C. McCroskey was the first to explore a more formal definition of communication apprehension in 1970. He defined it as "an individual's level of fear or anxiety associated with ... communication with another person or persons" (McCroskey 2009, 13). In the workplace, communication is critical to group function and lack of it has a negative impact. Consider the employee who is apprehensive about speaking up in meetings. Potential ideas, opinions, or even concerns from this voice will be missing. Additionally, a fear of conversing in work groups or one on one conversations may be perceived as uncivil or rude by co-workers, potentially leading to ostracization or even bullying. Research shows that individuals who display communication apprehension are more likely female, less powerful, racial minorities, have introverted personalities, or experience depression or anxiety (Cardon et al. 2023). As communication anxiety is quite common in the workplace, recognizing this condition is a starting point in navigating interactions.

For individuals overcoming communication apprehension, three traditional approaches are available—systematic desensitization, cognitive restructuring, and assertiveness training. Systematic desensitization involves learning relaxation techniques and practicing application of these methods in a communication setting (Cardon et al. 2023). For example, an individual can pause and breathe prior to speaking to a group. Second, cognitive restructuring is identifying communication stressors and learning to "identify, evaluate, and correct their inaccurate beliefs" (Ezawa and Hollon 2023a, 396). For example, in a work setting an employee may think their idea is not worthy of contributing. However, if that thought is restructured, it could become "my idea may help resolve the problem." Finally, learning to be more assertive and conveying one's thoughts helps mitigate social communication anxieties. Training in this area involves communicating emotion, making decisions, recognizing personal rights, and discerning how and when to convey thoughts and emotions. Along with this, assertive communication includes confident and strong nonverbal gestures including standing up straight, limiting fidgeting, and directly facing the listener (Kelly 2019). In addition to these traditional methods, the use of virtual reality training (VRT) has shown positive results with overcoming communication apprehension (Gorinelli et al., 2023). VRT simulates a variety of real-life communication scenarios for individuals to practice both informal conversations with another person and formal presentations in front of groups. Using one or more of these methods, communication anxiety can be improved and applied to worker interactions.

Some of the most emotional interactions between co-workers involve anger. While expressions of anger targeting organizational problems, inefficiency, or inequity can bring positive change, interpersonal anger negatively impacts the workplace. Research has found anger in the workplace results in reduced job satisfaction, trust, and performance levels (Callister et al. 2014). Those who witness or hear the angry exchange, especially when aggressive, may undergo emotional reactions, anxiety, or fear and find themselves mentally taking sides with one of the parties (Miron-Spektor and Anat 2009). Depending on the topic, it may even change the behavior of others witnessing the angry exchange. As an example, consider an employee called into their supervisor's office and reprimanded in a loud, angry tone. Employees outside the office hearing this exchange may feel anxious or even fearful of similar treatment. As a result, their workplace behaviors may change so they do not make the same mistake or provoke anger in their supervisor. Instead of the work environment becoming trusting and productive, it harms operations.

There are methods for navigating and reducing anger in the workplace. Much of these are based around emotion regulation led by the work of psychologist James J. Gross. Put simply, individuals identify a situation where emotion modification can be applied and through cognitive appraisal change emotional responses (Gross 2013). By modifying outlooks and intentionally reappraising or finding a new, positive aspect of the situation at the core of the exchange, negative emotions such as anger can be decreased and positive emotions increased (Gross 2013). This type of emotion regulation can take place while emotion is developing or after it has been induced (Gross 2013). For example, during a work conference, a co-worker is overheard criticizing a presentation by a colleague. The comments invoke anger, but by recognizing this response and redirecting thoughts, the presenter can determine if the criticism is valid, or some other factors triggered the remark. This might be followed by a cooling off period or deep breathing before approaching their colleague to discuss their perspective. Shifting from emotional reaction to cognitive change and response is one way to handle these types of anger-evoking situations.

Another method used to minimize anger is cognitive behavioral therapy (CBT). CBT is a technique where individuals can modify thinking patterns to alter emotions, including anger. The process of CBT involves assessment, intervention, and evaluation. During the assessment stage an individual would think about the anger incident and personal beliefs or attitudes relating to the exchange as well as how their response impacted the situation (Teater 2013). Depending on circumstances, a variety of interventions could be tried to alter thinking patterns such as training in areas of social skills, proper assertiveness, cognitive restructuring (changing negative thought patterns), or problem-solving (Teater 2013). This is followed by an evaluation of changes in thought, feelings, and behaviors as they relate to the original situational response (Teater 2013). For example, a verbal disagreement takes place when an employee puts forward a new idea that, despite a passionate justification, is dismissed by their supervisor. The employee experiences anger thinking the supervisor likes none of their suggestions. When applying cognitive restructuring, the employee could instead rethink the situation. Perhaps there was merit in the supervisor's decision? Was there a better idea available? Were there other factors which led to dismissing the idea such as cost, time, or staffing if implemented? This type of thinking allows the worker to reevaluate their thoughts and if anger was really justified or merely a defensive response when rejected. This kind of application of CBT illustrates how it can be used to turn anger into a more constructive mindset.

Relaxation techniques are another method for minimizing an individual's anger. Meditation and mindful practices have been shown to decrease feelings of anger and with continued practice even make changes to the brain related to anxiety and stress (Afonso et al. 2020). Jon Kabat-Zen created the mindfulness-based stress reduction (MBSR) program. MBSR has been studied and shown to decrease anxiety, stress, and rumination (Goldin and Gross 2010). Kabat-Zen's training program runs across eight weeks and involves learning to be present, improving perception, recognizing stressors and reactions to stress as well as improving interpersonal communication (Janssen et al. 2018). A more practical meditation approach for employees which has also shown positive impacts on anger is brief mindfulness meditation (BMM). This process involves only 15 minutes of daily meditation done for seven straight days. Gross suggests affective regulation training (ART). ART involves recognizing and identifying emotions and their cause in order to accept, modify, or confront when necessary (Gross 2013). ART also includes aspects of relaxation for coping with emotions (box 5.3). These and other similar types of relaxation and deep breathing techniques will reduce tension and mitigate feelings of anger.

---

**Box 5.3 ART Skills and Sequence**

Perform each step 3 seconds–3 minutes daily for 6 weeks

1   Muscle relaxation
2   Breathing relaxation
3   Nonjudgemental awareness
4   Acceptance [of thoughts]
5   Compassionate self-support
6   Analyzing emotions [felt]
7   Modify emotions

(Gross 2013, 536)

---

There are other response modifications which may also reduce levels of anger during an exchange. As mentioned, taking a break from the heated situation and returning to discuss the issues when tempers are cooled is one approach. Another is to take the other's perspective in order to understand the real issue and why it triggered an angry emotion (Gross 2013). Individuals can also reframe the emotional exchange and apply forgiveness to reduce it as a form of self-regulation (Ho, Van Tongeren, and You 2020). Distraction by drawing attention to an unrelated issue can also be used to temporarily relieve a tense situation, although the core issue still must be resolved to prevent a recurrence (Fabiansson and Denson 2012). Finally, focusing on what is being said and taking time in responding to the core issue helps maintain a calmer demeanor in hopes of finding resolution (Shukla and Shukla 2023). Using one or more of these varying responses modifications may help turn an angry work exchange towards understanding of real issues and shift conversations in a positive direction.

## Relational Communication

Relational communication and its role in the larger organizational operation is rooted, in part, in systems theory. In the 1940s, Norbert Wiener first introduced principles of the interconnectedness of communication, control, and feedback in the operation of technical systems (Strijbos and Mitcham

2005). Others expanded on this concept for application in multiple dis-ciplines, but it was Massachusetts Institute of Technology researcher Jay Forrester whose work in industrial dynamics connected system thinking to organizations in 1958 (Forrester 1968). Today's work relational systems are part of the larger theory as they are focused on the influence of work rela-tionships and behaviors on the larger work environment. Several areas can be identified and improved to promote a better workplace, and these include promoting functional connections, addressing differing perceptions of civi-lity, promoting positive communication exchanges, and emphasizing nur-turing relationships.

Work environments all involve some level of employee socialization and functional connections are a part of that dynamic. As chapter one illu-strated, when worker interactions go astray and exhibit some form of dis-ruptive, dysfunctional, or toxic behavior, it negatively impacts both the target and the larger work environment. However, functional connections can improve job satisfaction, employee commitment, and engagement (Bir-mingham et al. 2024). What employee actions make connections work? Some supportive functions are rooted in the friendships developed at work. These social connections provide task assistance, emotional support, and mentoring (Colbert, Bono, and Purvanova 2016). Co-workers who can lend a hand with a task or even listen to a co-worker's personal story of frus-tration contribute to interpersonal bonding and support. Supervisors also can contribute to an individual's positive relationships by providing oppor-tunities for career advancement and supporting personal growth in the workplace (Colbert, Bono, and Purvanova 2016). Those managers who help workers achieve their personal best or move forward with their careers bring growth and change into the workplace. Research also suggests other managerial actions may influence functional interpersonal connections. Lea-ders who exhibit the ability to handle stressful problems and get along with a variety of work personalities add to a positive, functional work group (Carson et al. 2012). While leadership is discussed in depth in chapter eight, important elements displayed for functional work connections include attri-butes of trust, inclusivity, decision making, adaptability, and accountability (Carson et al. 2012). The overall support, by both co-workers and super-visors, is an important element in creating positive interpersonal work connections.

Perception also plays a role in relational communications. A general defi-nition of perception is an individual's "interpretation of what is sensed" and interpersonal perception extends to a more dynamic environment involving communications from others ("Perception, Person" 2008, 205). The percep-tion of uncivil acts is influenced by aspects of personality and the social environment. In the workplace this involves the employees and the organizational norms. Research has found that some personality traits such as negativity, trait anger, and conscientiousness, are more likely to perceive instances of incivility as compared to agreeable, open, emotionally stable extroverts (Sliter, Withrow, and Jex 2015). Research also indicates individuals often perceive their own actions as polite and considerate when others on the receiving end have an opposite impression (Hess, Cossette, and Hareli 2016). When examining perception and the work environment, some theories posit the environment is created by perception and others the perception creates reality while recognizing that all perceptions are influenced by the organizational climate, gender, ethnicity, and frequency of uncivil acts (Kunkel and Davidson 2014). These elements of both personality and the work environment play a role in perceived incivility.

There are a number of ways to try to bring awareness or even improve perceptions of incivility from interpersonal exchanges. First among these is cognitive restructuring which is a process which "identifies, evaluates, and corrects inaccurate beliefs" (Ezawa and Hollon 2023b, 2). In a work setting, an employee might perceive a criticism as rude, but after thinking about the content the employee realizes it is an accurate correction rather than a personal insult. Similarly, positively reframing a negative statement into a more optimistic viewpoint in conversations can help. As mentioned in chapter two, meditation and mindful approaches may help workers interpret exchanges with reduced bias and controlled emotional responses. Finally, since thoughts can trigger emotions, simply paying attention to thoughts evolving during an interaction can help keep emotions in check and responses focused on fact.

Promoting positive communication exchanges between employees also helps foster a positive, engaged workforce and involves a variety of approaches. One method is filtering thoughts before being conveyed to a co-worker to determine their impact. Applying Alan Redpath's THINK questions (box 5.4) is one way to do this to keep remarks on a constructive path (1989). Another factor is employee bonding which is rooted in the social capital aspect of Pierre Bourdieu's Theory of Social Practice. Bonding involves "ties between individuals within a homogeneous group" (Tsounis et al. 2022, 558). In the workplace, this involves colleagues—those who interact in the immediate work group or across other groups and divisions. Concepts include creating work friendships and establishing trust; interacting with those in the work group over time all improve and strengthen relationships. As mentioned, reciprocity also plays a role in positive communications as co-workers providing help to others leads their colleagues to return the favor (Tsounis et al. 2022). Positively influencing and inspiring each other such as offering congratulations for meeting work goals or encouraging a worker to share a new concept is another method. Supervisors can also play a role in creating positive exchanges as well by being empathetic, supportive, sincere, supportive, and positively persuasive (Wahid, Halim, and Halim 2024). Other methods leaders can utilize include encouraging group or collaborative work, promoting tolerance in diversity, establishing a trusting environment, listening to employee suggestions, and encouraging employee efforts (Wahid, Halim, and Halim 2024). Creating a work environment of positive communication is the end result of many of these concepts coming together to form the larger interacting work environment.

---

**Box 5.4 THINK**

**T** Is it true?
**H** Is it helpful?
**I** Is it inspiring?
**N** Is it necessary?
**K** Is it kind?

(Redpath 1989, p. 160)

---

Along with promoting positive communication, emphasizing nurturing of work relationships also improves the workplace. The *Concise Oxford American Dictionary* (2006) defines nurture as "the process of caring for and encouraging the growth or development of someone or something" (608). Nurturing relationships are nonjudgmental, respectful, and supportive. Nurturing communication can be formal or informal but should be constant, especially involving collaborative efforts (Muda 2017). Such regular communication is also important to develop trusting and meaningful relationships from which nurturing plays a role in coping with work challenges (Muda 2017). Individuals who feel safe and supported by a co-worker are more likely to seek help or share concerns (Barden et al. 2024). Creativity in the workplace can be enhanced by nurturing relationships which exhibit "curiosity, courage, and patience" (Deutsch, Coleman, and Marcus 2006, 289). The interplay of these types of nurturing communications can strengthen the bond between employees and improve the work environment. Leaders are also players in the nurturing efforts and should work towards open and frequent communications and building bonds with their staff. Christine Porath, researcher and professor at the University of North Carolina at Chapel Hill, suggests utilizing a mentor for guidance and advice to thrive in the workplace (Porath 2016). Mentoring is another type of didactic work relationship which can be supportive and nurturing, especially to new employees. Lastly, as nurturing relationships are respectful relationships, during times of disagreement recognizing negative emotions but moving towards positive means problem solving is more likely. Nurturing relationships also involve the use of apologies. Apologies can heal negative interactions between individuals and provide "reconciliation and restoration of broken relationships" (Lazare 2004, 10). These aspects of nurturing which provide support, staff bonding, and trust play a role in the development of a positive and productive work environment.

## Conclusion

All members of a work group influence each other. As a result, this inter-woven mix of personality and socialization can be leveraged to create a civil and productive environment. Peers can actively play a role in this through bystander intervention when norms or moral codes are breached. Peers also provide opportunities for bonding and friendship which provides social support and support of others. Addressing worker emotions impacting the larger group such as communication anxiety and anger management can also shift things in a positive direction. Lastly, recognizing incivility is often rooted in perception helps co-workers move past disruptions and shift communications towards more respectful and nurturing interactions.

## Suggested Reads

Anderson, Janel. *Head On: How to Approach Difficult Conversations Directly*. Farmington Hills, MI: Gale House Publishing, 2018.
Kelly, Alex. *Social Skills: Developing Effective Interpersonal Communication*. Milton Park, Abingdon, OX: Routledge, 2019.
Keltner, Dacher. *Awe: The New Science of Everyday Wonder and How It Can Transform Your Life*. New York: Penguin Press, 2023.

## References

Afonso, Rui Ferreira, Inessa Kraft, Maria Adelia Aratanha, and Elisa Harumi Kozasa. "Neural Correlates of Mediation: A Review of Structural and Functional MRI Studies." *Frontiers in Bioscience-Scholar* 12, no. 1 (2020): 92–115. doi.org/10.2741/S542.
Anvari, Farid, Michael Wenzel, Lyndia Woodyatt, and S. Alexander Haslam. "The Social Psychology of Whistleblowing: An Integrated Model." *Organizational Psychology Review* 9, no. 1 (2019): 41–67. doi:10.1177/2041386619849085.
Aquino, Karl and Brent McFerran. "Moral Identify and the Experience of Moral Elevation in Response to Acts of Uncommon Goodness." *Journal of Personality and Social Psychology* 100, no. 4 (2011): 703–718. doi:10.1037/a0022540.
Bakker, Arnold B. and Evangelia Demerouti. "Job Demands–Resources Theory: Taking Stock and Looking Forward." *Journal of Occupational Health Psychology* 22, no. 3 (2017): 273–285. doi:10.1037/ocp0000056.
Barden, Sejal M., Ryan G. Carlson, Dalena Dillman Taylor, Ruiqin Gao, and Mrangelie Velez. "Fostering Health Relationships: A Preliminary Investigation of Relationship Education." *Journal of Counseling & Development* 102, no. 2 (2024): 137–152. doi.org/10.1002/jcad.12504.

Birmingham, Wendy C., Julianne Holt-Lunstad, Raphael M. Herr, and Abigail Barth. "Social Connections in the Workplace." *American Journal of Health Promotion* 38 no. 6 (2024): 886–891. doi:10.1177/08901171241255204b.

Callister, Ronda Roberts, Barbara Gray, Donald E. Gibson, Maurice E. Schweitzer, and Joo Seng Tan. "Anger at Work: Examining Organizational Anger Norms Impact on Anger Expression Outcomes." In *Handbook of Conflict Management Research*, Oluremi B. Ayoko, Neal M. Ashkanasy, and Karen A. Jehn, eds. Cheltenham, Gloucestershire, UK: Edward Elgar Publishing Limited, 2014.

Cardon, Peter, Ephraim A. Okoro, Raigan Priest, and Greg Patton. "Communication Apprehension in the Workplace: Focusing on Inclusion." *Business and Professional Communication Quarterly* 86, no. 1 (2023): 52–75. doi:10.1177/23294906221129599.

Carson, Marisa Adelman, Linda Rhoades Shanock, Eri D. Heggestad, Ashley M. Andrew, S. Douglas Pugh, and Matthew Walter. "The Relationship Between Dysfunctional Interpersonal Tendencies, Derailment Potential Behavior, and Turnover." *Journal of Business Psychology* 27 (2012): 291–304. doi:10.1007/s10869-011-9239-0.

Colbert, Amy, Joyce E. Bono, and Radostina K. Purvanova. "Flourishing via Workplace Relationships: Moving Beyond Instrumental Support." *Academy of Management Journal* 59, no. 4 (2016): 1199–1223. Doi.org/10.5465/amj.2014.0506.

*Concise Oxford American Dictionary*. New York: Oxford University Press, 2006.

Deutsch, Moron, Peter T. Coleman, and Eric C. Marcus, eds. *The Handbook of Conflict Resolution: Theory and Practice*. Hoboken, NJ: Jossey-Bass, 2006.

Ezawa, Iony D. and Steven D. Hollon. "Cognitive Restructuring and Psychotherapy Outcome: A Meta-analytic Review." *Psychotherapy* 60, no. 3 (2023a).

Ezawa, Iony D. and Steven D.Hollon. "Cognitive Restructuring." In *Psychotherapy Skills and Methods That Work*, Clara E. Hill and John C. Norcross, eds. New York: Oxford Academic, 2023b. Online edition July 20, 2023. doi:10.1093/oso/9780197611012.003.0022. Accessed 16 Oct. 2024.

Fabiansson, Emma C. and Thomas F. Denson. "The Effects of Intrapersonal Anger and Its Regulation in Economic Bargaining." *PLos One* 7, no. 12 (2012): e51595. doi:10.1371/journal.pone.0051595.

Forrester, Jay. "Industrial Dynamics–After the First Decade." *Management Science* 14, no. 7 (March1968): 398–415.

Goldin, Philippe R. and James J. Gross. "Effects of Mindfulness-Based Stress Reduction (MBSR) on Emotion Regulation in Social Anxiety Disorder." *Emotion* 10, no. 1 (2010): 83–91. doi:10.1037/a0018441.

Gorinelli, Simone, Ana Gallego, Päivi Lappalainen, and Raimo Lappalainen. "Virtual Reality Acceptance and Commitment Therapy Intervention for Social and Public Speaking Anxiety: A Randomized Controlled Trial." *Journal of Contextual Behavioral Science* 28 (2023): 289–299. doi.org/10.1016/j.jcbs.2023.05.004.

Gross, James J. ed. *Handbook of Emotion Regulation*. New York: Guilford Publications, 2013.

Haidt, Jonathan. "The Positive Emotion of Elevation." *Prevention & Treatment* 3, no. 1 (2000), Article 3c: 1–2. doi:10.1037/1522-3736.3.1.33c.

Harvey, Michael, Darren C. Treadway, and Joyce T. Heames. "The Occurrence of Bullying in Global Organizations: A Model and Issues Associated with Social/

Emotional Contagion." *Journal of Applied Social Psychology* 37, no. 11 (2007): 2576–2599. doi.org/10.1111/j.1559–1816. 2007.00271.x.

Heese, Jonas and Gerardo Perez-Cavazos. "The Effect of Retaliation Costs on Employee Whistleblowing." *Journal of Accounting and Economics* 71, no. 2–3 (2021): 101385. doi:10.1016/j.jacceco.2020.101385.

Hess, Ursula, Michel Cossette, and Shlomo Hareli. "I and My Friends are Good People: The Perception of Incivility by Self, Friends and Strangers." *Europe's Journal of Psychology* 12, no. 1 (2016): 99–114. doi:10.5964/ejop.v12i1.937.

Ho, Man Yee, Daryl R. Van Tongeren, and Jin You. "The Role of Self-Regulation in Forgiveness: A Regulatory Model of Forgiveness." *Frontiers in Psychology* 11 (2020). doi.org/10.3389/fpsyg.2020.01084.

Huntington, Tom. "The Great Feud." *HistoryNet.* August 19, 1998. Accessed January 25, 2025. https://www.historynet.com/the-great-feud-august-98-american-history-feature/.

Janssen, Math, Yvonne Heerkens, Wietske Kuijer, Beatrice van der Heijden, and Josephine Engels. "Effects of Mindfulness-Based Stress Reduction on Employees' Mental Health: A Systemic Review." *PLos One* 13, no. 1 (2018): e0191332. doi:10.1371/journal.pone.0191332.

Jennings, Laura, Kun Zhao, Nicholas Faulkner, and Liam Smith. "Mapping Bystander Intervention to Workplace Inclusion: A Scoping Review." *Human Resources Management Review* 34, no. 2 (2024): 1010174. doi:10.1016/j.hrmr.2024.101017.

Kelly, Alex. *Social Skills: Developing Effective Interpersonal Communication.* New York: Routledge, 2019.

Kelly, Janice R., Nicole E. Iannone, and Megan K. McCarty. "Emotional Contagion of Anger is Automatic: An Evolutionary Explanation." *The British Journal of Social Psychology* 55 (2016): 182. doi:10.1111/bjso.12134.

Kunkel, Danylle and Dan Davidson. "Taking the Good with the Bad: Measuring Civility and Incivility." *Journal of Organizational Culture, Communications and Conflict* 18, no. 1 (2014).

Lazare, Aaron. *On Apology.* Cary: Oxford University Press, 2004. Accessed October 21, 2024. ProQuest Ebook Central.

McCroskey, James C. "The Communication Apprehension Perspective." In *Avoiding Communication: Shyness, Reticence, and Communication Apprehension*, J. A. Daly and James C. McCroskey, eds. New York: Hampton Press, 2009.

Miron-Spektor, Ella and Rafaeli Anat. "The Effects of Anger in the Workplace: When, Where, and Why Observing Anger Enhances or Hinders Performance." *Research in Personnel and Human Resources Management* 28 (2009): 153–178.

Moisuc, Alexandrina and Markus Brauert. "Social Norms are Enforced by Friends: The Effect of Relationship Closeness on Bystanders' Tendency to Confront Perpetrators of Uncivil, Immoral, and Discriminatory Behaviors." *European Journal of Social Psychology* 49 (2019): 824–830. doi:10.1002/ejsp.2525.

MSU Prevention, Outreach and Education Department. "Be an Active Bystander." Michigan State University. June 2021. https://workplace.msu.edu/wp-content/uploads/2021/06/Be-an-Active-Bystander.pdf.

Muda, Suhaini. "Communication and Nurturing to Sustain Collaborative Partnership." *SHS Web of Conferences* 33, 00076 (2017). doi:10.1051/shsconf/20173300076.

Near, Janet P. and Marcia P. Miceli. "Organizational Dissidence: The Case of Whistle-Blowing." *Journal of Business Ethics* 4 (1985): 1–16. doi:10.1007/BF00382668.

Passon, Brian. "The Power of Storytelling for Behavior Change and Business." *American Journal of Health Promotion* 33, no. 3 (2019): 475–476. doi:10.1177/0890117119825525d.

"Perception, Person." In *International Encyclopedia of the Social Sciences*, 2nd edition, 205–207, vol. 6. William A. Darity, Jr., ed. Detroit, MI: Macmillan Reference USA, 2008. Gale eBooks. Accessed October 16, 2024. https://link.gale.com/apps/doc/CX3045301915/GVRL?u=horrygtc&sid=bookmark-GVRL&xid=e1437323.

Pohling, Rico and Rhett Diessne. "Moral Elevation and Moral Beauty: A Review of the Empirical Literature." *Review of General Psychology* 20, no. 4 (December 1, 2016). doi:10.1037/gpr0000089.

Porath, Christine. *Mastering Civility*. New York, NY: Balance, 2016.

Porath, Christine L. and Amir Erez. "Overlooked but Not Untouched: How Rudeness Reduces Onlookers' Performance on Routine and Creative Tasks." *Organizational Behavior and Human Decision Processes* 109 (2009): 29–44. doi:10.1016/j.obhdp.2009.01.003.

Redpath, Alan. "The Making of a Man of God." In *A Passion for Preaching*, David L. Olford, ed. Nashville, TN: Thomas Nelson Publishers, 1989.

Rosamund, Martha. "The Bitter Dinosaur Feud at the Heart of Palaeontolgy." BBC News. January 19, 2023. https://www.bbc.com/future/article/20230119-the-dinosaur-feud-at-the-heart-of-palaeontology.

Salancik, Gerald R. and Jeffrey Pfeffer. "A Social Information Processing Approach to Job Attitudes and Task Design." *Administrative Science Quarterly* 23, no. 2 (June1978): 224–253. http://www.jstor.org/stable/2392563.

Scherbarth, Sandra and Stefan Behringer. "Whistleblowing Systems: A Systematic Literature Review on the Design Specifications and the Consideration of the Risk for Organizational Insiders to Blow the Whistle." *Corporate Ownership & Control* 18, no. 2 (2021): 60–73. doi:10.22495/cocv18i2art5.

Schweitzer, Vera M., Wladislaw Rivkin, Fabiola H. Gerpott, Stefan Diestel, Jana Kuhnel, Roman Prem, and Mo Wang. "Some Positivity Per Day Can Protect You a Long Way: A Within-Person Field Experiment to Test an Affect–Resource Model of Employee Effectiveness at Work." *Work & Stress* 37, no. 4 (2023): 446–465. doi:10.1080/02678373.2022.2142987.

Shea, Christine M., Mary Fran T. Malone, Jennifer A. Griffith, Viktoriya Staneva, Karen J. Graham, and Victoria Banyard. "Please Feel Free to Intervene: A Longitudinal Analysis of the Consequences of Bystander Behavioral Expectations." *Journal of Diversity in Higher Education* 16, no. 4 (2023): 486–496. doi:10.1037/dhe0000348.

Shukla, Niharika and Archana Shukla. "Navigating Anger and Mastering its Management." *The International Journal of Indian Psychology* 11, no. 3 (July–September2023). doi:10.25215/1103.321.

Sliter, Michael, Scott Withrow, and Steve M.Jex. "It Happened, or You Thought It Happened? Examining the Perception of Workplace Incivility Based on Personality Characteristics." *International Journal of Stress Management* 22, no. 1 (2015): 24–45. doi.org/10.1037/a0038329.

"Social Exchange Theory." In *International Encyclopedia of the Social Sciences*, 2nd edition, edited by William A. Darity, Jr., 585–586, vol. 7. Detroit, MI: Macmillan Reference USA, 2008. Gale eBooks. Accessed October 4, 2024. https://link.gale.com/apps/doc/CX3045302490/GVRL?u=horrygtc&sid=bookmark-GVRL&xid=8fd57d1a.

Strijbos, Sytse, and Carl Mitcham. "Systems and Systems Thinking," In *Encyclopedia of Science, Technology, and Ethics, 1880–1884*, vol. 4, Carl Mitchem, ed. Detroit, MI: Macmillan Reference USA, 2005. Gale eBooks. Accessed October 14, 2024. https://link.gale.com/apps/doc/CX3434900660/GVRL?u=horrygtc&sid=bookmark-GVRL&xid=822bd0b6.

Teater, Barbara. "Cognitive Behavioural Therapy." In *The Blackwell Companion to Social Work*, 4th edition, Martin Davies, ed. Hoboken NJ: Wiley-Blackwell, 2013.

Tsounis, Andreas, Despoina Xanthopoulou, Evangelia Demerouti, Konstantinos Kafetsios, and Ioannis Tsaousis. "Workplace Social Capital: Redefining and Measuring the Construct." *Social Indicators Research* 165 (2022). doi.org/10.1007/s11205–11022–03028-y.

Vianello, Michelangelo, Elisa Maria Galliani, and Jonathan Haidt. "Elevation at Work: The Effects of Leaders' Moral Excellence." *The Journal of Positive Psychology* 5, no. 5 (October 21, 2010): 390–411. doi:10.1080/17439760.2010.516764.

Wahid, Rizwana, Shanjida Halim, and Tanzina Halim. "Positive Communication Skills in the Workplace." *Migration Letters* 21, no. S8 (2024): 59–70. https://migrationletters.com/index.php/ml/article/view/9229.

# Chapter 6

# Utilizing Connections

Connections are a part of the vibrant environment of the workplace. Beyond one-on-one interactions, connections are constantly flowing in all directions between groups and various sectors. How do these types of interactions influence workplace civility? How can cohesive and productive environments be facilitated through these connections? Before exploring these ideas, an example of connection failure provides a look at how complex these interactions sometimes are and how easily they can become flawed.

The full launch of the US government's Patient Protection and Affordable Care Act's health insurance marketplace, HealthCare.gov, failed on October 1, 2013, crashing within two hours after going live (Goldstein 2016). Although 2.8 million people visited the site that morning, only six individuals were able to complete and submit a healthcare application (Andrews and Werner 2013; Levinson 2016). A 2016 analysis of the failure was conducted by the US Department of Health and Human Services Office of Inspector General and while there were a number of contributing factors, among those were a breakdown in project collaboration and leadership (Levinson 2016). The report indicates policy development delayed subsequent project phases, geographic relocation of staff divisions negatively impacted communications, failure to assign a project leader led to poor decision making and collaboration, and breakdowns in coordination with contractors led to technical problems (Levinson 2016). The staff representing the Centers for Medicare & Medicaid Services (CMS), the final agency assigned to oversee the development and launch, also complained of policy coordination issues at the state level and policy development issues with the White House (Levinson 2016). While the CMS moved quickly to rectify issues in subsequent days and weeks, the initial full launch of HealthCare. gov was a disastrous day.

This failure of the healthcare marketplace's inaugural day provides insight into the importance of work group coordination, communication, and guidance. Not all recommendations of the Inspector General's report are covered in this chapter, but several concepts relating to work

DOI: 10.4324/9781003590149-6

connections are reviewed along with other ideas for promoting positive connectivity from the intergroup perspective. These ideas include improving information flow from and between work silos, addressing conflict between organizational divisions, facilitating connections between work groups, and leveraging support from senior leadership.

## Siloed Communication

Information sharing is an important, if not critical, aspect of a functional organization. However, this knowledge sharing can be absent when organizational silos are present. Every organization has work groups, departments, or cliques that form a natural part of its structure. Additionally, each of these various groups is focused on one aspect or area of the larger operation in some way and because of this information and knowledge often become compartmentalized. These groups are work silos. This failure to communicate, whether intentional or not, contributes to organizational dysfunction. Already reviewed in previous chapters are causes and solutions related to interpersonal exchanges, online interactions, and workgroup influences. Here, two additional solutions are explored geared more specifically to reducing information silos—enhancing interpersonal connections and utilizing boundary spanners.

In the structure of work organizations, social groups emerge both formally and informally in daily operations. These social groups form "silos" which retain "pockets of interaction and knowledge in organizations" (Bento, Tagliabue, and Lorenzo 2020, 1). Consider, for example, the potential for silos of information occurring in an organization with offices in different geographic locations. Communication would be critical if one location led on the development of new designs while another location dealt with customer needs and feedback impacting those designs. Another example comes from administrative or executive team decision making. While an organization's top leadership discussions may involve discretion, if there was a new initiative impacting employees, communication early and often down the line would be desired. Studies indicate the more complex the concepts are the more important communication becomes to prevent the formation of information silos (Bento, Tagliabue, and Lorenzo 2020). Knowledge solely retained by workplace silos can inhibit communication flow and may lead to issues and conflict.

To overcome silos in the workplace, several methods are available to organizations. As an overriding norm, open communication should be encouraged and prioritized. This kind of communication may include facilitating joint decision making of individuals across departments to promote more inclusive interactions (Jeske and Olson 2024). Organizations can also encourage information exchange by increasing visibility and highlighting the importance of roles played by all groups and departments

(Jeske and Olson 2024). This type of sharing gives all employees a better understanding of job functions of other areas which may lead to increased information exchanges or reaching out when problem solving. Another method involves mapping lines of communication from different sectors, groups, or divisions to learn where information is flowing or being inhibited (Jeske and Olson 2024). This type of mapping also identifies silos that may currently exist. Once identified, exploration as to how they developed may lead organizations to make changes which improve communication. In collaboration with other researchers, Drs. Derek Cabrera and Laura Cabrera of Cornell University, Ithaca, New York, also introduced the VMCL model (box 6.1) to assist organizational leaders with silo reduction (2018). Similarly, Cabrera and Cabrera introduced a relationship-driven systems approach to silos to overcome communication barriers. This approach, the relationship-distinction-system (RDS), involves identifying the distinctions (or functions) of organizational divisions, mapping relationships of employees or groups occurring between these divisions, and identifying individuals and methods for connection (Cabrera and Cabrera 2018). The significance of relationships is also emphasized by Dr. Ann C. Baker, Professor in the School of Policy, Government, and International Affairs at George Mason University, Fairfax, Virginia. Baker emphasizes the importance of facilitating catalytic conversations and the sharing and exploring of different fact-based ideas and experiences to promote innovation among employees (Baker 2010). These conversations occur across divisions, departments, and physical spaces to push past existing group boundaries. (Relationship mapping software is readily available to facilitate this technique.) All these approaches provide methods for promoting connections between isolated work groups and reducing information silos.

## Box 6.1  VMCL Model to Decrease Silos

*Vision*: Measurable goals are shared among different people or groups
*Mission*: Steps to reach goals are enacted
*Capacity*: Systems and resources are provided for task
*Learning*: Ideas and feedback are shared through the process

(Cabrera et al. 2018, 25–26)

Another important part of facilitating communication across isolated social groups and departments is to leverage boundary spanners. Boundary spanners are the individuals who can bridge two groups within an organization or even groups external to the workplace (such as contractors). Boundary spanner roles require managing relationships, coordinating collaborations, mediating between groups, and promoting innovation (Le

Croze and Journe, 2023). These characteristics all point to the importance of boundary spanners having excellent interpersonal skills and excelling at establishing rapport with others in the work environment. As an example, consider someone from a marketing division who reaches out to a department needing new product or event promotions. Aspects of market research, product information, promotional strategies, or branding must be coordinated between the two areas. While boundary spanners can come from any rank in the workplace, they should be trustworthy and will need to possess mediation or negotiation skills (Lomas 2007). These individuals can also assist with breaking down silos of information as they facilitate sharing and communicating across groups who otherwise may not be in touch. Boundary spanners facilitate essential cross-silo collaboration, but they also may be inclined to experience burnout. Organizations need to recognize the high demands of this role and set clear expectations in addition to providing adequate resources (such as special skills training or communication tools) (Quintane et al. 2024). Boundary spanners should be monitored by their managers as well for signs of burnout where an intervention such as a workload readjustment or break to disengage may be applied (Quintane et al. 2024). If carefully balanced and coordinated, such individuals are invaluable to breaking down workplace silos.

## Work Groups

Other methods for promoting a positive work connection involve various aspects of work group relations. Subcultures are the first of these areas. Researchers define subcultures as groups or units of an organization which share "a set of values, norms, and practices." (Lopez 2010, 9). Subcultures can be formed by an organization's formal divisions or departments, rank (such as administrators), job function, length of tenure, or physical location as well as basic demographics (age, religion, or gender.) Often subcultures may involve workers from the same country or the larger cultural influences. These various subcultures form their own methods of interacting, creating, and performing, often deeply rooted in the subculture's work evolution, which may be quite different from other groups in the larger organization. Because of this, conflicts can arise from differing principles, practices, or priorities.

There are several ways to manage subcultures to promote a positive work environment. As with work silos, encouraging open communication keeps information flowing beyond the boundaries of subcultures. Like the larger organization, supervisors can reward knowledge sharing both within and between work groups to promote its continuance. Organizational leaders may also have to implement conflict resolution techniques (discussed in chapter eight) when problems arise. In doing this, values, behaviors, and belief systems must be identified, compared, and considered (Schwarz

2016). This understanding not only aids in resolving issues at hand but provides information on potential areas of disagreement which can be pre-emptively addressed moving forward. Such conflicts may be related to cultural differences in areas of work communication, etiquette, and values. An understanding of Hofsetede's cultural dimensions theory (how culture impacts behavior) will help leaders navigate these types of dynamics (see box 6.2). These dynamics are also a part of a larger process of organizational subculture alignment which cycles from group identification to alignment needs (box 6.3) (Chandler, Csepregi, and Heidrich 2018). Finally, leaders should consider how new, work-related information passed down will be perceived by the various subcultures to facilitate correct interpretations (Chandler, Csepregi, and Heidrich 2018).

---

**Box 6.2 Hofstede Cultural Dimensions Theory**

Individualism v. Collectivism (importance of individual v. group achievements)
Indulgence v. Restraint (uninhibited v. restricted social norms)
Long Term v. Short Term Orientation (emphasis of immediate v. future rewards structures)
Masculinity v. Femininity (gender differences impacting assertiveness, caring, relationship quality)
Power Distance (rigid v. relaxed hierarchy)
Uncertainty Avoidance (comfort level with uncertainty)

(Hofstede 2011)

---

**Box 6.3 Steps to Subculture Alignment**

1   Identify subcultures
2   Identify culture types and perceptions
3   Identify misperceptions
4   Identify common characteristics
5   Assess homogeneity ... [Hofstede dimensions]
6   Identify areas of commonality [of subgroup and larger organization's]
7   Identify areas requiring alignment

(Chandler, Csepregi, and Heidrich 2018, 136)

---

Another aspect of work group management is rooted in relationship versus task conflict. Studies indicate that relationship-based conflict harms team-oriented work while task conflict does not (Lee et al. 2015). Consider a clash of personalities within a work group which distracts from task completion. This relationship conflict may unfold as sparring between two individuals who dislike each other, or criticism taken personally because of an underlying dislike. Relationship conflicts can lead to reduced productivity and job dissatisfaction (Lee et al. 2015). Conversely, task conflict may be a dispute of the best approach or a critique of a novel idea which may have faulty reasoning. These types of task conflicts are good and provoke healthy debates, increase creativity, and deliver a better end result (Bradley et al. 2012). Thus, one way to promote civility within team collaborations is to refrain from relational conflict. This involves interacting in a professional manner, respecting fellow workers, and operating teams in a productive and positive way as discussed in chapter seven. Conversely, task conflict within groups should be allowed provided members have an understanding that such clashes will be resolved and lead to a better and improved outcome. When relational versus task conflict is recognized and managed appropriately, the group and organization benefit.

Often in operations individuals form special groups to complete a task or project, and the structure of this collaboration impacts civility. Sociologist James D. Thompson's classic work on organizational behavior, *Organizations in Action*, considered the interdependencies of such work groups, and divided these collaborations into three types—pooled, sequential, and reciprocal (Barbini and Masino 2017). Pooled projects are tasks done separately but then combined to achieve the end goal (Thompson 1967). Projects structured in this way emphasize individual work with minimal communications. As a result, this structure may have less overt conflict, although issues attributed to the lack of communication may have to be navigated between workers. Sequential collaborations involve tasks, as the term implies, done in a defined order where each task relies on the completion of the one before it (Thompson 1967). Errors or delays with each stage of development may lead to exchanges of frustration or anger which must be overcome to move forward. Individuals in these types of groups should embrace patience, persistence, cooperation, and perseverance. Lastly, reciprocal alliances involve the output of one group becoming the input for another resulting in an interwoven dependency to reach task completion (Thompson 1967). Those working in this type of setting should be strong in areas of emotional intelligence and be receptive, flexible, and willing to take risks in idea creation. Thus, depending on the design flow of the special work group, approaches to maintaining civil interactions vary.

When individuals come together for a special work group assignment, how they bond becomes an important factor to success. These types of groups could include interdepartmental meetings, department head meetings, committees, advisory boards, or task forces with participating individuals bringing differences in talent, rank, tenure, experience, creativity, and knowledge among other attributes. When diverse individuals work together there is always a chance for conflict, but group bonding reduces its incidence. Such cohesion is facilitated when members connect on a social level through common interests or beliefs (Kolb, Collins, and Lind 2008). Sharing conversations about favorite sports teams, hobbies, music, food, or any other commonality connects individuals. Research indicates shared experiences, both positive and negative, also lead to group bonding (box 6.4) (Bastian et al. 2018). These types of sharing shift an initial liking to deeper connections of interpersonal trust and interdependence between individuals which contributes to group cohesiveness and cooperation (Lu and Fan 2017). Thus, opportunities to have social interaction should be made available. As covered in task interdependence, bonds also form when group members are individually impacted by the result of the collective actions. For example, if a sales agency team outperforms other firms, the members may all be rewarded with a bonus. This type of situation would encourage team bonding to accomplish their sales goal. Additional information on developing teams is found in chapter seven, but it is worth noting here that group bonding, including interdepartmental teams, is quite effective.

## Box 6.4 Facilitating Group Bonding

- Increase emotional intelligence of group members
- Offer social activities for group members
- Promote psychological safety
- Share "negative or adverse experiences"
- Share "positive" emotions with others

(Bastian et al. 2018, 2; Lu and Fan 2017)

In addition to bonding, group size impacts civility. Studies indicate smaller groups (3–5 individuals) typically share more quality exchanges and this minimizes conflict (Susskind and Odom-Reed 2019). Relative and useful information exchanged leads to better informed team members which may promote problem solving, answer questions, and reduce errors which leads to clearer understanding and dispute avoidance. Related to the quality of exchanges is the actual number of interactions with others in the group. Smaller groups have more exchanges and that has a positive impact on the dynamics whereas larger groups, with fewer exchanges, may have issues due to communication gaps. Smaller groups can also more easily balance the number of interactions with co-workers so there are not too many or too few. Too few communications provide inadequate information, and too many exchanges could result in information overload and be perceived as taking up too much time. When communication exchanges are balanced, they achieve optimal "connective flow" or "highly effective and highly efficient" exchanges which lends to the positive aspects of collaboration (Kolb, Collins, and Lind 2008, 183). Thus, smaller groups with bonding opportunities and more frequent, quality exchanges will tend to function in a more harmonious manner.

Task interdependence is typically a subset of group work and involves the interactions and reliance of group members on each other to accomplish their goal (Pandy and Karve 2020). Group members who share in this type of connection have increased team commitment and concern for the work done by other team members (Van Der Vegt, Means, and Van De Vliert 2000). Embracing individual differences of group members, especially in areas of their knowledge and skills, leads to organizational citizenship behavior and attributes of altruism, conscientiousness, positive attitude, participation, and courtesy (Janssen and Huang 2008; Robinson 2024). Other positives from task interdependence include increased job satisfaction and commitment, especially when both the tasks and outcomes impact all the individuals (Van Der Vegt, Means, and Van De Vliert 2000). Beyond creating opportunities for high task interdependence within group projects, leaders can facilitate positive and meaningful interactions through promoting autonomy and group decision making, delegating authority, providing employee support, and encouraging participation within the team (Lisak et al. 2022). Building trust among group members is another important factor for successful collaboration. For this, group members should agree upon purpose, share credit for accomplishments, distribute equal workloads, avoid individual domination, and move past territorial boundaries (Vangen and Huxham 2003). Through proper encouragement and facilitation of task interdependence, civil and productive group work can be accomplished.

## Senior Leadership

Work groups and teams typically have a leader or supervisor directly overseeing the work. More specifics on best practices for these team leads are covered in chapter seven. However, group leaders also have senior leaders or administrators above them in the hierarchy of the work organization which influence the functionality of work groups. These individuals impact groups with operational, cognitive, and emotional support, and by leveraging aspects of these areas positive group work can be shaped.

One of the most common ways senior leaders assist groups is by providing operational support. The functionality of teams is impacted when they are lacking in the proper resources. Often senior leaders, because of their rank and authority in the organization, are the individuals which can secure what is needed. For example, they may have power to make purchases or control supply inventories, and this authority is essential to obtaining materials necessary for proper team function. Senior leaders also assist with making available necessary technological support which could include methods for electronic communication, design creation, data collection and analytics, project management, and various other software as well as technological hardware needs of the group. With authority by position, senior leaders can deter or mitigate issues which may arise from the lack of proper resources or problem solve in this area if they arise.

Senior leaders also play a role in cognitive support. One of the critical roles of senior leadership is to provide the overall directives of the organization and connect these directives to the tasks assigned to the working groups (O'Leary and Gerard 2012). Having a clearly defined direction is an attribute of properly functioning work teams. Another aspect of cognitive support is simply the senior leader's knowledge and experience in the industry which can be shared and utilized by the work group. The senior leader may be viewed as a reliable person to respond to questions and provide guidance when issues arise. However, these individuals must also balance the group autonomy with their personal perspectives on how things should be done. Studies indicate there are many benefits from supporting work group autonomy even from a more distal senior leadership position (Slemp et al. 2018). Among these are prosocial, proactive, and engaged behaviors (Slemp et al. 2018). Leaders at this level or rank may also get involved with dispute resolution from conflict arising from those involved in the work group that cannot be settled by their immediate supervisor (more on leadership and conflict management is discussed in chapter eight). Another role includes understanding and facilitating connections across boundaries from the working group to supporting individuals, stakeholders, and departments. An organizational network analysis of who workers go to for advice and expertise exposes unseen bridges of communication which senior leaders can facilitate and support (Chen et al. 2024). Through these areas of cognitive support, these higher-ranking individuals can help smooth the path for group success.

A final area of impact from senior leaders comes in the form of emotional support. Showing interest and expressing support for the progress and accomplishments of the work group is important to team collaboration (Jassawalla and Sashittal 2001). As an example, imagine the positive impact that would occur with swing shift workers if a senior leader who normally works days took the time to visit and express their appreciation during the evening. This type of support is done with "inclusive engaging" through conversations with group members and personal encouragement (Ang'ana and Chiroma 2021). Senior leaders also can provide emotional support in times of crisis or conflict. These administrators often must manage disputes along with disgruntled or disengaged team members and empathy does play a role in resolution of these issues. Additionally, senior leaders can provide opportunities to celebrate team accomplishments. Positive collaboration is supported when senior leaders provide this type of ongoing emotional support and encouragement throughout the life of the work team.

## Conclusion

Connections evolving from work groups, including subcultures and specialized work teams, play an important role in work operations. To promote civility, organizations should embrace open information exchanges and opportunities for connection beyond typical group compositions. This approach includes concepts for utilizing boundary spanners to promote communication between different work groups. Additionally, leaders can identify how information flows between groups, departments, or divisions to promote better exchanges. Group connections can also be improved through social aspects of member bonding, embracing individual differences, and building trusting relationships. Lastly, senior leaders can facilitate civility within work groups by providing operational, cognitive, and emotional support while balancing their interventions with group autonomy.

## Suggested Reads

Fosslien, Liz and Mollie West Duffy. *No Hard Feelings: The Secret Power of Embracing Emotions at Work*. New York, NY: Portfolio, 2019.
Gardner, Heidi K. and Ivan A. Matviak. *Smarter Collaboration: A New Approach to Breaking Down Barriers and Transforming Work*. Brighton, MA: Harvard Business Review Press, 2022.
Willcock, David Ian. *Collaborating for Results: Silo Working and Relationships that Work*. New York, NY: Routledge, 2016.

## References

Andrews, Wyatt and Anna Werner. "Healthcare.gov Plagued by Crashes on 1st Day." CBS News. October 1, 2013. https://www.cbsnews.com/news/healthcaregov-plagued-by-crashes-on-1st-day/.
Ang'ana, Gilbert A. and Jane Adhiambo Chiroma. "Collaborative Leadership and its Influence in Building and Sustaining Successful Cross-Functional Relationships in Organizations in Kenya." *Journal of Business and Management* 23, no. 8 (2021): 23. doi:10.9790/487X-2308061826.
Baker, Ann C. *Catalytic Conversations: Organizational Communication and Innovation*. Oxford: Taylor & Francis Group, 2010. Accessed October 28, 2024. ProQuest Ebook Central.
Barbini, Francesco Maria and Giovanni Masino, eds. *J.D. Thompson's Organizations in Action 50th Anniversary: A Reflection*. Bologna: TAO Digital Library, 2017. https://amsacta.unibo.it/id/eprint/5737/1/ThompsonAnniversary.pdf.
Bastian, Brock, Jolanda Jetten, Hannibal A. Thai, and Niklas K. Steffens. "Shared Adversity Increases Team Creativity Through Fostering Supportive Interaction." *Frontiers in Psychology* 9 (2018): 2309. doi:10.3389/fpsyg.2018.02309.
Bento, Fabio, Marco Tagliabue, and Flora Lorenzo. "Organizational Silos: A Scoping Review Informed by a Behavioral Perspective on Systems and Networks." *Societies* 10, no. 3 (2020). doi:10.3390/soc10030056.

Bradley, Bret H., Bennett E. Postlethwaite, Anthony C. Klotz, Maria R. Hamdani, Kenneth G. Brown. "Reaping the Benefits of Task Conflict in Teams: The Critical Role of Teams Psychological Safety Climate." *Journal of Applied Psychology* 97, no. 1 (2012): 151–158. doi:10.1037/a0024200.

Cabrera, Derek and Laura Cabrera. "Connecting Silos: Solving the Problem of Organizational Silos Using a Simple Systems Thinking Approach." [White Paper No. 4] Cornell University for Public Affairs, February 2018.

Cabrera, Derek, Laura Cabrera, Erin Powers, Jeremy Solin, and Jennifer Kushner. "Applying Systems Thinking Models of Organizational Design and Change in Community Operational Research." *European Journal of Operational Research* 268, no. 3 (2018): 932–345. doi.org/10.1016/j.ejor.2017.11.006.

Chandler, Nick, Aniko Csepregi, and Balazs Heidrich. "The World I Know: Knowledge Sharing and Subcultures in Large Complex Organisations." In *Knowledge Management in the Sharing Economy. Knowledge Management and Organizational Learning*, vol. 6, E. M. Vătămănescu and F. Pînzaru, eds. Cham, Switzerland: Springer, 2018. doi:10.1007/978-3-319-66890-1_7.

Chen, Ximeng, Yiding Cao, Jiachen Liu, Danushka Bandara, and Hiroki Sayama. "Exploring Social Networks: An Analysis of Intra-organizational Networks." *Northeast Journal of Complex Systems* 6, no. 1 (2024), Art. 6. doi:10.22191/nejcs/vol6/iss1/6..

Goldstein, Amy. "HHS Failed to Heed Many Warnings that HealthCare.gov was in Trouble," *The Washington Post*. February 23, 2016. https://www.washingtonpost.com/national/health-science/hhs-failed-to-heed-many-warnings-that-healthcaregov-was-in-trouble/2016/02/22/dd344e7c-d67e-11e5-9823-02b905009f99_story.html.

Hofstede, Geert. "Dimensionalizing Cultures: The Hofstede Model in Context." *Online Readings in Psychology and Culture* 2, no. 1 (2011). doi.org/10.9707/2307-0919.1014.

Janssen, Onne and Xu Huang. "Us and Me: Team Identification and Individual Differentiation as Complementary Drivers of Team Members' Citizenship and Creative Behaviors." *Journal of Management* 34, no. 1 (2008). doi:10.1177/0149206307309263.

Jassawalla, Avan R. and Hemant C. Sashittal. "The Role of Senior Management and Team Leaders in Building Collaborative New Product Teams." *Engineering Management Journal* 13, no. 2 (2001): 33–39. doi:10.1080/10429247.2001.11415114.

Jeske, Debora and Deborah Olson. "Silo Mentality in Teams: Emergence, Repercussions and Recommended Options for Change." *Journal of Work-Applied Management*, ISSN 2205–2062. May 23, 2024. doi:10.1108/JWAM-07-2023-0064.

Kolb, Darl G., Paul Collins, and E. Allen Lind. "Requisite Connectivity: Finding Flow in a Not-So-Flat World." *Organizational Dynamics* 37, no. 2 (2008): 181–189. http://hdl.handle.net/2292/17163.

Le Croze, Jean-Christophe and Benoit Journe, eds. *Safe Performance in a World of Global Networks: Case Studies, Collaborative Practices and Governance Principles*. Cham, Switzerland: Springer, 2023. Accessed October 28, 2024. ProQuest Ebook Central.

Lee, Chun-Change, Yu-Hsni Lin, Hsin-Chung Huan, Wei-Wen Huang, and Hsu-Hung Teng. "The Effects of Task Interdependence, Team Cooperation, and

Team Conflict on Job Performance." *Social Behavior and Personality* 43, no. 4 (2015): 529–536. doi.org/10.2224/sbp.2015.43.4.529.

Levinson, Daniel R. "HealthCare.gov CMS Management of the Federal Marketplace: A Case Study." US Department of Health and Human Services Office of Inspector General. February 2016. https://oig.hhs.gov/reports/all/2016/healthcaregov-case-stu dy-of-cms-management-of-the-federal-marketplace/.

Lisak, Alon, Raveh Harush, Tamar Icekson, and Sharon Harel. "Team Inter-dependence as a Substitute for Empowering Leadership Contribution to Team Meaningfulness and Performance." *Frontiers in Psychology* 13 (February 11, 2022). doi:10.3389/fpsyg.2022.637822.

Lomas, Jonathan. "The In-Between World of Knowledge Brokering." *BMJ* 335 (2007): 129. doi:10.1136/bmj.39038.593380.AE.

Lopez, Enric Serradell. "Subcultures in Large Companies: An Exploratory Analysis" [Conference Paper]. In *Organizational, Business, and Technological Aspects of the Knowledge Society*, Miltiadis D. Lytras, Patricia Ordonez de Pablos, Adrian Ziderman, Alan Roulstone, Hermann Maurer, and Jonathan B. Imber, eds.. WSKS2010. Communications in Computer and Information Science, vol. 112. Berlin, Heidelberg: Springer, 2010. doi.org/10.1007/978-973-642-16324-1_2.

Lu, Lou and Hsueh-Lian Fan. "Strengthening the Bond and Enhancing Team Per-formance: Emotional Intelligence as the Social Glue." *Journal of Organizational Effectiveness: People and Performance* 5, no. 3 (2017): 182–198. doi:10.1108/ JOEPP-10-2016-0062.

O'Leary, Rosemary and Catherine M. Gerard. "Collaboration Across Boundaries: Insights and Tips from Federal Senior Executives." *IBM Center for the Business of Government*, 2012. https://www.businessofgovernment.org/sites/default/files/Colla boration%20Across%20Boundaries.pdf.

Pandy, Aparna and Shailaja Karve. "Task Interdependence and Communication Styles in Teams." *Indian Journal of Industrial Relations* 56, no. 1 (2020): 167–180.

Quintane, Eric, Sunny Lee, Jung Won Lee, Camila Umaña Ruiz, and Martin Kilduff. "Why Employees Who Work Across Silos Get Burned Out." *Harvard Business Review Digital Articles*, May 13, 2024, 1–8. https://search.ebscohost.com/login.asp x?direct=true&AuthType=shib&db=buh&AN=177501985&authtype=shib& site=ehost-live&scope=site.

Robinson, Cheryl "How to Impact Company Culture with Organizational Citizen-ship Behavior," *Forbes*. Last updated April 23, 2024. https://www.forbes.com/ sites/cherylrobinson/2024/04/23/how-to-impact-company-culture-with-organiza tional-citizenship-behavior/.

Schwarz, Roger. "Getting Teams with Different Subcultures to Collaborate." *Har-vard Business Review Digital Articles*, July 22, 2016, 2–4. https://search.ebscohost. com/login.aspx?direct=true&AuthType=shib&db=buh&AN=118683760&a uthtype=shib&site=ehost-live&scope=site.

Slemp, Gavin R., Margaret L. Kern, Kent J. Patrick, and Richard M. Ryan. "Leader Autonomy Support in the Workplace: A Meta-analyticRreview." *Motivation and Emotion* 42 (2018): 706–724. doi:10.1007/s11031–11018–9698-y.

Susskind, Alex M. and Peggy R. Odom-Reed. "Team Member's Centrality, Cohe-sion, Conflict, and Performance in Multi-University Geographically Distributed Project Teams." *Communication Research* 46, no. 2 (2019): 151–178. doi:10.1177/ 0093650215626972.

Thompson, James D. *Organizations in Action: Social Science Bases of Administrative Theory.* New York: McGraw-Hill Book Company, 1967.

Van Der Vegt, Gerben, Ben Means, and Evert Van De Vliert. "Team Members' Affective Responses to Patterns of Intragroup Interdependence and Job Complexity." *Journal of Management* 20, no. 4 (2000), 633–655. doi:10.1177/0149206300026004.

Vangen, Siv and Chris Huxham. "Nurturing Collaborative Relations: Building Trust in Interorganizational Collaboration." *Journal of Applied Behavioral Science* 35, no. 5 (2003): 5–31. doi:10.1177/0021886303039001001.

# Chapter 7

# Implementing Effective Teamwork

Many of today's companies are using teams in their organizational structure. One of these companies whose methods have been extensively reviewed is Zappos, an online shoe retailer. Zappos shifted from a top-down hierarchy in 2014 towards an employee self-management style using teams (termed circles) (Zhou 2023). While there were challenges and changes since the initial organizational switch, the company still embraces a microenterprise team concept today (Minnaar 2021). More importantly, Zappos has retained an emphasis on employee well-being and positive interactions. Among its ten core values are concepts of being open-minded, communicating honestly, embracing a family-like spirit, and displaying humility ("About Us" n.d.). All of these concepts have a positive impact on team civility.

Zappos is just one example of how organizations are incorporating team concepts. This type of group collaboration now impacts nearly all workers. A Gensler 2023 study of United States employees across various industries found 98% of them work in a team ("Work, Life" 2023). Office workers (both the US and global average) spend 42% of work time collaborating with others ("Global Workplace" 2023). Other research found employees spending 50% of their time on collaborative work and work teams (Cross, Rebele, and Grant 2015; Tagliaro, Zhou, and Hua 2022). In addition, a Gallup poll has found that of those who contribute to a work team, 84% serve on multiple teams ("Gallup State" 2017). These statistics indicate the important role of teamwork in workplaces today. Such work evolves in many forms from in-person to remote to hybrid and in a wide variety of team types. With so much time spent in team environments, factors influencing civility in this work dynamic become quite important. The extent of these influences can be explored by examining team leadership, member collaborations, and group identity.

## Team Leadership

Proper team leadership is an essential component of a successful team. As described in chapter six, the launch of HealthCare.gov illustrates how poor

DOI: 10.4324/9781003590149-7

team leadership can not only lead to failed goal achievement but also to dysfunctional or uncivil actions among its members. Effective team leaders understand and convey the vision of the organization and connect the team actions to this larger purpose. They organize and guide team members through meetings and phases of the team's work. Successful team leaders also share power and credit with their team members (O'Leary and Gerard 2012). These are just some aspects of effective team leadership. What other leadership attributes impact a team's civility? What can these leaders do to promote positive, cohesive group work? To answer this, an exploration follows of relevant leader characteristics as well as impacts of team norms, meeting organization, psychological safety, and group humility.

There are a number of team leader traits which result in improved group collaboration. As discussed in other chapters, the first of these is the ability to facilitate open and respectful communication among individuals in the group. One example of leader-facilitated collaboration comes from the Cleveland Clinic. This hospital uses short (15–30 minute), daily huddles of staff and supervisors at six different authority levels—from caregivers to CEOs—focused on improving care and addressing issues (Mathias 2019). This type of leader-led interaction facilitates communication with team members and utilizes these exchanges to strengthen relationships, increase trust, and troubleshoot issues.

Another area which is beneficial to team collaboration involves ethical leadership. As the term implies, individuals displaying this characteristic demonstrate fair and just actions and are role models for proper behavior. Studies indicate ethical leaders impact the team dynamic by maintaining motivation and citizenship behavior, even when a team's performance falls short (Martin et al. 2022). Ethical leadership leads to increased information sharing and pro social behaviors which positively contribute to group collaboration (Sun, Park, and Yun 2024). To increase ethical leadership, organizations can have team leaders engage in reality-based training. In this type of training, ethical case studies are presented, analyzed, discussed, and argued in a group setting over four to twelve weeks to increase awareness and promote moral decision making (Caldwell et al. 2020).

Along similar lines to ethics, studies indicate leader humility results in increased job satisfaction, affective organizational commitment, and psychological safety, and these attributes all contribute to positive worker interactions (Luo et al. 2022). Humble team leaders are unafraid to admit mistakes and display modesty rather than self-importance. These leaders listen, inspire, encourage, and respect team members. Methods for improving leader humility include increasing openness to ideas, elevating self-awareness, boosting capacity for forgiveness, practicing self-sacrifice, and keeping a gratitude journal (Lavelock et al. 2014).

Lastly, multi-cultural team research indicates that a leader's cross-cultural competencies "lead to more effective communication, conflict management, ... [and] trust building" (Stahl and Maznevski 2021, 10). The *American Journal of Medicine* provides guidelines ("5 Rs") for healthcare industry leaders on this topic emphasizing harmony and respect (box 7.1) (Robinson, Masters, and Ansari 2021). Improvements in this area also come from expanding one's understanding of different cultures through lectures and education, personal experiences, or professional development opportunities such as cultural intelligence training. Research has found these kinds of personal strengths-interpersonal communication, ethics, humility, and cultural competence-are developed over time and include a cognitive component (awareness and understanding), a behavioral component (concept application), and an organizational component (broader cultural training and support) (Getha-Taylor, Holmes, and Moen 2020). For team leaders lacking in some of these areas, change is possible with focused self-improvement efforts. Overall, team leaders acquiring these attributes facilitate a more civil, positive, and effective working group.

---

**Box 7.1  The 5 Rs of Cultural Humility in Interactions**

*Reflection:* (learn from interactions)
*Regard:* (be respectful)
*Relevance:* (be culturally responsiveness)
*Resiliency:* (cultural adaptability)
*Respect:* (treat others with dignity)

(Robinson, Masters, and Ansari 2021, 162)

---

When teams are formed, it is the team leader who initiates a discussion of workgroup norms. These norms are important as they provide the guidelines to group function and participant interaction and many of these norms directly impact group civility (box 7.2) (Peng 2023). These criteria may involve methods for both logistics (meetings, communication methods, or timelines) and social interactions (group exchanges and participation). Clearly outlined norms defining expectations, frequency and methods for communication, and task assignments may minimize confusion and disagreements among group members. For example, "We will respect each other's time and arrive promptly to meetings" or "We will maximize group efficiency by keeping cell phones on silent and refraining from texting or taking calls" are examples of norms relating to conduct. To create such team norms, the group may spend several hours brainstorming and debating which guidelines will be in place for team operation. Included in these guidelines should be specific norms for civility. Acceptable interpersonal interactions can be a part of group norms (box 7.2), and these guidelines have a direct impact on team civility since they define how group members work together. Civility norms define not only respectful interactions but broader norms such as being non-judgmental and open minded, how disagreements are handled, or how non-conforming behavior will be handled. For example, a civility norm may state, "We will listen to other group members without interruption and be respectful of their opinion." Research supports the use of civility norms finding that when incorporated into teams, there is less deviant behavior among the members (Clark and Walsh 2016). While creating norms initially takes time and debate, they do provide the necessary boundaries for positive interaction as the team moves forward.

## Box 7.2 Team Norms Impacting Civility

- Allow balanced participation
- Avoid negative body language
- Communicate openly and honestly
- Refrain from personal attacks
- Respect differing perspectives
- Utilize consensus decision making

(Peng 2023)

Another role of a team leader is to conduct effective meetings. It is the team leader whose job is to ensure members comply to agreed norms and to maximize the meeting's effectiveness while keeping dysfunctional behavior in check. This is no easy task. The leader must manage both logistical and relational aspects of meetings to accomplish this. From the logistic perspective, research into team meetings has found that planning and structure are part of an effective group interaction. Thus, leaders must utilize a meeting agenda with clear objectives, share the agenda in advance, keep to scheduled start and end times, and prioritize agenda topics (Odermatt, König, and Kleinmann 2015). Along with that, during the meeting team leaders are sometimes tasked with leading discussions. This may include allotting appropriate time for each topic, giving equal voice to all participants, asking open-ended questions, or redirecting off topic discussions (LeBlanc and Nosik 2015). For online meetings, this may involve monitoring chat questions or responding to a raised hand from an attendee. While providing clear communication, matching work to individuals with appropriate skill sets and assigning individual goals is also important. Individual assignments are even more critical for online meetings where non-verbal feedback is limited (Maduka et al. 2018). Team leaders should also ensure equal workload distribution and follow up with team members in between meetings on their progress. From the relational perspective, team leaders may have to navigate disputes. Striving for civility should not limit open discussion and disagreements during team meetings. However, a team leader may have to intervene if disagreements turn personal or become too heated. In these instances, several approaches may be invoked such as restating norm guidelines, redirecting the discussion, pausing for a break, engaging other participants' opinions, or speaking privately to disrespectful individuals (LeBlanc and Nosik 2015). Leaders can improve their understanding of methods for running effective meetings through training workshops or courses.

There are other aspects of team leadership which can positively impact team collaboration and one of these involves psychological safety. When the team leader promotes a group dynamic where sharing and debating ideas can be done without negative repercussions, they are creating a psychologically safe workspace. In such work environments, team members are more likely to share information and coordinate efforts to accomplish goals, and this type of engagement contributes to positive interactions (Mogard, Rorstad, and Bang 2022). The American Psychological Association suggests leaders promote psychological safety by using mistakes as learning opportunities, complimenting risk taking, encouraging idea sharing, and openly acknowledging individual contributions to the group (Schwartz 2023). Another example comes from a clinical teaching environment which utilizes "CENTRE" as guidelines for psychologically safe group interactions (Cave et al. 2016). Along with this, leaders can guide difficult discussions by inviting team members to communicate their perspectives and ideas with a focus on content followed by group input.

> **Box 7.3  CENTRE for Group Psychological Safety**
>
> (A)  C "Confidentiality" of others' input outside of group
> (B)  E "Equal" opportunity to speak in the group
> (C)  N "Non-judgmental ... listening" to others
> (D)  T "Timeliness" with meeting attendance
> (E)  R "Right to pass" in discussions
> (F)  E "Engage[ment]" of all members is encouraged
>
> (Cave et al. 2016, 3)

Another attribute a leader can leverage to promote respectful team collaboration is group humility. Group humility is based on the individual humility of its members. Individual attributes of humility include acknowledging personal weaknesses, learning from others' strengths, and being open to new ideas for growth (Owens and Hekman 2012). As members of teams spend more time together, they begin to form a "collective attitudinal and behavioral expression" which evolves into a type of team personality (Chiu, Marrone, and Tuckey 2021, 363). Humble individuals are the foundation these humble groups and individual characteristics spread to a larger group perspective and approach. Studies indicate these humble groups experience less incivility, stress, and anxiety while increasing cooperation, kinship, and achievement (Chiu, Marrone, and Tuckey 2021; Norcross 2019). This group perspective has a positive impact not only with how the members interact with each other, but how the group responds to other employees or divisions of the larger organization. As with developing personal humility, leaders can extend similar strategies to their team. Such ideas include crediting team member accomplishments, promoting open communication, celebrating group achievements, and recognizing members who contribute to the good of the group.

## Collaboration

In addition to attributes of team leaders, positive group dynamics are impacted by other facets of collaboration. The first of these is balanced autonomy. Team autonomy can be reflected from two perspectives—individuals on a team and the team itself. For both, balanced autonomy reflects an even distribution of independence versus group authority. Studies in individual autonomy indicate increased creativity, motivation, cognitive flexibility, and self-regulation when given decision making abilities (Ryan, Kuhl, and Deci 1997). All of these attributes add to a positive social interaction in teams. Positive social impacts also result from self-directed or autonomous teams. Because of the shared vision and group oversight responsibilities, these members work more collaboratively and are open to participating in problem-solving discussions (Zychova, Simova, and Fejfarova 2023). While team autonomy can foster positive team interactions, how exactly is this balance struck?

Individual team autonomy begins with assigned tasks, and these assignments are accomplished when they are embraced by skilled workers. If given too much independence and decision-making authority, these team members may adopt a slightly dysfunctional authoritative role within the group and position themselves as experts whose opinions carry greater weight leaving less room for others to contribute. As a result, disagreements may occur if their opinion or method is challenged or questioned by other team members. Additionally, if team members perceive their skills are not valued, a loss of autonomy or self-direction may result, and these individuals, upset that their self-worth is not recognized by the other members, disengage from work (Bates et al. 2023). To maintain balanced autonomy within the team, groups should have regular discussions which reflect on methods or approaches to be utilized, recognize value in differing methods, and welcome all team member perspectives (Bates et al. 2023).

Along with this, clarifying procedures or processes, utilizing trial approaches when applicable, and reflecting or assessing progress along the way encourages group involvement and equalizes authority (Bates et al. 2023). While individuals should be given some degree of autonomy for task completion, a balance must still be struck between group participation and individual input.

With the larger team autonomy or the self-directional authority given to the group as a whole, a balance must be struck with the larger organization or even external partners. If there is misalignment between the team and their larger environment, disputes may arise. To minimize this, needed project information and agreed upon objectives with the larger collective should be defined at the start of a team's activity (Ravn et al. 2022). This type of early clarification sets the team up for strategic congruence. As the team proceeds towards their goal, the degree of autonomy varies. One approach gives the team total control for goal achievement, oversight, and conflict resolution. Another design brings in oversight from above where operational rules and procedures are defined by higher ranking individuals (Moe et al. 2021). A less invasive approach has oversight in place, but only to monitor and guide the team when necessary. Lastly, teams may have some input to the decision-making process from a bottom-up perspective with supervisory staff to ensure the group maintains its external alignment (Moe et al. 2021). Through these various approaches, balanced team autonomy can be maintained.

Along with traditional, human team composition, more recent research has been conducted with the integration of an artificially intelligent (AI) team member. The role of AI may vary from support for the team or team members to being a fully integrated member with equal authority (Lyons et al. 2021). Research indicates its influence is both negative and positive. Some studies show AI's presence on teams results in lower trust, reduced human communications, and lower team cognition (Zercher, Jussupow, and Heinzl 2023). However, other studies point to AI's influences contributing to positive team dynamics. As it relates to civility, one attribute an AI member brings to the whole is psychological safety. As machines contribute and exchange information with human partners, there is safety in its relatively objective responses (Lyons et al. 2021). However, such objectivity may change in the future as affective computing incorporates improved emotional simulation into AI responses. Several other studies have found additional AI benefits relating to positive team interaction. AI can detect "potential direct and indirect conflict" and as a result alert the team and aid in resolution (Khakurel and Blomqvist 2022). For example, AI can detect differing opinions of human team members and invite a sharing of perspectives. Other areas of impact include improving proactive team communication, task interdependence, project oversight, and team cohesion (Khakurel and Blomqvist 2022). AI's impact on team civility will continue to be explored as it is increasingly integrated into the workforce and work teams.

## Group Identity

The bond formed by team members is part of what makes these groups successful. The positive aspects of this kind of group cohesiveness were laid out in chapter six. However, along with the benefits, comes the possibility of team deviance. This type of team deviance can be defined as "norm-violating behaviors" which are perceived as a threat to the best interest or goal attainment of the group (Spoelma and Chauhan 2023, 86). Individuals who are grouped together over time form a team morality, a justice perspective which, if violated, may lead to a negative interaction. This type of response can impact two different targets. First, team members can turn on someone within their group who they view as a threat. Internal team deviance is similar to mobbing as multiple people target an individual. However, this targeting occurs exclusively within the boundaries of a formal team. For example, team members may call out and turn on a member who fails to contribute fairly and misses essential task deadlines. Second, team deviance can involve a groupthink perspective with multiple team members playing a role in harmful behavior targeting the larger organization or external group. An illustration of this could be a group which perceives being given an unfair workload and in retaliation may find ways to slow production that negatively impact the organization. Both types of deviant team behaviors create uncivil situations and are best avoided.

Beyond the suggestions for improved collaboration already reviewed, there is also a larger team construct to consider if minimizing team deviance. First, team members should be aligned with larger organizational objectives to keep the perspective of group importance and its supporting role for the larger good. Also, organizations should consistently address unfair practices and address any grievance which may trigger a group's collective action to right a wrong (Thornton and Rupp 2016). Using the previous example, team grievances of a heavy workload should be recognized and addressed by the organization, not ignored. This type of response, both to groups, individuals, and other teams, as well as equal resource distribution has been shown to reduce negative group behaviors (Thornton and Rupp 2016). Supervisory style can also impact team deviance. More harmonious group behaviors result when supervisors are democratic and supportive of team needs. Thus, organizations should encourage team oversight that falls in more inclusive or participatory styles. These types of approaches can be applied to promote positive team function within the organization.

Other team elements related to group identity also play a role in minimizing deviant team behavior. Team members who are engaged, open to new learning opportunities, and avoid procrastination are less dysfunctional (Van Hooft and Van Mierlo 2018). Innovation and idea creation should be encouraged and embraced as part of the team collective. To limit procrastination, leaders can facilitate task completion with regular check-ins and breaking up larger tasks into smaller segments. This manageable approach to task completion equates to more readily accomplishable goals. Stretch goals, or goals set beyond a reasonable level of achievement, have been shown to negatively impact group dynamics resulting in increased conflict, unethical behavior, reduced motivation, stress, and fear of failure (Ahmadi, Jansen, and Eggers 2022). Thus, leaders can help promote positive group identity through supporting realistic goal setting and team innovation while providing individual assistance when needed.

Teams which take on the identity of a clan culture also display less deviant behavior. Clan culture is a "tribal, group, and family culture" in which team members are loyal and committed (Aichouche et al. 2022). Members of a group who form this type of family perspective become supportive of each other and display more positive relational behaviors. Teams who come together like a work family also are more loyal, engaged, and happy (Bujang et al. 2024). Spotify, a streaming music platform, utilizes this type of group culture. At the lowest level they form autonomous "squads" of six to twelve individuals who have their own "huddle room" and leverage an agility coach to improve collaboration (Kniberg and Ivarsson 2012, 3). These squads are then grouped into tribes that work in close proximity to maximize interactions and have a tribe leader who delivers in-person, informational updates regularly (Kniberg and Ivarsson 2012, 5–6).

While forming a tight, family-like bond has positive impacts on behaviors, it must be balanced with the group being receptive to new participants and external input while steering clear of deviant behaviors in defense of the team. Developing clan-like cohesiveness is accomplished by encouraging open collaboration, idea sharing, empowering employees, and supporting employee needs. Revisiting Spotify, this company accomplishes this by forming "chapters" or groups of individuals of different squads with similar skills in addition to organizing "guilds" or grouped individuals of varying skill sets serving different tribes who come together to share information and best practices (Kniberg and Ivarsson 2012, 9–10). This type of sharing of accomplishments, something learned, mistakes made, or feelings of uncertainty facilitates the family-like dynamic among team members (Matsudaira 2019). Lastly, teams should avoid a groupthink mentality and include a nonconformist or dissenter. Teams who have utilized this type of cognitive diversity improve group creativity and problem solving, especially when group members have bonded on a social level and are open to new ideas or approaches (Paulus, Baruah, and Kenworthy 2018).

## Conclusion

As the concept of teams continues to play a dominant role in the workplace, the importance of positive and civil collaboration should be highlighted. Team oversight begins with proper team leadership and self-inspection of personal skills in areas of communication, ethics, humility and culture for this role. The establishment of team norms which include aspects of civil interactions creates the boundaries for effective and respectful collaborations. Beyond running effective meetings, leaders also lay the foundation for psychological safety and promote team humility. Balancing the proper team autonomy and aligning the team properly within the larger organizational goals is also essential to minimize dysfunction. Thus, by reviewing approaches by leadership, group collaboration, and the team's role as part of a larger vision, civility within this group dynamic can be achieved.

## Suggested Reads

Edmondson, Amy C. *Teaming: How Organizations Learn, Innovate and Compete in the Knowledge Economy*. Hoboken, NJ: Jossey-Bass Pfeiffer, 2012.
Gostick, Adrian and Chester Elton, with Anthony Gostick. *Anxiety at Work: 8 Strategies to Help Teams Build Resilience, Handle Uncertainty, and Get Stuff Done*. HarperCollins Publishers, 2021.
Stanier, Michael Bungay. *How to Work with (Almost) Anyone*. Vancouver, British Columbia: Page Two Books, 2023.

## References

"About Us." Zappos.com (n.d.). Accessed January 8, 2025. https://www.zappos.com/c/about.
Ahmadi, Saeedeh, Justin J. P. Jansen, J. P. Eggers, "Using Stretch Goals for Idea Generation Among Employees: One Size Does Not Fit All!" *Organization Science* 33, no. 2 (2022): 671–687. doi:10.1287/orsc.2021.1462.
Aichouche, Riad, Khalil Chergui, Said Khalfa Mokhtar Brika, Mohammed El Mezher, Adam Musa and Ahmed Laamari. "Exploring the Relationship Between Organizational Culture Types and Knowledge Management Processes: A Meta-analytic Path Analysis." *Frontiers in Psychology* 13 (2022). doi:10.3389/fpsyg.2022.856234.
Bates, Geoff, Anna Le Gouais, Andrew Barnfield, Rosalie Callway, Md Nazmul Hasan, Caglar Koksal, Heeseo Rain Kwon, Lisa Montel, Sian Peake-Jones, Jo White, Krista Bondy, and Sarah Ayres. "Balancing Autonomy and Collaboration in Large-Scale and Disciplinary Diverse Teams for Successful Qualitative Research." *International Journal of Qualitative Methods* 22 (2023): 1–15. doi:10.1177/1609406922114459.
Bujang, Muhammad Amin, Salawati Mat Basir, Shalini Munusamy, and Hee Jhee Jiow. "Impacts of Workplace Culture on Deviant Workplace Behavior: A Systematic Review." *Sage Open* 14, no. 2 (2024). doi:10.1177/21582440241247976.

Caldwell, Jame L., Alisha Y. Ortiz, Erin R.Fluegge, and Michael J. Brummett. "The Effectiveness of Ethics Training Strategies: Experiential Learning for the Win." *International Journal of Business and Management Research* 8, no. 4 (2020): 124–131. doi.org/10.37391/IJBMR.080407.

Cave, Douglas, Hilary Pearson, Paul Whitehead, and Sherin Rahim-Jamal. "CENTRE: Creating Psychological Safety in Groups." *The Clinical Teacher* 13 (2016): 427–431. doi:10.1111/tct.12465.

Chiu, Chia-Yen (Chad), Jennifer A. Marrone, and Michelle R. Tuckey. "How Do Humble People Mitigate Group Incivility? An Examination of the Social Oil Hypothesis of Collective Humility." *Journal of Occupational Health Society* 26, no. 5 (2021): 361–373. doi:10.1037/ocp0000244.

Clark, Olga L. and Benjamin M. Walsh, "Civility Climate Mitigates Deviant Reactions to Organizational Constraints." *Journal of Managerial Psychology* 31, no. 1 (2016): 186–201. doi:10.1108/JMP-01-2014-0021.

Cross, Rob, Reb Rebele, and Adam Grant. "Collaborative Overload," *Harvard Business Review*, January–February(2015). https://hbr.org/2016/01/collaborative-overload.

"Gallup State of the American Workplace." Gallup Inc., 2017. https://www.gallup.com/workplace/238085/state-american-workplace-report-2017.aspx.

Getha-Taylor, Heather, Maja Husar Holmes, and Justin R. Moen. "Evidence-Based Interventions for Cultural Competency Development Within Public Institutions." *Administration & Society* 53, no. 1 (2020): 57–80. doi:10.1177/00953997187643.

"Global Workplace Survey Comparison 2023." Gensler Research Institute, 2023. https://www.gensler.com/gri/global-workplace-survey-comparison-2023.

Khakurel, Jayden and Kirsimarja Blomqvist. "Artificial Intelligence Augmenting Human Teams. A Systematic Literature Review on the Opportunities and Concerns." In *Artificial Intelligence in HCI*, Helmut Degen and Stavroula Ntoa, eds. HCII 2022. Lecture Notes in Computer Science, vol. 13336. Cham, Switzerland: Springer International Publishing, 2022. doi:10.1007/978-3-031-05643-7_4.

Kniberg, Henrik and Anders Ivarsson. "Scaling Agile @ Spotify with Tribes, Squads, Chapters & Guilds." *Crisp's Blog*, Crisp. October2012. http://www.agileleanhouse.com/lib/lib/People/HenrikKniberg/SpotifyScaling.pdf.

Lavelock, Caroline R., Everett L.Worthington, Jr., Don E. Davis, Brandon J. Griffin, Chelsea A. Reid, Joshua N. Hook, and Daryl R. Van Tongeren. "The Quiet Virtue Speaks: An Intervention to Promote Humility." *Journal of Psychology and Theology* 42, no. 1 (2014): 99–110. doi:10.1177/0091647114042001.

LeBlanc, Linda A. and Melissa R. Nosik. "Meeting Preparation and Design Characteristics." In *The Cambridge Handbook of Meeting Science*, Joseph A. Allen, Nale Lehmann-Willenbrock, and Steven G. Rogelberg, eds. Cambridge, UK: Cambridge University Press, 2015: 49–68.

Luo, Yifei, Zeyu Zhang, Qishu Chen, Kairui Zhang, Yijiang Wang, and Jianfeng Peng. "Humble Leadership and Its Outcomes: A Meta-Analysis." *Frontiers in Psychology* 13 (December 20, 2022). doi:10.3389/fpsyg.2022.980322.

Lyons, Joseph B., Katia Sycara, Michael Lewis, and August Capiola. "Human–Autonomy Teaming: Definitions, Debates, and Directions." *Frontiers in Psychology* 12 (May 28, 2021): 589585. doi:10.3389/fpsyg.2021.589585.

Maduka, Nnamdi, Helen Edwards, David Greenwood, Allan Osborne, and Solomon Babatunde. "Analysis of Competencies for Effective Virtual Team

Leadership in Building Successful Organisations." *Benchmarking* 24, no. 2 (2018): 696–712. doi.org/10.1108/BIJ-08-2016-0124.

Martin, Sean R., Kyle J. Emich, Elizabeth J. McClearn, and Col.Todd Woodruff. "Keeping Teams Together: How Ethical Leadership Moderates the Effects of Performance on Team Efficacy and Social Integration." *Journal of Business Ethics* 176 (2022): 127–139. doi:10.1007/s10551-020-04685-0.

Mathias, Judith M. "Daily Tiered Huddles Help Prioritize and Resolve OR Problems." OR Manager, November 18, 2019. https://www.ormanager.com/daily-tiered-huddles-help-prioritize-resolve-problems/.

Matsudaira, Kate. "How to Create a Great Team Culture (and Why It Matters)." *Communications of the ACM* 62, no. 6 (2019): 42–44. doi:10.1145/3316778.

Minnaar, Joost. "Zappos's Evolution: From Holacracy to Market-Based Dynamics." Corporate Rebels, October 2, 2021. https://www.corporate-rebels.com/blog/zappos-market-dynamics.

Moe, Niles Brede, Darja Šmite, Maria Paasivaara, and Casper Lassenius. "Finding the Sweet Spot for Organizational Control and Team Autonomy in Large-Scale Agile Software Development." *Empirical Software Engineering* 26, no. 101 (2021). doi:10.1007/s10664-021-09967-3.

Mogard, Emil Viduranga, Ole Bendik Rorstad, and Henning Bang. "The Relationship between Psychological Safety and Management Team Effectiveness: The Mediating Role of Behavioral Integration." *International Journal of Environmental Research and Public Health* 20, no. 1 (2022): 406. doi:10.3390/ijerph20010406.

Norcross, Melissa. "The Power of Enabling Humility in Teams." *The Journal of Character & Leadership Development* 6, no. 1 (2019). https://jcldusafa.org/index.php/jcld/article/view/144.

Odermatt, Isabelle, Cornelius J. König and Martin Kleinmann. "Meeting Preparation and Design Characteristics from Meeting Setup." In *The Cambridge Handbook of Meeting Science*, Joseph A. Allen, Nale Lehmann-Willenbrock, and Steven G. Rogelberg, eds. Cambridge, UK: Cambridge University Press, 2015.

O'Leary, Rosemary and Catherine Gerard. "Collaboration Across Boundaries Insights and Tips from Federal Senior Executives." IBM Center for the Business of Government, 2012. Accessed December 16, 2024. https://www.businessofgovernment.org/report/collaboration-across-boundaries-insights-and-tips-federal-senior-executives.

Owens, Bradley P. and David R. Hekman, "Modeling How to Grow: An Inductive Examination of Humble Leader Behaviors, Contingencies, and Outcomes." *Academy of Management Journal* 55, no. 4 (2012): 787–818. doi:10.5465/amj.2010.0441.

Paulus, Paul B., Jonali Baruah, and Jard B. Kenworthy. "Enhancing Collaborative Ideation in Organizations." *Frontiers in Psychology* 9 (October 21, 2018). doi:10.3389/fpsyg.2018.02024.

Peng, Xue. "Advancing Workplace Civility: A Systematic Review and Meta-analysis of Definitions, Measurements, and Associated Factors." *Frontiers in Psychology* 14 (November 8, 2023): 1277188. doi:10.3389/fpsyg.2023.1277188.

Ravn, Johan E., Nils Brede Moe, Viktoria Stray, and Eva Amdahl Seim. "Team Autonomy and Digital Transformations: Disruptions and Adjustments in a Well-established Organizational Principle." *AI & Society* 37 (2022): 701–710. doi:10.1007/s00146-022-01406-1.

Robinson, Dea, Christie Masters, and Aziz Ansari. "The 5 Rs of Cultural Humility: A Concept Model for Health Care Leaders," *The American Journal of Medicine* 134, no. 2 (2021): 161–163. doi:10.1016/j.amjmed.2020.09.029.

Ryan, Richard M., Julius Kuhl, and Edward L. Deci. "Nature and Autonomy: An Organizational View of Social and Neurobiological Aspects of Self-regulation in Behavior and Development." *Development and Psychopathology* 9 (1997): 701–728. doi:10.1017/S0954579497001405.

Schwartz, Beth M. "What is Psychological Safety at Work? Here's How to Start Creating It." *American Psychological Association.* December 4, 2023. https://www.apa.org/topics/healthy-workplaces/psychological-safety.

Spoelma, Trevor and Tamanna Chauhan. "Expanding the Dimensionality of Team Deviance: An Organizing Framework and Review." *Small Group Research* 54, no. 1 (2023). doi:10.1177/10464964221127982.

Stahl, Gunter K. and Martha L. Maznevski, "Unraveling the Cultural Diversity in Teams: A Retrospective of Research on Multicultural Work Groups and an Agenda for Future Research." *Journal of International Business Studies* 52 (2021): 4–22. https://doi.org/10.1057/s41267-020-00389-9.

Sun, Ui Young, Haeseen Park, and Seokhwa Yun. "Ethically Treated Yet Closely Monitored: Ethical Leadership, Leaders' Close Monitoring, Employees' Uncertainty, and Employees' Organizational Citizenship Behavior." *Journal of Organizational Behavior* 45, no. 5 (June 2024). doi:10.1002/job.2760.

Tagliaro, Chiara, Yaoyi Zhou, and Ying Hua. "Work Activity Pattern and Collaborative Network: New Drivers for Workplace Space Planning and Design." *Journal of Interior Design* 47, no. 3 (September 2022): 29–46. doi:10.1111/joid.12226.

Thornton, Meghan A. and Deborah E. Rupp. "The Joint Effects of Justice Climate, Group Moral Identity, and Corporate Social Responsibility on the Prosocial and Deviant Behaviors of Groups." *Journal of Business Ethics* 137 (2016): 677–697. doi:10.1007/s10551-015-2748-4.

Van Hooft, Edwin A. J. and Heleen Van Mierlo. "When Teams Fail to Self-Regulate: Predictors and Outcomes of Team Procrastination Among Debating Teams." *Frontiers in Psychology* 9 (2018): 464. doi:10.3389/fpsyg.2018.00464.

"Work, Life, and the Workplace A 2023 Survey of Office Workers in Six US Cities." Gensler Research Institute, 2023. https://www.gensler.com/gri/work-life-workplace-2023-survey.

Zercher, Desiree, Ekaterina Jussupow, and Armin Heinzl. "When AI Joins the Team: A Literature Review on Intragroup Processes and their Effect on Team Performance in Team-AI Collaboration." *ECIS 2023 Research Papers* (2023): 307. https://aisel.aisnet.org/ecis2023_rp/307.

Zhou, Wenhau. "Adapting to Change: Exploring Zappos' Self-Management Structure and Its Impact on Innovation and Cultural Diversity." *Modern Economy*, 14 (2023): 293–304. doi.org/10.4236/me.2023.143017.

Zychova, Kristyna, Tereza Simova, and Martina Fejfarova. "A Bibliometric Analysis of Team Autonomy Research." *Cogent Business & Management* 10, no. 1 (2023). doi:10.1080/23311975.2023.2195024.

# Chapter 8

# Leading with Civility

In 2012, Marissa Mayer took over the leadership role at Yahoo and shortly afterwards implemented a Quarterly Performance Review stack ranking system. This system forced managers to rate employees on a scale of one to five in "buckets" of percentages—10% greatly exceeds, 25% exceeds, 50% achieves, 10% occasionally misses and 5% misses (Feloni 2015). Those ranking in the bottom 5% were at risk of being fired for underperforming (roughly 1,100 Yahoo employees lost their jobs), and while an initial purge may have removed low performers, its ongoing use resulted in a climate of fear and disengagement (Feloni 2015; Goel 2016). Other potential behaviors that may result from such a system could include unethical behaviors, reduced cooperation between employees, and reduced trust. From the perspective of civil leadership, some leader decisions, such as the Yahoo ranking system, may have an opposite impact.

While this chapter highlights various aspects of leadership related to civility it should be stated at the outset that a leader's civility overall has a significant impact on organizations. More specifically, recent research has proven that leaders that act with civility can impact organizational commitment (Sharifirad 2024). Or, conversely, leader incivility can cause damage to organizational commitment. One of the most important things a leader can do therefore in creating a positive environment is to create a psychologically safe workspace.

## Leadership Traits

Psychological safety relating to teams was explored in chapter seven, but other aspects of the concept apply directly to leadership itself. Psychological safety begins with being open and vulnerable. According to the results of one recent study, "Vulnerable leadership represents a significant shift in leadership paradigms, emphasizing modeling vulnerability, investing time, and displaying empathy. It offers numerous benefits for organizational dynamics, including enhanced trust, collaboration, and innovation" (McAdoo 2025). This comes in stark contrast from past ideas about

DOI: 10.4324/9781003590149-8

leadership when vulnerability and openness were seen as weaknesses. Achieving this is more a way of being than a task to accomplish. While leaders should not always wear their emotions on their sleeve or share everything that comes to mind, being authentic and real comes with acknowledging one's own faults, shortcomings, and personal challenges. It also comes with acknowledging on a very practical level when one has made a mistake, whether that pertains to a mistake in a general work setting or, more pertinently for the discussion here, in relation to a leadership mistake or error. It helps to consider a couple of concrete examples as to how this may apply. Leaders often get to where they are by being very driven. Oftentimes leaders are born problem solvers and "doers." In a leadership role, however, one might need to learn to become more patient and give others room to grow and accomplish goals. This could be something shared as a leader when mentoring or counseling others. One might share examples in this case where they lacked patience and did not allow team members to grow and contribute to a project or solution. Conversely, leaders also need to, at times, be decisive. This, too, could be a shared lesson. One could discuss a time when more direct intervention and action was needed but they failed to provide it. This kind of openness and vulnerability does not necessarily provide easy solutions for others, but does provide perspective and, importantly for the context here, demonstrates a willingness to acknowledge that they do not always have all the answers. Recent research by McAdoo also emphasizes the knowledge-sharing aspect as being critical in that it provides followers with not just an understanding that it is acceptable and safe to share mistakes but also that these are valuable learning opportunities. The value to the workplace is clear as stated by McAdoo, "When leaders share knowledge, they transform their environment by creating work-related tacit knowledge among organizational members" (McAdoo 2025).

Authenticity and consistency are other critical elements in creating a psychologically safe workspace. The leader in particular needs to be both of these. In the case of the latter, a leader who is inconsistent and erratic can absolutely destroy psychological safety in an organization. People need to know where their leader stands and know that they will adhere to their values even under difficult or stressful situations. Leaders that can be caring one minute but spiteful or uncivil the next do irreparable damage to trust and safety and also cause dysfunction in communication within the organization. They also need to be authentic and true to themselves. It is a bit harder to pin down exactly what this means as it differs by individual. According to Aldijana Bunjak, Robert G. Lord, and Bryan P. Acton (2024), "honesty concerning one's identity and core values reflects an essential aspect of what is seen as being authentic." This requires leaders to lay their cards on the table so to speak. They need to explicitly share their values and demonstrate those values in their behavior. It does no good to speak of democratic decision making and empowerment, for example, if one is going to micromanage and dictate solutions without input. Others in the organization can see immediately through this and will label the leader as inauthentic. It also relates to a significant extent to the previously made point about vulnerability. People want leaders who are human even if that means they have flaws and shortcomings at times.

## Communications

Another important element is the development of a leader's listening skills and the use of those in developing feedback channels. A highly functional, civil organization has leaders that find multiple ways to listen and receive feedback. One-to-one, face-to-face interactions are the best although not the only way for this to occur. While deep listening is best done face-to-face and one-on-one, leaders can also develop other feedback channels as well. These can include anonymous feedback channels and team debriefs. Leaders should actively seek input from employees. This involves building relationships and trust over time. When one considers older theories or ways of approaching management that focus on extreme efficiencies, this requires much more patience and a willingness to allow relationships, conversations, and feedback to occur naturally even when it is not always obviously productive along the way. Having conversations over time, getting to know others, understanding their drives, their body language, and their concerns all takes time, and it is not something that can be forced. This is why authenticity is so important. Ideally, listening and building relationships comes from a genuine desire to understand others and this can only be done through deep listening. As stated by the author of *Be Your Own Leadership Coach: Self-Coaching Strategies to Lead Your Way*,

> The leaders who made the greatest impression on me were those who were skilled listeners. These leaders made me feel like I mattered by listening to my contributions. It wasn't that they always agreed with what I said. Rather, they reflected on what I said and furthered our conversations. Most importantly, they were mentally present and engaged in the conversation—whether physically or virtually.
>
> (Stein 2023)

### Box 8.1 Psychological Safety

- Be consistent and authentic
- Be open and vulnerable
- Develop listening skills and feedback channels
- Encourage civil dissent

- Foster inclusive communication
- Respond productively to failure
- Set clear boundaries

Another aspect of creating a psychologically safe workplace regarding communication, which may seem a bit counterintuitive, is that a leader needs to encourage dissent. The key here is to allow and even foster the idea that one can differ with the leader in a respectful manner. Too often leaders say that they have an open door or are willing to hear concerns or problems. And yet, when those problems or concerns are raised, they "shoot the messenger." Nothing is more damaging to an organization than a leader who punishes those who raise concerns. This is not, to be noted, to condone blatant insubordination. Sometimes individuals can push beyond when a decision is made and even sabotage decisions made by the leader. That kind of behavior needs to be corrected. While the focus here is on the leader it is incumbent on followers to agree to disagree at some point. That said, feedback, especially negative feedback, should be considered a *gift* by a leader. Even if the leader cannot directly or immediately address a concern, knowing that they will be heard and not attacked for sharing concerns is very important for employees in any organization. According to one group of authors, "It's not enough for leaders to give people permission to dissent; they must demand it of people" (Fletcher et al. 2023, 4). These authors go on to point out that people need to be able to speak up, which can be a personal risk, for the benefit of a given discussion. Not to belabor the point, but this is a very big problem in many organizations. When leaders over-react with a defensive response to dissent, especially if it is done publicly, it creates a decidedly non-psychologically safe space.

Related to the idea that a leader should encourage dissent to create a civil and psychologically safe workspace, they also need to create an overall inclusive environment related to communication. This can be done in a variety of ways. The important point here is for a leader to be proactive. It is not enough to just be available to listen. A leader needs to get together with people they lead and actively seek their thoughts and ideas. Any organization will have a group of people that vary in how outspoken they are. It is important for leaders to make sure that those who tend to speak up less are heard. Guiding principles for embracing employee voice include establishing effective methods for employee expression and training leaders in appropriate response (Olson-Buchanan, Boswell, and Lee 2019). Celia Moore and Kate Coombs have also identified key ways to make this happen. One should ask questions that are clearly seeking different or dissenting views, acknowledging when someone raises a legitimate specific concern, keeping meetings casual or informal using humor when appropriate to lighten the mood, take time and do not rush discussions, and getting everyone to explicitly state or own their views or perspectives on the topic or challenge being discussed (Moore and Coombs 2024). Understanding that some individuals may be more willing than others to speak up, this may require a concerted effort on the part of the leader to make sure all voices are heard. Research shows that these efforts are especially critical for leaders who are more extroverted and tend to dominate discussions (Grant, Gino, and Hoffman 2011). In these circumstances it is helpful for a leader to be a bit quieter and more reserved in interacting with quieter or more reserved employees.

---

**Box 8.2 Principles of Employee Voice**

- Establish a continuous cycle of voice communication
- Provide multiple methods for employee voice (direct/indirect or formal/informal)
- Respond to employee comments and concerns
- Train leaders to recognize and utilize employee voice

(Olson-Buchanan, Boswell, and Lee 2019)

---

## Establishing Group Climate

Yet another key aspect in creating a psychologically safe workspace is to always respond productively to failure. Oftentimes failures cause people to become defensive and hoist blame on to others. Yet, the most productive thing to do with failure is to step back and analyze what can be learned from it. This type of review can incorporate cognitive, emotional, and motivational elements (box 8.3) (Zhou et al. 2023). While openness and vulnerability are important, finding a productive way to address problems or failures without gossip or blame is one of the cognitive elements. This is not to say that a leader does not have to hold people in the organization accountable. There will be more on the importance of accountability throughout this book. However, the key distinction here is to emphasize what can be learned from a failure from a problem-solving focus and provide motivational support through the correction process. One step to approaching things in a more constructive manner is to ask pertinent questions. These questions should be framed in such a way as to interrogate the problem or challenge that was faced as opposed to finding or emphasizing fault in any individual or workgroup. In other words, instead of asking why a person, workgroup, or organization failed, the leader can ask what the relevant elements were leading to failure that could possibly be addressed or avoided in the future. This may still be uncomfortable but puts the emphasis on growth and away from emotions associated with blame, which can create an entirely different psychological space. Some research also suggests that leaders tend to do just that, place emphasis on blame and not on problem solving. One other problem with this is that where the blame is placed can lie in deep rooted beliefs that may or may not be correct (Sinnema et al. 2021). This suggests that leaders need to better interrogate their assumptions about the nature and cause of problems while remaining open to novel or unique solutions. This harkens back to the discussion of mindfulness and the need to sometimes also apply a "beginner's mind" to determining the reasons for failure. These are points to be considered more generally regarding leadership every bit as much as they are related more specifically to creating a civil environment.

> **Box 8.3 Leader Support of Work Failures**
>
> **Cognitive:** provide clear standards, definitions, communication, and feedback
> **Emotional:** display kindness, caring, and concern for employee
> **Motivational:** convey encouragement, intrinsic motivators, identify value of failure
>
> (Zhou et al. 2023)

Another facet of leadership influencing the creation of a safe and civil environment involves setting boundaries. There are a couple of key dimensions here. One aspect of this is making it absolutely clear that decisions within the organization will be ethical. It is apparent that in organizations such as Enron, who filed for bankruptcy in 2001 due to fraudulent accounting to cover money laundering and failed deals, that conversations at the top levels can actively ignore moral and ethical standards ("The Enron Scandal" 2021). It is important therefore to understand what the ethical and moral standards are in any given sector. The other more urgent and practical aspect of this to consider here is the need to establish boundaries of behavior for those involved in conversations and discussions. For example, personal attacks should never be tolerated. The focus needs to be kept on the issue at hand. If a slight such as this occurs the leader needs to speak up and restate acceptable norms. According to The Institute for Local Government some ways that decorum and civility can be maintained include not allowing interruptions, encouraging everyone to listen to one another, immediately intervening if someone is being attacked or heckled, separating people from the problem or issue being discussed, taking a break in the discussion if necessary, and even ejecting or removing someone from the meeting or organization if they continually violate norms of civility (Institute for Local Government 2011). Of course, any leader has a responsibility to coach employees that fall short in this area. This can include direct conversations about how norms have been violated as well as outside coaching or disciplinary action short of termination.

All the above elements which contribute to a climate of safety also contribute to trust. It would be very unusual for employees to give their best effort or fully engage without trusting leadership. As stated by the authors of *Leadership in Higher Education: Practices That Make a Difference*, "Leaders put trust-building on their agendas; they don't leave it to chance. It is the central issue in human relationships within and outside organizations. Without trust you cannot lead" (Kouzes and Posner 2019). Trust, it should be noted, is a two-way street. Leaders need to trust their employees and they need to engender trust as well. In some ways trust is less a goal than a byproduct of many of the elements mentioned above. Demonstrating genuine concern and caring for the individuals one leads, along with being vulnerable, authentic, willing to listen, empathetic, and consistently showing these qualities leads to a trusting and civil environment.

## Flexibility and Situational Awareness

Leaders need to be flexible but especially as it relates to handling a wide variety of different situations which can involve incivility. Flexibility in large part relates to one's own ability to embrace not just one's knowledge and experience but being willing to actually let go of those very things to explore new approaches to difficult problems. In the book *What Got You Here Won't Get You There: How Successful People Become Even More Successful* authors Marshall Goldsmith and Mark Reiter demonstrate how leaders need to learn new approaches throughout their career. This is especially true for anyone new to a leadership position. Oftentimes, people are successful due to technical skills, for example, whereas leadership, especially at higher levels, requires exceptional emotional intelligence and soft skills. With regard to civility, leaders can use these skills to demonstrate and model basic and advanced civility. Simple pleasantries even matter in this context. They become even more important when addressing incivility and making sure that the boundaries that have been established by the leader and organization are adhered to. Leaders need to be able to size up a situation and understand numerous contextual and situational factors. These factors can include knowledge of the organization, understanding of the individuals involved, being able to understand root causes of problems, and a willingness to gather additional facts and information.

## Managing Conflict

Successfully managing conflict is one of the most challenging and important tasks of any leader. The first step is to have policies in place that define behaviors and boundaries as well as procedures for handling violations. Not all conflict involves explicit violations so understanding organizational norms is also key. Research on leadership which examines the different approaches of transactional, transformational, and laissez-faire leadership has identified aspects of each that can be useful. Transformational leaders can emphasize and model group or organizational norms while also demonstrating understanding of individual needs. Transactional leaders can also reward specific instances of good behavior or performance and develop neutral solutions as specific instances of conflict arise. Laissez-faire leaders have a place as well, albeit more limited. In some circumstances it is appropriate to allow employees to work out conflict directly with minimal leader involvement (Doucet, Poitras and Chênevert 2009). Much of the research on this topic indicates a lack of training and even a lack of acknowledgement as to the importance of leaders being savvy in conflict management and resolution (Katz and Flynn 2013). While approaches may differ, the first step in addressing conflict is identifying that it exists. In the more egregious examples this may be obvious but that is not always the case. Developing an understanding of the conflict comes next. This requires the leader to gather facts and ask questions. It requires an understanding of issues, emotions, and systems that may be involved or contributing to the conflict. Regarding emotions, one study concluded more specifically that leaders need to "help subordinates reappraise events that led to the conflict in a less affectively threatening way" (Thiel et al. 2018, 377). At this point, in some rare cases a leader may decide to not become too directly involved or provide suggestions or thoughts to consider for the parties in conflict. It usually, however, involves bringing the parties to the conflict together in a manner prescribed by the given organization, getting individuals to understand if norms have been violated, and helping them understand the overarching goal or vision for the organization and how it is impacted by the conflict. Ideally resolutions can then be achieved and tested. It is important for leaders to also follow up on conflict to make sure issues have truly been resolved over time.

While the steps for addressing conflict have been highlighted above, it should be noted that these often require difficult conversations. It is important for the leader to emphasize the problem or issue be resolved without allowing personal attacks. This is especially true in interpersonal conflict. It is helpful when possible, to highlight the strengths that each party brings to the organization and to the issue at hand while also acknowledging transgressions. When trust is damaged between parties this is no easy task and is usually not a quick fix. Conversations may occur one on one or with all involved. The leader needs to set aside an appropriate amount of time and a safe place where interruptions can be avoided or minimized while engaging in these conversations. It also helps for leaders to follow up afterwards with the parties on agreed upon steps forward.

Documentation of some kind is often important or even required in many organizations as is some involvement from human resources departments. Employees, even those that have violated norms of civility, need to understand that, in conflicts which involve disciplinary action every effort will be made to provide support and guidance to get them back on track.

## Treatment of Workers

There are a number of other important issues that come into play in making sure that leaders promote a positive and civil workplace. While not an exhaustive list, the few that will be considered here are the balance of workloads, the need to address nepotism or favoritism, and the equal treatment of employees as regards both transgressions and rewards. All of these can be challenging because they do not have a simple, one size fits all solutions.

While individuals often have varied workloads these need to be balanced over time. This is challenging because it is not always clear as to how this balance can occur. For example, in higher education a vice president or dean will have more responsibility both during and after hours than, say, a part-time office assistant. In a hospital setting doctors may put in more hours than administrative staff. However, in these instances compensation serves to an extent as a balance. Divisions within an organization can also vary in workload and this can shift over time. Additionally, work sectors may be impacted seasonally being extremely busy and overwhelmed in summer months due to workflow while others are busier in fall or spring for example. Regardless of work sector, the idea here is that balance occurs over time. This can be very challenging for leaders as employees do not always have an understanding of other people's or department's work or roles. To the extent possible then developing an understanding of how every person and department contributes to the organization can mitigate perceptions.

Nepotism is a significant concern in many organizations. One recent study has indicated, for example, that nearly one third of all individuals will work in an organization that a parent works in by the age of 30 (Krupnick 2023). That does not even account for other familial relationships in the workplace. In many sectors it is fairly common for spouses to work for the same organization. And yet again, this does not account for nepotism in the form of friendships that exist outside the workplace. Having strong relationships and connections can be a benefit in the workplace, but this can be detrimental if individuals are given preferential treatment, promotions, or raises based more on these connections than actual workplace needs and qualifications. It is important that individuals are treated fairly regardless of their connections to others in the organization. This can get messy at times when individuals who are eminently qualified and capable are given plum assignments or promotions while the perception of others is that treatment is more about the relationship. This is why it is important for leaders to raise awareness of the strengths and qualifications of individuals in these circumstances. One other aspect of favoritism that gets confusing is that, while leaders should treat everyone fairly, they do not have to treat them the same. People have specific skills and strengths, and so it is entirely appropriate for a leader to recognize this and make choices along these lines. For an overly simplistic example, a leader may turn to or give greater weight to the feedback of an employee who has extensive experience on a specific issue when crafting a new related policy than a less experienced employee with little or no experience.

## Conclusion

The role of a leader in fostering civility within an organization cannot be overstated. In most organizations, leaders are present at all levels and across various areas. While many aspects of leadership are important, creating an environment of psychological safety is central. This includes being open and vulnerable, responding constructively to failure, encouraging civil dissent, fostering inclusive communication, setting clear boundaries, being consistent and authentic, and developing effective listening skills and providing for feedback channels. Additionally, building trust, demonstrating flexibility and situational awareness, navigating difficult conversations (especially in conflict management), and adopting a positive and fair approach to the involvement and treatment of workers are crucial. By prioritizing these elements, leaders can cultivate a supportive, civil, and productive organizational culture.

## Suggested Reads

Bolman, Lee G. and Terrence E. Deal. *Reframing Organizations: Artistry, Choice, and Leadership.* 7th edition. Hoboken, NJ: Jossey-Bass, 2021.
Goldsmith, Marshall, and Mark Reiter. *What Got You Here Won't Get You There: How Successful People Become Even More Successful.* New York: Hyperion, 2007.
Kouzes, James M., and Barry Z. Posner. *The Leadership Challenge: How to Make Extraordinary Things Happen in Organizations.* 7th edition. Hoboken, NJ: Jossey-Bass, 2021.

## References

Doucet, Olivier, Jean Poitras, and Denis Chênevert. "The Impacts of Leadership on Workplace Conflicts." *International Journal of Conflict Management* 20, no. 4 (2009): 340–354. doi:10.1108/10444060910991057.

Feloni, Richard. "Why Stack Ranking Systems, Like the One Marissa Mayer Instituted at Yahoo, Are Completely Outdated." *Business Insider*. Insider Inc., January 22, 2015. https://www.businessinsider.com/yahoo-marissa-mayer-stack-ranking-2015-1.

Fletcher, Ben, Chris Hartley, Rupe Hoskin, and Dana Maor. "Into All Problem-Solving, a Little Dissent Must Fall." McKinsey & Company, 2023. https://www.mckinsey.com/business-functions/organization/our-insights/into-all-problem-solving-a-little-dissent-must-fall.

Goel, Vindu. "Yahoo's Brain Drain Shows a Loss of Faith Inside the Company." *The New York Times*. The New York Times Company, January 10, 2016. https://www.nytimes.com/2016/01/11/technology/yahoos-brain-drain-shows-a-loss-of-faith-inside-the-company.html.

Grant, Adam M., Francesca Gino, and David A. Hofmann. "Reversing the Extraverted Leadership Advantage: The Role of Employee Proactivity." *Academy of Management Journal* 54, no. 3 (2011): 528–550. doi:10.5465/amj.2011.61968043.

Institute for Local Government. 2011. *Tips for Promoting Civility in Public Meetings*. Accessed January 14, 2025. https://www.ca-ilg.org/sites/main/files/file-attachments/tips_for_promoting_civility_in_public_meetings_2.pdf.

Katz, Neil H. and Linda T. Flynn. "Understanding Conflict Management Systems and Strategies in the Workplace: A Pilot Study." *Conflict Resolution Quarterly* 30, no. 4 (2013): 393–410. doi:10.1002/crq.21070.

Kouzes, Jim and Barry Posner. *Leadership in Higher Education: Practices That Make A Difference*. [N.p.] Berrett-Koehler Publishers, 2019. https://research.ebsco.com/linkprocessor/plink?id=443917f0-f8a6-302e-8ac1-4a9999dd3b62.

Krupnick. Max. "Nepotism's Impact in the Job Market." *Harvard Magazine*, 2023. https://www.harvardmagazine.com/2023/06/right-now-nepotism.

McAdoo, Justice. "The Impact of Vulnerable Leadership on Employee Empowerment." *Open Journal of Business and Management* 13, no. 1 (2025): 45–67. doi:10.4236/ojbm.2025.131004.

Moore, Celia and Kate Coombs. "Five Ways Leaders can Get People to Speak Up." *MIT Sloan Management Review (Online)* 11 (2024): 1–3. https://login.libproxy.uncg.edu/login?url=https://www.proquest.com/scholarly-journals/five-ways-leaders-can-get-people-speak-up/docview/3150321853/se-2.

Olson-Buchanan, Julie, Wendy R.Boswell, and Young Eun Lee. "Toward a Workplace that Facilitates Civility While Encouraging Prosocial and Remedial Voice." *Industrial and Organizational Psychology* 12, no. 4 (2019): 400–404. doi:10.1017/iop.2019.74.

Sharifirad, Mohammad Sadegh. "Surviving Supervisor Incivility: Can Age-related Coping Strategies Attenuate its Negative Effect on Commitment?" *Interdisciplinary Journal of Management Studies* (Formerly known as Iranian Journal of Management Studies) 17, no. 2 (2024): 521–538. doi:10.22059/ijms.2023.349131.675400.

Sinnema, Claire, Frauke Meyer, Deidre Le Fevre, Hamish Chalmers, and Viviane Robinson. "Educational Leaders' Problem-Solving for Educational Improvement: Belief Validity Testing in Conversations." *Journal of Educational Change* 22, no. 4 (2021): 567–589. doi:10.1007/s10833-021-09437-z.

Stein, Karen. *Be Your Own Leadership Coach: Self-Coaching Strategies To Lead Your Way.* Highett, Victoria: Major Street Publishing, 2023. https://research. ebsco.com/linkprocessor/plink?id=dd6056ca-48ca-3dd4-a2c8-c177eb9911e2.

"The Enron Scandal (2001)." International Banker. September 29, 2021. https:// internationalbanker.com/history-of-financial-crises/the-enron-scandal-2001/.

Thiel, Chase E., Jennifer A. Griffith, Jay H.HardyIII, David R. Peterson, and Shane Connelly. "Let's Look at this Another Way: How Supervisors can Help Subordinates Manage the Threat of Relationship Conflict." *Journal of Leadership & Organizational Studies* 25, no. 3 (2018): 368–380. doi:10.1177/1548051817750545.

Zhou, Qiwei, Jih-Yu Mao, Shuting Xiang, Ran Huang, and Bowei Liu. "How Can Leaders Help? A Mediated Moderation Influence of Leader Consideration and Structure Initiation on Employee Learning from Work Failures." *Journal of Knowledge Management* 27, no. 3 (2023). doi:10.1108/JKM-05-2021-0401..

# Chapter 9

# Navigating Middle Management

While leadership was discussed in some depth in the previous chapter, this chapter will address the specific challenges faced by middle managers. Some research indicates that while middle management is often hard to distinctly define it does have some common elements. Much of the research on middle management tends to focus on the specific strategic role of middle managers or the role they play in instituting change (Rezvani 2017). While there is undoubtedly a great deal of overlap with senior management, middle managers face unique challenges. These include balancing the conflicting expectations of senior leadership and direct reports, having to work with limited autonomy, working through communication challenges or with limited information, potential workload issues while staying motivated and avoiding burnout, and handling conflicts. Aspects of all these roles can influence the workplace tenor. Additionally, middle managers must oversee their work group effectively which involves additional aspects of fair treatment, resource allocation, periodic evaluations, and handling internal problems.

An example of middle management failure is found in a 2017 blog post by Susan Fowler who brought attention to managerial issues at Uber. During her one year with the company as an engineer, Fowler's post reflected a toxic workplace identifying issues regarding harassment, discrimination, retaliation, and in-fighting taking place at the middle management level (Fowler 2017). In response to the post, Uber hired a law firm to investigate the allegations. After over 200 interviews were conducted, their recommendations focused on changes in oversight, staffing, training, culture, diversity, and processes (Balakrishnan 2017). Specifically for managers, recommendations in the areas of civility included training in communication with employees, displaying proper managerial relationships, handling complaints, providing employee feedback and reviews, and supporting individual goal setting (Balakrishnan 2017).

While extreme, the issues at Uber illustrated not only the importance of the middle management role, but also how significantly this position can impact an organization's culture and level of civility. Middle management

DOI: 10.4324/9781003590149-9

is challenged with balancing expectations and needs of direct reports while also being beholden to senior leadership and the larger organization. Middle managers steer the knowledge and activities that occur at the operational level as well as the dynamics of the work group. No organization is perfect, however, and this is often an area ripe with dysfunction. In examining this position, it helps to initially consider the various roles played by middle managers.

## Overview of Middle Management Roles

There are several important roles played by middle managers. Middle managers have the unique position of switching power positions or roles from low (reporting to a higher-ranking supervisor) or high (overseeing staff) which can be both challenging and stressful (Anicich and Hirsh 2017). From a high position, middle managers must lead a work group effectively and solve problems within the group as they arise. Additionally, these individuals monitor and evaluate the performance of employees and allocate resources effectively. Regarding communications, these middle players in an organization must communicate effectively down to their work group and upward with senior leadership or a supervisor. How a middle manager handles these areas impacts the climate of their work environments and resulting level of civility. Each of these will be considered here briefly in turn.

Leading a work group effectively comes first by setting expectations. This includes providing a deep understanding of what the manager expects of their direct reports, including a vision for the department or unit. This should be inspirational and, if aligned properly, connect in a meaningful way to the inspirational goals of the larger organization. Defining this alignment promotes employee engagement and lays the groundwork for a positive organizational culture while minimizing confusion and conflict which may otherwise develop (Alagaraja and Shuck 2015). Workgroup alignment also includes providing more specific expectations for subunits of the group or specific group members. In an ideal scenario, a middle manager helps those under their supervision understand their connections to the whole at a multitude of levels. Leading the workgroup also includes motivating its members. While extrinsic rewards do count and will be addressed further, understanding how each team member is intrinsically driven is most important. For the manager, this involves getting to know each direct report as an individual. This takes time, patience, and a genuine interest and curiosity in others. It also requires the manager to know what a healthy work–life balance is for each employee they oversee. Tasks need to be spread effectively and fairly across the workgroup accounting for roles and individual strengths. Managing direct reports also includes developing the group as well as individual members. This can be done through direct coaching but also through access to professional development opportunities inside and outside the organization. This type of guidance from middle management sets a foundation for a positive, productive work climate.

Communicating with senior leadership constitutes yet another central role for middle managers and directly relates to workplace civility. Flexibility is required when communicating with senior leadership or a supervisor, but such correspondence is most effective when it can be tailored to suit the style of the leader. Research indicates that effective middle managers often do just that (Cable and Judge 2003). Since senior management is often tasked with several areas of responsibility it helps for messaging to be concise (Weiss 2022). Data can also be especially important when communicating with senior leadership as it aids in the decision-making process (Stobierski 2019). Communication is also most effective when it is in agreement with larger organizational goals. If the middle manager can express their need for resources, for example, within the broader context, they will tend to be more effective in getting those resources for their team, department, or area. Perhaps the most important piece is one that takes time and that involves building relationships and trust with senior leadership through communication.

In addition to upward information exchanges, middle management communicates with direct reports. As with senior leaders, the establishment of trust as a best practice allows for the expression of thoughts, concerns, and feelings without fear of reprisal. Other critical communication components with direct reports which promote a respectful and engaged workplace include active listening, providing clear instructions, and recognizing and rewarding employees. Intrinsic rewards work best over time, but recognition has its place as well. One study, for example, "showed that employees regardless of their seniority level need their efforts and achievements duly recognized by their seniors" (Khan, Zarif, and Zhan 2011). It should be noted that recognizing the work of others on a consistent basis has the benefit of increasing engagement within the organization which in turn increases employee satisfaction, productivity, and perceived value (Jo and Shin 2025).

Yet another key role of middle managers is the monitoring and evaluation of employees. This process often begins and ends with formal periodic evaluations, often annually but sometimes within other shorter time frames. It is important for managers to have meaningful conversations with employees to establish goals, regularly check the progress of those set goals, and then provide a summative evaluation of achievement in a set time frame. Numerous tools can be employed for this with organizations often having developed or adapted their own over time (Moniz 2010). It should be noted for our purposes here that civil and positive behavior can be one element considered in these evaluations. Where some managers fall short is in not utilizing the time between formal evaluations to conduct regular check-ins. According to one recent study, "Though it may seem like too much, our survey data and conversations showed that employees are actually more engaged when managers conduct daily check-ins" (Garr 2022). Checking in and observing employees on a regular basis are critical parts of a middle manager's duties.

Another role of the middle manager involves allocating resources effectively. Research has indicated adequate resources impact an employee's well-being and performance (Nielsen et al. 2017). In nearly every circumstance or situation resources, whether they be financial or human, are limited. Managers need to understand the processes and outcomes for their department or division and balance resources to accomplish what is needed by the larger organization. This inevitably involves trade-offs and situations where individual subunits or members of the team may not get all of the resources they desire. It is important, however, that they get what they need to minimize stress and promote a positive work environment. Prioritizing is perhaps the most important element of this. This follows from the overall vision for the organization and department or division. While the importance of communicating has already been mentioned, it plays a critical role here as well. Managers should be open and transparent with employees as to how and why resources are being allocated in a specific way. This is also a great opportunity to foster collaboration to make best use of resources as well. Sometimes this collaboration can occur within the team or unit, but it can also include encouraging collaboration with other units or areas within the organization. This is when it is helpful for both the manager and team members to have established relationships in the organization that extend beyond the immediate working group. As mentioned in chapter six, these individuals are called boundary spanners and are the glue that holds organizations together, especially in terms of interpersonal relationships. As an example, a recent report on wildlife risk management demonstrated how boundary spanners help to coordinate resource sharing which positively impacted wildfire governance (Davis et al. 2021). The importance of boundary spanners highlights just how far reaching and how many domains this can apply to.

The last role mentioned here for middle managers refers to the need to address problems when they arise. Every unit or team will experience difficulties. These can vary considerably. While resources and access to them can create challenges, one of the most significant problems a manager can face is interpersonal conflict within the division or sometimes between members of their division and another within the organization. While methods for handling interpersonal conflicts were reviewed in chapter eight, conflicts stemming from other work issues may require other approaches for resolution. Prioritization is one important aspect here. Some problems are simply more pressing than others and a middle manager needs to know how to contextualize these. Problems can also be more immediate or long term. While communication has already been mentioned in several instances, it is especially important on a variety of levels when handling problems. A middle manager in particular needs to know when to involve senior leadership. Sometimes this needs to happen to simply keep them in the loop. Other times, senior leadership can be a significant resource. This is especially the case in handling human resource (HR) issues that cannot be discussed with direct reports for example. This has the effect of both getting real advice and assistance but also buy-in when difficult steps need to be taken to fix or solve an issue, HR-related or otherwise.

**Box 9.1  Critical Middle Manager Roles**

- Allocating resources advantageously for smooth operation
- Communicating effectively both to the work group and upward to senior leadership
- Leading a work group effectively and aligning goals
- Monitoring and evaluating the performance and behavior of employees
- Solving problems within the work group

Developing a civil workplace requires everyone's help and contribution but middle managers play a special role. They do this first and foremost by modeling civil behavior and strongly adhering to principles associated with integrity and civility. Additionally, they show respect for all employees, reward good behaviors and accomplishments, and set clear boundaries as to what will and will not be acceptable within the department or division. Middle managers also recognize the need for a work–life balance, and they develop an environment of trust where employees feel free to share concerns and challenges. Fostering inclusivity, making sure each team member feels a sense of belonging is another meaningful role. Lastly, they also show they care for the individuals within the unit by supporting and investing in their development.

## Importance of Adaptability and Flexibility

While adaptability and flexibility are important in any leadership role, they are uniquely critical for middle managers. As mentioned, these individuals serve as a bridge and need to be able to convey and translate the overall strategic mission to their group to facilitate work alignment. More will be discussed later in the chapter on this topic, but they serve a critical role when changes are being made within the organization. They need to be able to determine how and when those changes will impact the employees they oversee to facilitate smooth transitions and overcome resistance. Conflict is never one-size-fits-all, therefore, middle managers need to be able to adapt and apply novel solutions to difficult issues or problems. They also need to apply flexibility and adaptability to resources. While resource allo cation may occur on an annual basis, for example, unexpected events and changes may require a reshuffling of these and middle managers play key roles in making these decisions. This is especially the case in monitoring and adjusting to maintain operational efficiency in the face of unforeseen challenges. As noted already, everyone is unique, and managers must be able to adapt their approach based on the individual employees' needs and capabilities. This is true for a variety of issues but most especially when considering the development of staff as well.

## Leadership Styles and Cognitive Flexibility

There are many different leadership styles all of which apply to middle managers. They can be deconstructed in various ways but one common way the research on leadership style is broken down is by considering the following: transformational leadership, transactional leadership, servant leadership (sometimes referred to as laissez-faire although there are some differences between this and servant leadership), democratic leadership, and autocratic leadership (Karie and Kulmiye 2023). These will be considered each in turn.

Transformational leadership is often held up as one of the most impactful styles, especially as it relates to work civility. It focuses on creating a vision. It also focuses on motivating employees and developing trust. Since relationships are one of the most important elements for transformational leadership it can take time and patience to utilize this approach. While transformational leadership can be found in the research literature more frequently applying to senior leadership, middle managers can build a more stable team over time often utilizing this approach as well (Notarnicola et al. 2024).

Transactional leadership focuses on a more short-term approach to leadership. The emphasis is on getting things done and utilizing extrinsic rewards and punishments. A middle manager using this approach is less focused on building relationships and more on making sure specific outcomes are met. Again, there can be overlap in styles utilized but transactional leadership is all about results. While transformational leadership is generally preferred, one recent study that considered a multitude of research publications on this topic overall stated conclusively that "transactional leaders can positively influence organizational performance and drive high performance" (Dong 2023).

Servant leadership has become more popular in recent decades. Coined by Robert Greenleaf in the 1970s the emphasis for the leader is on serving those who follow or report to them (Letizia 2020). Humility and a desire to serve more generally characterize this approach. A middle manager using this approach consistently asks what their employees need in order to be successful at their jobs. Relationships and caring for employees as people are very important considerations. Sometimes this style is categorized as laissez-faire in that the manager may allow employees to operate more freely.

Democratic leadership has its roots in various places. Kurt Lewin is one key figure in exploring democratic decision making in the workplace as he showed the benefits over time of involving employees in this way (Moniz 2010). A democratic or collegial approach can often be seen in higher education as multiple voices are allowed to weigh in on decisions. This does result in more buy-in but can be challenging for a middle manager to employ. With regard to direct reports, democracy does not mean everyone will get their way so a consensus needs to be built, and this can be time consuming. With regard to senior leadership, the decision arrived at by the group may or may not have the support of top leadership creating challenges for the middle manager.

Lastly, autocratic leadership is a style that may be employed. This is often thought of as the "old school" way of thinking where employees may have little say and are told what to do. There are times, however, when this style is still appropriate. Common examples might include issues associated with safety concerns or regulatory compliance. In these circumstances employees may need to be told exactly what is expected and held accountable.

### Box 9.2 Styles of Leadership and Their Impact on Civility

*Autocratic leadership:* reduced stress with clear directives
*Democratic leadership:* employee voice in decision making
*Servant leadership:* open, relationship-driven, caring
*Transactional leadership:* positive impacts of increased performance
*Transformational leadership:* increased motivation and trust

Some examples were already provided but it is important to consider that, for middle managers, all of these styles have a time and place. Most managers will tend to drift towards a particular approach. However, it is important to be able to have cognitive flexibility and shift into different styles based on circumstances and situations. For example, in addition to the examples above, in the case of an immediate crisis a leader might need to be more autocratic. When a decision requires more time and creative input a democratic or collegial approach is often best. If members of a team are highly skilled and competent, servant leadership might be ideal with its focus on support. With its emphasis on specific outcomes or results, transactional leadership can be applicable to meeting specific targets or quotas.

Lastly, transformational leadership can be especially useful to build a team over time, especially when trying to foster long-term, strategic change within an organization or unit. All of these require a middle manager to utilize cognitive flexibility, which researchers boil down to an ability to know when to rely on one's managerial or leadership habits or tendencies and when to apply different or novel approaches in style when solving problems (Laureiro-Martínez and Brusoni 2018). Cognitive flexibility can be improved, and some training applications utilizing gaming techniques show promise for behavioral change (box 9.3) (Lee et al. 2024; Olfers and Band 2018). Understanding, therefore, the context, situation, and organization as a whole are central to knowing which style or styles apply from moment to moment.

---

**Box 9.3 Elements of Cognitive Flexibility Training**

- Encountering unexpected variables
- Rule learning and rule switching
- Task switching patterns
- Timed response times for speed required

(Lee et al. 2024; Olfers and Band 2018)

---

## Overcoming Resistance and Implementing Change

Change in the workplace often brings increased stress and negative emotions amongst employees. Therefore, it is worth considering more intently the position of a middle manager when it comes to overcoming resistance to change. Research on this topic indicates the importance of middle managers broadly in two key areas, the pre-implementation stage by helping senior leadership understand what is feasible and in the implementation stage where changes are communicated to direct reports (Hermkens 2021). There are a number of critical factors here. Perhaps the most important thing is to communicate why change is needed. Often this involves understanding changes expected by senior leadership and being able to translate those expectations to the unit or team. While often given a directive from above, the middle manager needs to be able to involve the team as much as possible in decision making and be able to address concerns or fears. Again, this is difficult territory to navigate. The manager may need to share their own concerns and fears, and it is appropriate for them to be transparent in this regard. In the implementation of change, employees will pay as much or more attention to what a manager does as what they say so leading by example is also very important. Likewise, a middle manager can build on incremental progress by highlighting even small achievements by team members that align with the desired changes. Lastly, a middle manager must overall be patient when implementing changes. One of the most common mistakes is to expect change to be quick and/or easy. Depending on the circumstances, when larger, deeper changes are sought this will occur slowly over time. Some research suggests that developing patience, not just in this context, but more generally can have significant positive ramifications for an organization or group's performance (Holt 2014).

## Managing Conflicts

As one study notes, "While conflict is inherent to workplaces, its management is crucial" (Peng 2023). For middle managers, managing conflicts can involve unique challenges depending on whether these involve direct reports, senior leadership or other departments. While some principles of conflict management can apply to all situations, where the conflict is situated matters. When handling conflict among subordinates, understanding the root cause or causes of conflict is of paramount importance. This requires a willingness to observe and, most importantly, listen. It is very easy to jump to conclusions without gathering all of the information. When possible, a manager needs to take the time to have conversations with all of the parties in conflict and place the situation in context. Open dialogue is a necessity as is a degree of neutrality. Being aware of one's own biases and emotions as discussed in chapter two is critical. It is not always possible to find a win–win situation as Stephen Covey might suggest from his book, *The Seven Habits of Highly Effective People*, but an attempt should be made to find common ground whenever possible (Covey 2020). This can include reminders to the parties about shared goals of the unit or team. Once a resolution has been determined, it is very important for the manager to set clear expectations for what comes next. Following up to make sure those expectations are followed and providing ongoing coaching, professional development, or training opportunities when appropriate are also important. Lastly, in some circumstances, as noted above in solving problems, it is helpful to involve or at least consult with senior leadership about the conflict and the measures taken to resolve it.

Dealing with conflict when it is above the level of a middle manager is uniquely challenging. Due to the power differential, it can be intimidating to raise concerns. However, it is important to be open and honest when sharing these with senior leadership. While sharing those concerns it is essential to actively listen, especially understanding the myriad of other responsibilities and challenges that those senior leaders face. If there are misunderstandings, seeking to better understand senior leadership is important. Most critical is to focus on solutions and to stay professional. While all leaders are different, most will respond better if the middle manager can be poised and collected in how they approach and present concerns. In some circumstances middle managers may need to enlist outside support such as from HR. If this occurs it is important to have a record and documentation of any conversations that have occurred.

In some instances, middle managers will deal with conflicts that involve other areas or divisions. This could be a direct conflict or one involving subordinates from their own and another area or unit. As with handling conflict that involves two subordinates or senior leadership, the manager should be clear in sharing concerns while actively listening. The focus should be on finding common ground whenever possible. In some cases, senior leadership may need to be enlisted as a mediator. It is best, however, if the middle manager can establish long-term trusting relationships with other divisions. This makes it much easier to resolve conflicts.

## Navigating Autocratic Leadership

Navigating autocratic leadership can be a unique challenge for any employee but especially someone in middle management which is why it is worth addressing this in more detail here. At the outset, it should be noted that for a manager whose style tends towards collegial and democratic, having a supervisor who is autocratic could be very taxing. It is not uncommon for different leadership styles to be prevalent from one individual to another and this needs to be taken into account. It is important, therefore, for all types of leaders to fully understand their options and what the best course of action is. Understanding why a heavy-handed leader employs an autocratic approach can be helpful but not always possible. Usually, in the case of working with an autocratic leader who prefers direct interactions, one should remain professional and calm, clarify their intentions, and communicate in a concise manner (Zhou et al. 2023). It is important, to the extent one can, to develop thick skin and leverage mindfulness to assist with reducing emotional responses. That is not to condone behavior where autocratic behavior becomes bullying. It is a difficult distinction but not taking things too personally is important. In any case, it helps to have a trusted support network in the workplace that one can turn to, especially if abusive behavior occurs. Taking care of oneself is paramount in both managing one's own workload and dealing with an autocratic decision maker whose behavior could be characterized as bullying. It is important when communicating decisions that come from above that direct reports have some understanding of the autocratic style from which these decisions may arise. This is a tricky balancing act for the middle manager who needs to be as transparent as possible to their employees while not maligning their superior. In these cases, stick to the facts at hand as best as possible. For example, if a mandate has been declared on an issue and no staff input is sought by the administration a manager might communicate in firm language. For example, "based on the strategic decision to pursue x goal our division has been informed that we *must* ..." For the well-being of the manager and the staff, the manager needs to differentiate what they can control and what they cannot and have some peace of mind in knowing this. In the case of an autocratic leader who is abusive or bullying, working with HR can be important and maybe even necessary. If HR is not helpful, one may need to consider finding a different place to work.

## Conclusion

Middle managers play a critical role in organizations by balancing the expectations of senior leadership with the needs of their direct reports. Their responsibilities or roles include leading teams, communicating effectively, monitoring performance, allocating resources, and solving problems. Effective middle managers must be adaptable and flexible, especially when dealing with challenges such as limited autonomy, competing pressures, and communication barriers. Leadership styles for middle managers can vary and overlap depending on the situation, ranging from transformational and servant leadership, which focus on relationships and long-term development, to transactional or autocratic leadership, which emphasize efficiency and compliance. Strong communication skills are essential for both advocating for resources and fostering trust with employees and senior leaders. Ultimately, middle managers bridge the gap between strategic goals and day-to-day operations, playing a critical role in creating a more civil and productive workplace overall.

## Suggested Reads

Mautz, Scott. *Leading from the Middle: A Playbook for Managers to Influence Up, Down, and Across the Organization.* Hoboken, NJ: Wiley, 2021.
Scott, Kim. *Radical Candor: Be a Kick-Ass Boss Without Losing Your Humanity.* New York: St. Martin's Press, 2017.
Sinek, Simon. *Leaders Eat Last: Why Some Teams Pull Together and Others Don't.* New York: Portfolio, 2014.

## References

Alagaraja, Meera and Brad Shuck. "Exploring Organizational Alignment-Employee Engagement Linkages and Impact on Individual Performance: A Conceptual Model." *Human Resource Development Review* 14, no. 1 (2015): 17–37. doi:10.1177/1534484314549455.
Anicich, Eric M., and Jacob B. Hirsh. "The Psychology of Middle Power: Vertical Code-switching, Role Conflict, and Behavioral Inhibition." *Academy of Management Review* 42, no. 4 (2017): 659–682.

Balakrishnan, Anita. "Here's the Full 13-Page Report of Recommendations for Uber." CNBC. Updated June 13, 2017. https://www.cnbc.com/2017/06/13/eric hol der-uber-report-full text.html.

Cable, Daniel M. and Timothy A.Judge. "Managers' Upward Influence Tactic Strategies: The Role of Manager Personality and Supervisor Leadership Style." *Journal of Organizational Behavior: The International Journal of Industrial, Occupational and Organizational Psychology and Behavior* 24, no. 2 (2003): 197–214. doi:10.1002/job.183.

Covey, Stephen R. *The 7 Habits of Highly Effective People: Powerful Lessons in Personal Change.* New York: Simon & Schuster, 2020.

Davis, Emily Jane, Heidi Huber-Stearns, Antony S. Cheng and Meredith Jacobson. "Transcending Parallel Play: Boundary Spanning for Collective action in Wildfire Management." *Fire* 4, no. 3 (2021): 41. doi:10.3390/fire4030041.

Dong, Bo. "A Systematic Review of the Transactional Leadership Literature and Future Outlook." *Academic Journal of Management and Social Sciences* 2, no. 3 (2023): 21–25. doi:10.54097/ajmss.v2i3.7972.

Fowler, Susan. "Reflecting On One Very, Very Strange Year at Uber." Susan Fowler (blog). February 19, 2017. https://www.susanjfowler.com/blog/2017/2/19/reflectin g-on-one-very-strange-year-at-uber.

Garr, Stacia. 2022. "Why Your Team Members Need Daily Check-Ins." *Harvard Business Review*, September 19, 2022. https://hbr.org/2022/09/why-your-team-mem bers-need-daily-check-ins.

Hermkens, Freek. "Middle Management: A Reinforcement on Change." *IOSR Journal of Business and Management* 23, no. 2, Ser. III (2021): 20–28. doi:10.9790/ 487X-2302032028.

Holt, Karen. "Taking Time for Patience in Organizations." *Journal of Management Development* 33, no. 10 (2014): 1012–1025. https://www.emerald.com/insight/con tent/doi/10.1108/jmd-11-2013-0132/full/html.

Jo, Hyeon and Donghyuk Shin. "The Impact of Recognition, Fairness, and Leadership on Employe Outcomes: A Large-scale Multi-group Analysis." *PloS ONE* 20, no. 1 (2025): e3012951. doi:10.1371/journal.pone.0312951.

Karie, Omar Hussein and Bashir Abdi Mohamed Kulmiye. "Leadership Styles and Organizational Performance: A Literature Review." *European Journal of Social Sciences Studies* 9, no. 2 (2023). doi:10.46827/ejsss.v9i2.1574.

Khan, Shazia, Tayyaba Zarif, and Bilqees Zhan. "Effects of Recognition-based Rewards on Employees' Efficiency and Effectiveness." *IBT Journal of Business Studies (JBS)* 2, no. 2 (2011). doi:10.46745/ilma.ibtjbs.2011.72.1.

Laureiro-Martínez, Daniella and Stefano Brusoni. "Cognitive Flexibility and Adaptive Decision-Making: Evidence from a Laboratory Study of Expert Decision Makers." *Strategic Management Journal* 39, no. 4 (2018): 1031–1058. http://www. jstor.org/stable/45105306.

Lee, Liz Y., Máiréad P. Healy, Nastassja L. Fischer, Ke Tong, Annabel S. H. Chen, Barbara J. Sahakian, and Zoe Kourtzi. "Cognitive Flexibility Training for Impact in Real-world Settings." *Current Opinion in Behavioral Sciences* 59 (2024): 101413. doi:10.1016/j.cobeha.2024.101413.

Letizia, Angelo. 2020. "Servant Leadership." In *The SAGE Encyclopedia of Higher Education*, 1st edition, Marilyn J. Amey and Miriam E. David, eds. Sage UK.

https://search.credoreference.com/articles/Qm9va0FydGljbGU6NTE1ODA=?
aid=96519.

Moniz Jr., Richard. *Practical and Effective Management of Libraries: Integrating Case Studies, General Management Theory and Self-Understanding.* Chantilly: Elsevier Science & Technology, 2010. Accessed February 5, 2025. ProQuest Ebook Central.

Nielsen, Karina, Morten B. Nielsen, Chidiebere Ogbonnaya, Marja Känsälä, Eveliina Saari, and Kerstin Isaksson. "Workplace Resources to Improve Both Employee Well-being and Performance: A Systematic Review and Meta-analysis." *Work & Stress* 31, no. 2 (2017): 101–120. doi:10.1080/02678373.2017.1304463.

Notarnicola, Ippolito, Blerina Duka, Marzia Lommi, Eriola Grosha, Maddalena De Maria, Laura Iacorossi, Chiara Mastroianni, Dhurata Ivziku, Gennaro Rocco, and Alessandro Stievano. "Transformational Leadership and Its Impact on Job Satisfaction and Personal Mastery for Nursing Leaders in Healthcare Organizations." *Nursing Reports* 14, no. 4 (2024): 3561–3574. doi:10.3390/nursrep14040260.

Olfers, Kerwin J. F. and Guido P. H. Band. "Game-based Training of Flexibility and Attention Improves Task-switch Performance: Near and Far Transfer of Cognitive Training in an EEG Study." *Psychological Research* 82, no.1 (2018): 186–202. doi:10.1007/s00426-017-0933-z.

Peng, Xue. "Advancing Workplace Civility: A Systematic Review and Meta-analysis of Definitions, Measurements, and Associated Factors." *Frontiers in Psychology* 14 (2023): 1277188. doi:10.3389/fpsyg.2023.1277188.

Rezvani, Zahra. "Who is a Middle Manager: A Literature Review." *International Journal of Family Business and Management* 1, no. 2 (2017). doi:10.15226/2577-7815/1/2/00104.

Stobierski, Tim. "The Advantages of Data-Driven Decision-Making." *Harvard Business School Online.* August 26, 2019. https://online.hbs.edu/blog/post/data-driven-decision-making.

Weiss, Amy. "10 Strategies to Communicate Better with Your Boss." *Psychology Today.* March 1, 2022. https://www.psychologytoday.com/us/blog/working-with-difficult-people/202203/10-strategies-to-communicate-better-with-your-boss.

Zhou, Chengxu, Guilan Yu, Ying Meng, and Ang Li. "The Influence of Authoritarian-Benevolent Leadership on Subordinates' Work Engagement: A Social Information Processing Perspective." *Psychology Research and Behavior Management* 16 (2023): 3805–3819. doi:10.2147/PRBM.S422961.

# Chapter 10

# Improving the Workplace Environment

The Washington Commanders football team can serve as a warning for how a workplace environment can become toxic. Under the leadership of Dan Snyder, the Washington organization was investigated extensively in 2020 into 2021. Sexual harassment, blatant racism and the use of anti-gay slurs were found to be rampant and common (Saul 2021). Importantly, the organization provided little to no remedy for addressing employee concerns. According to a final report issued in 2021, "bullying and intimidation frequently took place and many described the culture as one of fear, and numerous female employees reported having experienced sexual harassment and a general lack of respect in the workplace" (Saul 2021). Unfortunately for the employees in this organization at the time, the only safety came in getting out. This does not have to happen. In fact, there are many ways that organizations can promote a productive approach to workplace conflict that encourages a positive as opposed to a toxic environment.

While improving the workplace environment includes a number of different elements, one of the most significant factors and a central focus in this chapter is minimizing dysfunction by taking a strong, proactive, institutional disposition to addressing conflict. Approaches utilizing human resources, judicial teams, unions, or ombudsmen may play a role in this conflict management. The work environment can also be improved by organizational support for new hires while guiding existing employees towards positive interactions through leadership and constructive policy creation. Lastly, encouraging the application of a service mindset to internal communications can make positive workplace impacts.

## Addressing Conflict

Interest in conflict resolution in the workplace has never been higher. According to one study, graduate programs in conflict resolution have ballooned in recent years showing the distinct need within government, profit, and non-profit organizations to address issues that frequently arise (Brubaker et al. 2014). According to the American Management Association

DOI: 10.4324/9781003590149-10

(AMA), "The definition of conflict resolution is to resolve an issue or problem between two or more people..." (American Management Association 2023). The AMA generally breaks conflict resolution into five steps which include defining it, determining if the incident alone is the cause of the problem as opposed an underlying issue or problem, seeking solutions from the parties in conflict, identifying solutions that can work for both parties, and finally, coming up with an actual agreement (American Management Association 2023).

Why is addressing conflict proactively so important? It may seem obvious, but it needs to be clearly stated that addressing conflict leads to a more productive workplace, improves decision making, creates a more satisfying workplace for individual employees, and creates a better overall workplace culture. Allowing conflict to fester causes damage in all of these areas. For example, one recent study demonstrated conclusively that conflict, when left unaddressed, negatively impacts productivity (Adeyemi 2022). Most managers learn this through experience. There are times when things can be left to work themselves out but, more frequently, issues involving conflict in an organization require a leader's direct intervention. Furthermore, literature on conflict resolution demonstrates that conflict, when handled properly, can actually improve decision making throughout the organization. For example, one author states, "There are times that conflicts—when handled right—can create an atmosphere for creativity and innovation" (Scharlatt 2016, p. 5). Diverse views are much better for making decisions, but this comes with the need to positively manage conflict. Workplaces that have limited, well-managed conflict are healthier for employees and a more positive overall culture.

Human resource (HR) departments have an important role to play in managing conflict within organizations and in improving the work environment. This includes setting up clear communication channels, providing training for conflict management and overall leadership development, and providing regular assessments of workplace culture. Each of these will be considered here briefly in turn.

One way that HR departments can improve the workplace environment and foster positive outcomes is by establishing ways for everyone in the organization to raise concerns. In most organizations this translates at first to an employee being able to bring a concern to an immediate supervisor. If necessary, they should then have the opportunity to escalate those concerns to HR and/or senior leadership. Trusting that their voice will be fairly heard is a common challenge, however, as HR departments are often seen as more friendly to senior leadership. It is, therefore, important for HR to develop trust among all employees (Harrington, Rayner, and Warren 2012). Having a clear process for escalating concerns delineated and spelled out is important. One avenue taken by some organizations is to have a way for employees to raise concerns anonymously, perhaps through some form of digital reporting system. HR departments can also play a key supporting role by encouraging supervisors at all levels to have regular conversations and check-ins with their direct reports.

Another critical role played by HR in many organizations involves training all employees, but especially those in leadership positions, to handle difficult problems. This can occur in a variety of ways. HR departments with larger staffs can provide direct training on key skills such as conflict management for example. They can also provide additional training by utilizing outside facilitators. FranklinCovey is just one example of an organization that provides excellent, comprehensive training and development for organizational leaders (FranklinCovey 2025). HR departments can additionally offer leadership training programs that occur over lengthier periods of time. These can involve a creative mix of both in-house and external talent. Research indicates that these programs are most effective when the skills taught can be directly utilized in the workplace and when there is a firm understanding that leadership development takes time (Day et al. 2021).

Another proactive way that HR departments can positively impact their organizations is by periodically assessing the workplace environment. The use of employee surveys is one well-documented approach that can be taken. Oftentimes surveys can be utilized to pinpoint problems or at least discover areas where the organization seems to be struggling. According to Jennifer Sumiec in *The Journal of Employee Assistance*, "When possible, gear organizations toward using tools that are scientifically validated, behaviorally-focused, and produce data that drives action" (Sumiec 2016). Surveys do not usually provide solutions in and of themselves, but they could suggest areas to probe further through the use of focus groups or some other means of digging deeper into issues. More systematic metrics could also be utilized studying turnover in particular departments or divisions, as well as promotion and transfer rates. Exit interviews can also be a rich source of data and information as well.

### Box 10.1 Proactive Measures by HR

- Ensure clear communication channels
- Provide regular assessments of workplace culture
- Provide training for conflict resolution and leadership development

While the above-mentioned proactive measures can be taken, HR can play a key role in directly managing conflict and resolving problems. One way HR can do this is by serving as a neutral third party to resolve conflicts. Sitting outside the conflict they can guide the parties in conflict in identifying root causes and emphasizing shared concerns or interests. They can also help manage emotions and document critical information related to conversations and meetings. HR can establish ground rules for conversations when things get heated. They can make sure all voices are heard and, according to research, can play a significant role in addressing power imbalances in the mediation process (Bennett 2014). Critically, HR can also make sure that actual, demonstrable, concrete goals and steps can be taken for future action. Overall, a skilled HR representative can set the tone for civil and productive resolution of problems and issues.

## Resolution Through Judicial Teams, Unions, and Ombudsmen

One unique way that organizations can approach conflict and improve the workplace environment is by implementing internal judicial teams. These teams consist of a mix of individuals at various levels and with different roles within the organization. In creating the team, it is important for members to have a clearly defined role or scope. This includes an understanding of how the team may fit into other elements of an organization. In higher education, for example, a judicial team might handle a student complaint or appeal (Lee 2025). They may have a final say or they may simply provide a report to an administrator who has the final say. The important element is that they understand what their role is and what authority they have in handling issues or conflicts. They also need to understand what types of issues or cases they might handle and what issues or cases would be outside their purview.

Another important element of internal judicial teams to consider is procedure and process. Conflicts of interest need to be considered and consistent standards need to be applied. Documentation needs to be understood and discussed as well as timelines. In most cases, a judicial team leader needs to be determined and, since internal judicial teams are generally impermanent, terms of service or rotations need to be considered. There also needs to be standards for collecting and evaluating any evidence or information that is shared. Confidentiality should be understood to the extent that anyone outside the team needs to be involved in gathering additional information. A team must also have a way to protect individuals that are parties to this process as team members or parties involved in conflict could potentially experience retaliation of various kinds.

Lastly, teams need to be diverse. The diversity of the team will depend on two key elements, the nature of the organization and the nature of the issue being considered. It should also carefully consider demographics and overall bias. High quality internal judicial teams can leverage expertise across an organization to provide broader insight into problems. This is perhaps their greatest value. The work required and extent to which team members need to dedicate time to this process is also important to consider.

Utilizing existing members of the organization can involve pulling team members from other work. While some individuals may excel as team members, it would not be fair to continue removing them from other assigned duties.

### Box 10.2 Internal Judicial Teams

- Composition includes a diverse membership
- Guidelines clearly defined role and scope
- Members maintain confidentiality
- Resolutions have a set, specific timeline
- Standards are in place for collecting evidence

External judicial teams can provide similar remedies to internal judicial teams but are made up of individuals outside the organization. They can address any number of potential conflicts such as misconduct or ethical violations. External judicial teams are usually only utilized when all internal means of solving a problem have been exhausted. They can be used to issue advisory or even binding resolutions depending on how they are established. Like internal judicial teams they often are constituted by people with varying expertise and backgrounds. For example, if a company were to have a challenge of bias in its hiring practices in a specific instance, they could empower an external panel or judicial review that might consist of individuals with experience in employment law, hiring practices, and/or the industry that they serve. External judicial teams can exist for longer periods of time or if tasked with evaluating a single problem might just last a few months in duration.

Unions do not exist in every circumstance and labor laws guiding how they may be utilized are often complex, but when they are available they can play a key role towards improving the workplace environment and solving conflicts in the workplace. Unions tend to be strong advocates for workers' rights and can make sure organizational policies regarding conflict are implemented fairly. In fact, they can often file grievances for employees and work alongside them as advocates, usually based on any bargaining agreements that may exist. They can provide additional legal resources and expertise and protect workers from retaliation in the long run. Unions are different from some of the other entities already mentioned in that they can also lead systemic change beyond any single incident or problem. They can push for significant policy or procedural reform and serve as a conduit between management and staff. Again, access to a union is not available to everyone, but they can provide a unique layer of protection in many cases when addressing workplace conflict and overall workplace conditions (Daniels and Hoffman 2013).

Ombudsmen are yet another potential resource when handling conflict within an organization. While prominent within institutions of higher education, an ombudsman can be found in many industries such as healthcare and the government for example. Ombudsmen tend to be hired by an organization, often by senior leadership. They often work alone and have extensive training in conflict management and a deep knowledge of an organization's policies and procedures. In some cases, these types of positions are dictated by legislative or some other mandate. An example might help to illustrate what their unique role is. In healthcare, for example, two nurses might come into conflict over scheduling and patient care. Despite talking with their supervisor, tension remains, and communication is inadequate. An ombudsman could step in, listen to both nurses, and involve them in a well thought out process to both address the current conflict and improve future communication. Craig Mousin, author and former ombudsman, has referred to a model where the ombudsman could be thought of as a "helpful stranger" (Mousin 2025, p. 4). Mousin sees a special role for ombudsmen in fostering diversity and inclusion, "Ombuds embody a profession that calls for empathy and creativity that is well served to encourage belonging resulting in more harmony and justice in the workplace. Thus, ombuds serve to honor that dignity as helpful strangers" (Mousin 2025, p. 19). While they can be utilized for any instance of conflict, research indicates that an ombudsman can be especially helpful in dealing with incivility or bullying in an organization (Wajingurt 2019).

## Transitioning New Employees

Bringing new employees into an organization represents a unique point in time whereby the workplace environment may be improved by setting the right tone at the outset. While dating back to the 1970s, John Van Maanen's views on the socialization process continue to serve as an extremely useful guide. He posits that there are six dimensions to consider when bringing a new employee on board in an organization. These dimensions play a key part in how they will be socialized into the workplace. For example, collective versus individual socialization refers to whether or not an individual is brought in on their own or as a cohort (Van Maanen 1978). Individuals in cohorts can form initial and lasting social bonds that can impact the organization positively in the long run. Formal versus informal socialization refers to the extent that the onboarding process is left up to chance versus how much is laid out in very specific steps (Van Maanen 1978). The nature of the role and organization are important considerations here. The sequential versus random dimension is relevant in that it determines if an individual should learn specific aspects of a job before others (Van Maanen 1978). Likewise, fixed versus variable socialization considers the time frame that an individual is in training for (Van Maanen 1978). The serial versus disjunctive dichotomy or dimension refers to whether or not an individual is trained by their predecessor (Van Maanen 1978). If the workplace environment is a healthy one and the people doing the training have the right attitude, experience, and skills, then having this process be serial makes the most sense. But, if the position requires novel thinking or problem solving, then it might be best to have a disjunctive process. If a new employee is trained not only with method but also civil behavior, this element is of special consideration when seeking to build a positive culture within organizations. Lastly, one might consider investiture versus divestiture in the socialization process. In the case of investiture, the organization is hoping for the individual to bring their own creative, authentic self to the position (Van Maanen 1978). In divestiture, individuals are expected to conform to organizational standards which may not always be based in civility (Van Maanen 1978). There is not one simple answer for integrating new hires. Rather, the main point made is that leaders need to be mindful and aware of how the socialization process occurs when transitioning new employees into the organization.

As employees enter an organization they are socialized and made aware of general and role-specific expectations. While various entities assist in this process, the importance of role modeling and providing ongoing support cannot be overstated. According to some interesting research, leaders who have had good role models and are readily able to reflect upon that past experience are in turn good at role modeling (Brown and Treviño 2014). Likewise, as noted in chapter two, leaders that are self-reflective and self-aware are more effective at role modeling (Cook and Macaulay 2014). The process of role modeling will differ considerably depending on the role and type of organization as well as the values of that organization. In a dysfunctional organization where results are sought at all costs, leaders may exhibit bullying or rude behavior. In most organizations though much more constructive values prevail. If communicating openly and freely to achieve tasks is an organizational value, then leaders can exemplify this by being open and honest with staff. Leaders can lead by example when they acknowledge that they do not have all of the answers and are willing to grow and learn alongside their employees. By encouraging professional development while also engaging in it themselves, they can create a mindful organization that emphasizes positive qualities. They can likewise model the importance of work–life balance by showing they are proactively managing their own. Again, not every organization will be healthy in this regard. However, in an organization with strong, principled leadership focused on long-term success, care is exhibited toward employees as well as open encouragement of self-care. Lastly, leaders lead by example when they hold themselves accountable. This implies a willingness to acknowledge mistakes and apologize when appropriate.

Role modeling is helpful, but it needs to go hand in hand with ongoing empathetic support for employees. One way that leaders accomplish this is by actively listening on an ongoing basis. Active listening has numerous benefits but here it applies specifically to how it provides critical support. That support should also be personalized. Leaders need to know who their employees are as individuals in order to understand what kinds of support they specifically may need. Ongoing coaching, even when it is sharing something with an employee that they may not wish to hear, is also an important way to assist and support staff. Leading with empathy is essential. When circumstances warrant this might involve any number of things such as adjusting an employee's schedule, getting the employee help they need from another department, connecting the employee to an employee assistance program, or encouraging the employee to take breaks.

For most employees to thrive, managers need to do all these things stated above and also develop deep ongoing communication and relationships. This, for one, goes back to having regular check-ins. It is ideal when staff are willing to bring concerns to leadership as they arise but leaders cannot always count on that happening. Having regular points of communication opens the door to learning more about what is happening and being ready to help. Trust and relationships can also be built over time by showing that the leader values the input of their employees and regularly includes them in the decision-making process. They can also build relationships and communications through team building whereby relationships are not just strengthened with the leader or manager but across the entire team.

## Guiding Behavior Through Policy

While the proper handling of conflict and paying attention to bringing in new staff and supporting them over the long run are important, policies also provide a powerful way to guide behavior and create a more positive workplace environment, especially when they have clear and strong enforcement mechanisms. Well-written policies can provide consistency, clarity, reduce risk, and entail legal compliance associated with a given industry.

Civility policies are ones that are particularly worth considering in this context. These types of policies can specify respectful communication for example. They can also provide avenues for conflict resolution and outline professional behavior. A key policy to have is one that prohibits bullying, harassment, sexual harassment, and discrimination. While these are often dictated by law, a healthy organization should take as proactive a stance as possible. This means not just having a policy but providing employees with good and bad examples through ongoing training and documentation. Employees should understand who they can turn to for assistance when encountering such toxic behaviors and know that they have strong institutional support. Consequences for deviating from civil behavior need to be spelled out clearly and action needs to be taken by leadership when norms are violated. In the case of sexual misconduct, a review of literature has identified several areas organizations should focus on to effectively improve on written policy (box 10.3) (Salabay, Nurbaeni, and Wahyunengseh 2024). It is also not enough to simply have these policies or convey them on a single occasion. Rather, an organization should regularly convey positive expectations. Many organizations have annual training for issues associated with IT and data security. Having refresher sessions on civility is of equal importance. While embodying much of what has already been stated, some organizations take the additional step of having a good citizenship policy that emphasizes civic responsibility. Some companies such as Starbucks have gone so far as to hold the organization itself responsible for good citizenship through programs hiring refugees (Chezuba 2022).

---

**Box 10.3 Sexual Assault Policies Areas of Focus**

- Training for sexual assault focused on recognizing, preventing, reporting
- Develop a safe method for reporting
- Provide psychological and legal support for victims
- Promote understanding of regional and cultural norms

(Salabay, Nurhaeni, and Wahyunengseh 2024)

---

## Applying a Customer-based Mindset

One powerful way that organizations have gone about improving the overall work environment is through creating a customer-based mindset when working with others within the organization. The concept is fairly straightforward and involves treating each other as one would a customer. Since most organizations already understand the explicit and implicit importance of how important it is to care for customers or clients, this approach can increase civility internally. One study definitively connected such an approach to better job performance, greater overall productivity, and greater satisfaction with one's job (Kennedy et al. 2002). According to that same study, "When the requirements of each successive organizational member are met and ultimately linked with external customers, the organization can truly be said to have a customer orientation" (Kennedy et al. 2002, 167). This points to a very holistic approach to workplace civility that extends through peers, direct reports, supervisor, and the client or customer. Other benefits of this approach also include improved collaboration, better problem solving, and better alignment with institutional goals.

**Box 10.4 Benefits of a Customer-based Mindset**

- Better job performance
- Greater alignment with organizational goals and mission
- Greater job satisfaction
- Improved collaboration
- Increased problem solving

## Conclusion

Improving the workplace environment and handling conflict in a positive manner are critical elements for an organization to become and remain successful. Constructive approaches to conflict resolution with the assistance of HR, internal or external judicial teams, unions, or an ombudsman can all be helpful. Taking a proactive stance with clear communication channels, the provision of appropriate levels of training on conflict resolution, and regular assessment of the environment all play a role. Role modeling and empathetic leadership is also important in maintaining a high quality of achievement and satisfaction within the organization. Having specific policies that delineate good citizenship can bolster these efforts. Lastly, having a customer-based mindset when working with others within the organization can be the final piece in creating a positive and productive workplace environment.

## Suggested Reads

Chapman, Gary, Paul White, and Harold Myra. *Rising Above a Toxic Workplace: Taking Care of Yourself in an Unhealthy Environment.* Chicago: Moody Publishers, 2014.

Grant, Adam. *Give and Take: A Revolutionary Approach to Success.* New York: Viking, 2013.

Sutton, Robert I. *The No Asshole Rule: Building a Civilized Workplace and Surviving One That Isn't.* New York: Business Plus, 2007.

## References

Adeyemi, Joseph Kayode. "Workplace Conflict on Productivity and Emotional Stability of Employees." *International Journal of Management and Business Applied* 1, no. 2 (2022): 103–109. doi:10.54099/ijmba.v1i2.216.

American Management Association. "The 5 Steps to Conflict Resolution." Last modified January 25, 2023. https://www.amanet.org/articles/the-five-steps-to-conflict-resolution/#:~:text=Compromising%20is%20when%20both%20parties%

20come%20to,works%20to%20a%20peaceful%20resolution%20quicker.%
20Competing.

Bennett, Anthony. "The Role of Workplace Mediation: A Critical Assessment." *Personnel Review* 43, no. 5 (2014): 764–779. doi:10.1108/PR-02-2012-0036.

Brown, Michael E. and Linda K.Treviño. "Do Role Models Matter? An Investigation of Role Modeling as an Antecedent of Perceived Ethical Leadership." *Journal of Business Ethics* 122 (2014): 587–598. doi:10.1007/s10551-013-1769-0.

Brubaker, David, Cinnie Noble, Richard Fincher, Susan Kee-Young Park, and Sharon Press. "Conflict Resolution in the Workplace: What Will the Future Bring?" *Conflict Resolution Quarterly* 31, no. 4 (2014): 357–386. doi:10.1002/crq.21104.

Chezuba. "What Does It Mean To Be A Good Corporate Citizen?" Last modified September 8, 2022. https://www.chezuba.com/blog/what-does-it-mean-to-be-a -good-corporate-citizen.

Cook, Sarah and Steve Macaulay. "Making a Difference: Role Modeling." *Training Journal* (April2014): 34–38.

Daniels, Allen and Ruth J. Hoffman. *Labor Relations: Major Laws & A Guide to the National Labor Relations Act.* New York: Nova Science Publishers, Inc., 2013. https://research.ebsco.com/linkprocessor/plink?id=9b4cf6fb-a9e7-34b8-a 0eb-618b394c1297.

Day, David et al. "Unlocking Human Potential through Leadership Training & Development Initiatives." *Behavioral Science & Policy* 7, no. 1 (2021): 41–54. doi:10.1177/237946152100700105.

FranklinCovey. "Homepage." *Franklin Covey Co.*, 2025. Accessed February 24, 2025. https://www.franklincovey.com/.

Harrington, Susan, Charlotte Rayner, and Samantha Warren. "Too Hot to Handle? Trust and Human Resource Practitioners' Implementation of Anti-bullying Policy." *Human Resource Management Journal* 22, no. 4 (2012): 392–408. doi:10.1111/1748-8583.12004.

Kennedy, Karen Norman, Felicia G. Lassk, and Jerry R. Goolsby. "Customer Mind-Set of Employees Throughout the Organization." *Journal of the Academy of Marketing Science* 30, no. 2 (2002): 159–171. doi:10.1177/03079459994407.

Lee, Barbara A. "Judicial Review of Student Challenges to Academic Misconduct Sanctions." *Journal of College and University Law* 39, no. 3 (2025): 511–536. http s://www.nacua.org/docs/default-source/jcul-articles/volume-39/39_jcul_5119a 63f98add196525b0c1ff0000265210.pdf?sfvrsn=b87a9cbf_7.

Mousin, Craig B. "Facilitating Belonging: Ombuds as the Helpful Stranger." *SSRN Electronic Journal* (2025). doi:10.2139/ssrn.5101487.

Salabay, Desy Natalia, Ismi Dwi Astuti Nurhaeni, and Rutiana Dwi Wahyunengseh. "Development of Policies for Preventing and Handling Workplace Sexual Harass-ment: Systematic Literature Review." *E3S Web Conferences* 593: 01004 (2024). Paper presented at International EcoHarmony Summit (IES 2024): Navigating the Threads of Sustainability, Pekanbaru, Indonesia, September 26, 2024. doi:10.1051/e3sconf/202459301004.

Saul, Derek. 2021. "Congress Requests Information From NFL: Everything We Know About Washington Football Team's Email Scandal." Forbes.com, October, 22, 2021. https://research.ebsco.com/linkprocessor/plink?id=f68cb878-2f7a-3fcb-bfe9-615f07a b15a2.

Scharlatt, Harold. *Resolving Conflict: Ten Steps for Turning Negatives to Positives.* Greensboro, NC: Center for Creative Leadership, 2016.

Sumiec, Jennifer. "Is That an Elephant in the Room? Assessing Workplace Culture." *The Journal of Employee Assistance* 46, no. 1 (2016): 26+. Gale Academic One-File. Accessed February 24, 2025. https://link.gale.com/apps/doc/A441161969/AONE?u=horrygtc&sid=bookmark-AONE&xid=20b2aa34.

Van Maanen, John. "People Processing: Strategies of Organizational Socialization." *Organizational Dynamics* 7, no. 1 (1978): 19–36. doi:10.1016/0090-2616(78)90032-90033.

Wajingurt, Clara. "The Faculty Ombudsperson: Maintaining Civility and Academic Freedom in Higher Education." *Journal of the International Ombudsman Association* 12, no. 1 (2019). https://www.ombudsassociation.org/assets/docs/JIOA_Articles/JIOA-2019-B.pdf.

# Chapter 11

# Offering Training and Development

In 2016 Wells Fargo was called out for egregious business practices. The bank began promoting cross-selling strategies called "gaming" to increase sales in 1998, but it was not until 2002–2016 that unethical practices were used to meet the unrealistic quotas set by bank leaders (Office of Public Affairs 2020). When the scandal broke, over 5,300 employees were terminated for creating fake customer online banking accounts and credit card applications to boost numbers and receive employee compensation awards (Corkery 2016). The scope of this fraudulent behavior was enormous. According to *The New York Times*, "In all, Wells Fargo employees opened roughly 1.5 million bank accounts and applied for 565,000 credit cards that may not have been authorized by customers" (Corkery 2016). Employees later reported that they felt extreme pressure by their leadership to create these fake accounts. As a result of this breach of trust, Wells Fargo implemented new enhanced training programs and regular ethical reviews for positions and decisions related to the breach. They publicly addressed the wrongdoings by acknowledging mistakes and transparently stating how they would be addressed in the future in their 2017 annual report (Wells Fargo 2017). While Wells Fargo finally rectified their issues, they failed to proactively correct unrealistic sales expectations and the resulting unethical practices of bank staff for over a decade.

Wells Fargo presents an example of an organization's misstep in recognizing its vital role in creating an ethical, positive workplace. This chapter focuses squarely on methods for organizations to do just the opposite and be preemptive in preparing employees for work success while promoting a culture grounded in principled behaviors. To accomplish this, organizations and their employees must be able to grow and adapt. Organizations can focus on personal development plans and have organized, ongoing employee training to minimize rude or hostile actions and boost emotional intelligence. Also, while training and professional development have been mentioned throughout this book, it is important to focus on the importance of offering formal sessions to maintain employee engagement, individual development, and continually promote a positive and civil workplace

DOI: 10.4324/9781003590149-11

environment. As work environments of the future are built on the actions of the present, success depends on actions taken now.

## Individual Development Plans

One of the most fundamentally important layers of training and development is the individual development plan. While such plans can be used by organizations for assessment, when implemented from the formative perspective they can positively impact self-reflection and growth (Beausaert et al. 2011). Individual development plans have a number of components or elements such as an employee's overall profile and career goals, development objectives, an action plan, and performance metrics (box 11.1) (Greenan 2016). When plans are self-directed, focused, and combined with feedback from a mentor or supervisor, they can bring positive results (Beausaert et al. 2011).

According to the popular job matching and hiring platform Indeed there are eight key reasons why these plans matter. They allow for adaptation, help with goal achievement, improve morale, assist with branding, nurture future leaders within the organization, improve performance, and allow for correcting mistakes (Indeed 2025).

---

**Box 11.1 Individual Development Plans: Key Elements**

- Personal assessment
- Profile and career goals
- Development objectives
- Action plan and timeline
- Ongoing support
- Performance metrics

(Greenan 2016)

---

When considering an employee's profile, a number of factors come into play. This is the base point from which a plan is developed. It includes consideration of the employee's education, current skills, and competencies. For a pragmatic approach, any manager attempting to assist an employee should start with their resume or CV. Employees should be encouraged to keep records or documentation of any training or new competencies they acquire so that their resume or CV can always be kept up to date. The career goals of an employee may not always match up with their current or future role but, to the extent that the organization seeks to develop them, those goals should be matched with both present and possible future duties, roles, or responsibilities within the organization. They should also be connected to the broad mission of the organization and the department or division in which the employee is situated.

Once an employee's background, current skill set, and past experiences are taken into consideration, a development plan can be constructed. This should involve meaningful ongoing conversations between a supervisor and employee. Again, taking into consideration the individual and the needs of the organization, clear goals should be stated. These could build on strengths and address weaknesses or any shortcomings in the employee's skills. According to one study, an attempt "to determine the strengths and shortcomings of workers and encouraging workers are the most critical factors that affect the performance of employees" (Vuong, Ngoc, and Nguyen 2022). Ideally, these should be as concrete as possible to be able to measure progress regularly on both a formative and summative basis. Objectives should flow to specific activities such as workshops, on-the-job training, or opportunities for mentoring. Supporting resources should also be considered, whether this means assigning a mentor or allocating financial resources for training for example. While there is often room for flexibility, a timeline should also be considered and delineated. Specific proactive steps should be defined to make sure everything that needs to occur does. This includes follow ups and evaluations.

It is worth considering a few additional key points from the research regarding individual performance plans. According to one recent study regarding performance plans, "Role content and scope should be clearly defined to avoid role ambiguity and role conflict" (Nduati and Wanyoike 2022, p. 375). That same research emphasizes the critical importance of regular employee performance reviews to make sure progress is ongoing (Nduati and Wanyoike 2022). Yet another study notes the importance of time management relative to the individual performance plan and goal achievement. This investigation specifically examined the impact of interruptions in one's individual performance plan and the usefulness of having contingency plans for dealing with interruptions in one's work (Parke et al. 2018). One last point, coming from a systematic review found in the *International Academic Journal of Human Resource and Business Administration*, notes that organizational structures and processes need to be considered as important factors in establishing employee performance plans (Muriuki and Wanyoike 2021).

## Position-Specific Training

While individual performance plans are probably the most recognized way to provide training and support, position-specific training can also be very effective and efficient as it can be applied to more than one employee within the organization over time. One great benefit of role-specific or job-specific training is that it can cut down on the onboarding process. Also, rather than being left up to chance or mixed in with too much general information, knowledge of a role and clear instructions for that role or position are targeted. Such plans also impact the overall work environment as such training will minimize mistakes and more quickly connect the employee to aspects of respect, support, and communication within the workgroup.

A good example of role-specific training comes from professional or semi-professional sports where training tends to be very intricately tied to one's position. According to one study, "While 'specialist coaching' has emerged in various team sports over the past years, the optimal integration of these specialists into organisational structures may offer substantial opportunities for improvement of the work of sports organisations" (Otte et al. 2020, 22). This is a lesson for organizations of all types, not just those within the sports industry. By focusing on specialized knowledge and tasks, individuals who receive this training alone or in a cohort gain expert knowledge and skills that generally surpass that of more general approaches. This points back to previously covered leadership training programs for example that while a bit more general than the sports example, cater to very role-specific skills. Evidence indicates that such focus in leadership training provides for more effective training and onboarding (Day et al. 2021).

Another area that can be positively impacted by role-specific training is employee engagement. By seeing the direct connection to specific job tasks, employees will be more likely to immediately understand their relevance and connect on a deeper level to what is learned. Everyone who has been to school knows that it is more difficult to understand why education through courses such as algebra may seem less engaging or relevant than other more practical coursework. Having immediately relevant learning take place not only enhances work engagement, but, as research indicates, also enhances commitment to the organization and its goals as well (Ali et al. 2024). If placed in context, specialized training also has the benefit of better team performance as individuals understand the role they play relative to others.

Lastly, another approach which can be relevant to the role is skill-based training. Again, as with other training, there is some overlap, especially with role-specific training. That said, role-specific training is sometimes narrower, while skill-based training focuses on skill sets that may be more general or transferable. The key elements of skill-based training come in its focus on skills that are practical, specific, measurable, and that can be improved over time. While one might consider basic skills across a wide variety of disciplines, this type of training can include fairly high-level skills and knowledge. For example, one study exploring the use of this approach to training for counselors "demonstrated that skill-based training can facilitate superior skill acquisition, retention, and transfer to the applied setting and, in addition, bring about higher client satisfaction than conceptual-based training (Baumgarten and Roffers 2003, p. 290)." The key is that these trainings, being skill-based, included "demonstrations or experiential practice of the skills" that were not required in their control group (Baumgarten and Rotters 2003, 290). Thus, a hands-on approach to applying what was learned is essential in skill-based training.

## Professional Development and Job Satisfaction

Listening to employees and providing high-quality training and development opportunities is critically important for job satisfaction. While all employees will differ in terms of the various kinds of training development opportunities they prefer, it has been shown that providing training and development are very important in creating a productive work environment. One recent study, for example, showed that workplace training and development opportunities were connected to not just job satisfaction but were also significantly connected to loyalty and retention as well (Mampuru et al. 2024). An examination of nurses showed that they exhibited greater overall job satisfaction when professional development opportunities were provided, especially if those trainings were offered in flexible ways such as online (Hariyati and Safril 2018). Yet another study that examined the impact on job satisfaction of training for teachers showed that it did increase job satisfaction for teachers that had either a high or low need. One interesting side note from this study was that merely having *access* to training was impactful, so, in other words, knowing it was available in and of itself can impact job satisfaction (Smet 2021).

## Changing Roles and Adapting to Technology

There are two special cases that need to be considered when training or professional development play a crucial role. These include employees transitioning roles and employees encountering new technology. These are special cases because they reflect a need distinct from onboarding new employees or providing more general training opportunities.

When transitioning to a new position, individuals experience changes in several areas (box 11.2), three of which can be influenced by training—relational, behavioral, and psychological (George, Wittman, and Rockmann 2022). An employee entering a new role may be knowledgeable about the organization but lack key skills or information for taking on a new role. Oftentimes, it is taken for granted that someone who is familiar with the organization will quickly be able to fill a new role. While they may have useful insider knowledge, one should not make this assumption. Certainly, coming into a role with existing institutional knowledge and relationships is extremely helpful. In fact, building on strengths and leveraging both existing and new, helpful relationships when taking on a different role is critical to success (Cross, Pryor, and Sylvester 2021). Training impacting this relational area may include numerous areas, such as improved listening or empathy, which contribute to successful connections with other workers. For new tasks, it may be that some information could be provided in a more succinct format, and that training and development could, thus, be more targeted to the specifics of a new role (Gurchiek 2022). There can, however, be negative consequences to not being more proactive. For example, the individual might experience self-doubt if not properly trained. They might also experience added stress if they are not able to identify just what it is they are missing or if others in the organization assume they should have role-specific knowledge that they lack. One solution is to provide at least some role-specific training that, to an extent, mirrors that of hiring an external candidate.

> ### Box 11.2 Impact Areas of Role Transitions
>
> **Behavioral:** changes to routines and tasks
> **Physical:** change of workspace and resources
> **Psychological:** self-identification in new role
> **Relational:** new co-workers and contacts
>
> (George, Wittman, and Rockmann 2022, 104)

Another situation where special attention needs to be paid to professional development is in regard to technology. Most organizations deal with technology on a variety of levels. It would be unusual for someone to come into an organization without at least some basic skills relative to a given job. The fact is, however, that most software platforms and other technologies experience regular, incremental development at minimum and sometimes radical development or changes. In both cases, employees need to be provided with the skills and information they need to adapt. This also needs to be extremely timely. It is not uncommon for an organization to offer training too early or too late. For example, sometimes training will be provided but then setbacks cause the implementation of a new system or software to be delayed by months or even years. Under such circumstances, employees will likely have forgotten much of what they have learned. In other cases, an organization may roll out new software only realizing after the fact that training was missed. Another final factor to consider is how an employee's specific role intersects with technology changes. In higher education or retail environments for example, different roles may require very different usage of shared systems. All of this needs to be considered before implementing new changes in technology.

It would be remiss to not consider the impact of AI on the future of workplace training and development initiatives here. It is likely that most jobs will be impacted by this new technology in ways as or more impactful than the development of computers and the internet. One recent study exploring the communications industry in particular noted that,

> communication organisations and universities that want to secure a front-line position need to assume that from now on life-long learning and constant re-skilling are fundamental to face the current acceleration of technology. Training should focus on improving unique human traits and skills related to social interaction and gaining experience with current AI and automation tools.
>
> (Jiménez, Alejandro, and Ouariachi 2021)

Another study focused on education noted, "In the field of professional development in education, there is a need for comprehensive research into the necessary skills and competencies for educators and researchers to integrate GAI" (Al Naqbi, Bahroun, and Ahmed 2024, 29). That same study, taking a comprehensive view of professional development, noted that AI's impact will cut across all work sectors "revolutionizing how work productivity is increased" (Al Naqbi, Bahroun, and Ahmed 2024, 29). The authors of this text can speak to the fact that colleges and universities of all types and kinds have recently prioritized professional development programming for faculty associated with AI and how it will impact teaching, learning, and student preparedness across all fields of study.

## Promoting Civility through Formal Training Programs

Central to the purpose of this text, training programs that promote civility are important for healthy organizations. While sometimes targeting specific groups such as leaders, this type of training and development can be useful across an organization. In fact, it can be much more successful to the extent that everyone within the organization can be included. This might incorporate elements such as anti-bullying workshops as well as training on bias and microaggressions, conflict resolution, emotional intelligence, and ethics.

Workshops that address bullying are becoming more common either as a stand-alone effort or an overall effort to improve the workplace environment. One comprehensive Swedish study detailed a variety of ways that organizations are addressing bullying in the workplace. Its findings noted, interestingly, that one of the biggest problems was in defining exactly what bullying is. They note at the outset that "Bullying is a nebulous phenomenon, without a firmly established description concerning its parties, intensity, duration, frequency, severity, and intent (Cicerali and Cicerali 2015, 88)." Expanding on the definition of bullying introduced in chapter one, according to *The SAGE Encyclopedia of Higher Education,*

Workplace bullying (WB) refers to the systematic targeting of a worker through aggressive or hostile behavior or neglect which has negative consequences for the health and/or welfare of the person targeted and others, such as her or his family.

(Biglia and Toledo 2020)

According to Cicerali and Cicerali (2015) most organizations are not doing enough to both define bullying within their organization or to provide training to curb or address it. Some suggestions that come from their research include, in addition to better defining the boundaries of what constitutes bullying, creating greater awareness by helping all employees in the organization understand the impact it has on workers, having more clearly defined policies and procedures for addressing bullying, prompt intervention by managers when bullying occurs, and providing for support systems such as counseling when employees experience bullying (Cicerali and Cicerali 2015). The organization should approach anti-bullying with an ongoing perspective and incorporate awareness as part of regular training.

While these recommendations are directed at the organization or leadership, there are three distinct approaches that may be taken as an individual. These include "confrontation, avoidance, and reporting" (Henry et al. 2020, 36). Confrontation is the most difficult approach for many employees because it involves confronting a bully directly. This can be successful but should only be done when the victim feels safe enough to take this more direct action. Avoidance is yet another strategy that could be employed. While it may provide some measure of safety for the victim in the short run, it does not usually solve the problem and can prolong a toxic situation if the behavior is ongoing. Lastly, reporting is another option. This could be to one's supervisor, judicial team, or human resource department. This approach may work when the overseeing individual or group has earned the trust of the employee, and the employee can be assured that they will not face retribution. Unfortunately, many employees do not trust this process leaving them with limited options other than to leave the organization (Henry et al. 2020).

While bullying may constitute more obvious transgressions, bias is more subtle. The types of bias that can exist in the workplace are numerous. These can include racism, sexism, ageism, and ableism, but also more subtle forms of bias such as affinity bias where people from similar backgrounds or views can receive favorable treatment over others. Everyone has biases. Harvard University's Implicit Association Test is fairly well-known and an interesting tool for an individual to explore their own biases. One can go to their Project Implicit web site and take a number of different tests to determine which unconscious biases they may have (Project Implicit 2025). Being aware of one's biases can go a long way towards addressing them. A number of different approaches to training and development can also have a significant impact. This can include training that increases awareness of bias and its impact, providing more structured approaches to hiring and employee evaluation that take bias into account, encouraging overall diversity across hiring and decision making, developing more inclusive policies, and encouraging managers especially to address bias when its outward manifestations occur. Authors Gino and Coffman (2021) also offer several very useful suggestions or additional considerations for training and development to address workplace bias. It is worth noting that where they see organizations failing is when they think that just creating awareness that bias exists is the beginning and end of training. They also caution against taking measures without tracking their impact. One recommendation is to get employees to overcome a fixed mindset, realizing that they have the power to change their behavior which might be influenced by bias. This includes elements such as bringing up examples that counter stereotypes and providing concrete examples of biased behaviors. Another suggestion includes creating empathy which can be done by working in groups and sharing individual experiences and stories. Organizations can also encourage continued improvement which, for individuals, could include utilizing the ongoing assistance of a mentor, or for the organization, conducting regular audits of the environment. Lastly, reviewing and revising policies associated with hiring and performance evaluations will ensure they remain relevant (Gino and Coffman 2021).

Microaggressions are yet another challenge in the workplace. According to the American Psychological Association, microaggressions can be defined as "commonly occurring, brief, verbal or nonverbal, behavioral, and environmental indignities that communicate derogatory attitudes or notions toward a different 'other.' Microaggressions may be intentional or unintentional, and the perpetrators may possibly be unaware of their behavior" (American Psychological Association n.d.). One of the more interesting components of microaggressions is that they are often unintentional. This indicates that there is a significant opportunity through training and development to improve the workplace by developing awareness, empathy, and sensitivity. One approach to training, for example, focused on raising awareness, could involve exploring scenarios where microaggressions take place or even role playing such scenarios. Since much of the problem can be related to unconscious bias, bringing concrete scenarios into consciousness can be very effective. Role playing could also incorporate scenarios that include bystander intervention (Byrd 2018). Having employees willing to intervene on behalf of others can be very powerful. While perhaps not as active or engaging, providing online training through videos could also be useful. Again, while this type of training and development would be good for all employees, leaders can be trained to make an especially powerful impact by modeling inclusive behavior and having regular check-ins with affected employees.

While managing conflict has been a theme through and tackled more extensively in the previous chapter, the context here requires special consideration for providing training and development opportunities for employees when they encounter conflict. It almost goes without saying that for individuals in a management or human resource role training in conflict management and resolving conflict is essential. It should really be at a minimum available to all employees. As stated earlier in this text, there is no way to avoid conflict entirely and some conflict, when constructive, can even be helpful in moving an organization forward. Having workshops for employees can have numerous benefits including improved communication, better teamwork, better problem-solving, and improved retention. There are numerous options for handling conflict and, thus, approaches to training. They tend to focus on mediating, negotiating, and communicating. More specifically, three popular models are the Thomas-Kilmann Conflict Model, the Holton Model for Conflict Management, and the Interest-Based Relational (IBR) Approach.

The Thomas-Kilmann Conflict Model starts by first considering two dimensions. These center around assertiveness (towards one's own position) or cooperativeness. Beyond these dimensions, it further considers the individual's favored dispositions as fitting into five styles. These include competing, collaborating, compromising, avoiding, and accommodating (Trippe and Baumoel 2015). Training for this model would start with understanding the model and the styles but then move towards individuals understanding which style they gravitate towards. Role playing and the exploration of various scenarios could be used to give trainees the opportunity to explore how different styles would be applied in different situations. While a collaborative approach is ideal, one study indicated that most individuals, while claiming to be collaborative, tend towards avoidance (Lorelle et al. 2010). Again, this implicitly demonstrates an opportunity for learning and growth.

The Holton Model for Conflict Management is another approach to handling conflict that could be a part of employee training. Much like the Thomas-Kilmann Conflict Model, the Holton Model for Conflict Management idealizes collaboration. It starts by identifying the conflict. This could involve deeper investigation to explore root causes. From there, solutions are considered brainstorming ideas that address all sides of the conflict. This method also considers the implementation of the solution along with follow up. One intriguing aspect to this approach is what Holton refers to as the perceptual filter. This refers to viewing conflict or its resolution from the perspective of the specific role held within an organization (Holton 2003). While it seems obvious, it is not something always considered within conscious thought process. Holton (2003) further posits that all conflicts have three elements which include—content, relationship, and identity. Content is fairly straightforward as it is more or less the conflict itself. The relationship between the parties in conflict matters quite a bit though as well. Identity refers to the role of the employee or the category of employee. This, too, is worth considering. In practice, brainstorming with an open mind is essential. Training would, therefore, emphasize understanding how all these elements come into play in managing a conflict. Individuals trained in this method could work together considering all these layers as they creatively seek solutions to workplace conflict.

While there are many more approaches to conflict resolution that could be provided in employee training, the last one that will be considered here is the Interest-Based Relational (IBR) Approach. Developed by Fisher and Ury, the Interest-Based Relational (IBR) Approach starts by separating the people from the problem. In doing so, it seeks to maintain positive relationships and place the emphasis on the conflict as a problem to be solved collectively (Fischer, Ury, and Patton 2011). Thus, its emphasis is similar to the other two models in its focus upon collaboration. The most interesting part of the IBR approach is that it seeks to explore underlying interests as opposed to fixed positions which tend to be one of the biggest stumbling blocks in managing conflict. Brainstorming is also a key element with an emphasis on creative solutions. While the focus is centered on the problem, parties in conflict are encouraged to be open in expressing concerns. The maintenance of relationships for the long term is singularly important in developing a solution using this approach (Fischer and Ury 2011). Training in the IBR approach is especially useful for building and maintaining a healthy work environment over the long run. Again, if all employees can have access to training in this or any of the other methods, it will be easier within the organization to find solutions to vexing problems.

Training for employees in emotional intelligence can encompass many of the other training and development opportunities already mentioned, however, it is generally broader and all encompassing. In its most basic form, *The Gale Encyclopedia of Psychology* defines emotional intelligence as "an individual's ability to identify and manage his or her own emotions and to handle interpersonal relationships by recognizing the emotions of others" (Longe 2016). Therefore, training could be instituted to improve self-awareness, self-regulation, motivation, empathy, and social skills across the organization. Digging a little deeper, self-awareness, as discussed in chapter two, could help one better understand their own emotions and triggers as well as their strengths and weaknesses. The latter are especially important in relation to the individual performance plans already mentioned. Likewise, self-regulation points to building skills to control one's own impulses and manage workplace stressors. Emotional intelligence's emphasis on resilience and a growth mindset can also improve employee motivation. Finally, empathy and social skills can be improved by developing communication skills, especially deep listening, as well as helping the employee to establish and develop workplace relationships.

There are numerous specific training or professional development approaches that could be employed to improve emotional intelligence. For example, training could include the use of journaling and reflection or an introduction to mindful practices such as meditation. Role playing with active listening could be employed to better understand others. While already mentioned in this chapter, emotional intelligence may also include communication workshops that focus on resolving interpersonal conflicts. One recent study, which examined numerous prior studies on emotional intelligence training across a variety of professions, found it to be very effective and those effects lasted over time. They noted that "regardless of the nature of the work or the specific aspect of emotional competency being targeted, these interventions yield beneficial outcomes across diverse professional contexts" (Mehler et al. 2024, 12).

## Box 11.3 Emotional Intelligence Training: Skills to be Developed

- Self-awareness
- Self-regulation
- Motivation,
- Empathy
- Social skills

The final type of training that will be considered here is ethics training which can deter workplace misconduct and encourage doing the right thing. Depending on the industry, the focus of such training will vary and a number of methods are available via individual, group, or computer-based training (Box 11.4), (Martin, Kolomitro, and Lam). Studies are mixed on the best approach. However, mixed methods work well with general, less emotionally charged case studies and analysis providing the most benefit (Watts et al. 2017). Other research points to the effectiveness of active learning training methods. During her time as professor at Harvard, Mary C. Gentile first laid out her Giving Voice to Values (GVV) approach to ethical education. This involves not only ethical awareness of circumstances and analysis to aid decision making, but also "how to enact our values" through action (Gentile 2012, p. 190.) The GVV method focuses on role playing and a team approach to determining the best course of action (Gentile 2012). Yet another study found that defining ethical guidelines followed by practical work applications was effective (Caldwell et al. 2020). Additionally, ethics training which focuses on imparting "knowledge [of standards and procedures], ethical decision-making, and moral reasoning skills" has a stronger impact on learning (Watts et al. 2021).

**Box 11.4 Ethics Training Methods**

- Behavior modeling
- Case studies
- Computer-based instruction
- Group-based training
- Lecture
- Reality-based decision-making tasks
- Role play
- Simulation (virtual reality)

(Martin, Kolomitro, and Lam 2014, 16–17)

## Collecting Employee Feedback

Obtaining feedback from employees is essential for decision making and as part of the ongoing training and development process. It ensures that there is a two-way conduit related to training and development which can provide important feedback regarding the effectiveness of the program as well as areas for additional learning. Incorporation of feedback should be planned in advance of the training and include aspects of event organization, objectives, effectiveness, and outcomes (Armstrong with Taylor 2023). Methods for feedback can be achieved in a number of ways, but the most common are through surveys, suggestion boxes, one-on-one meetings, focus groups, or team meetings or workshops (box 11.5).

Surveys and suggestion boxes are similar and can be considered together. Surveys could consist of multiple-choice questions, ratings, or open-ended questions. While open-ended questions may provide more detail, multiple choice and ratings questions can be especially useful for tracking feedback over time. Suggestion boxes provide a similar function but allow employees more latitude in that they can raise an issue at any time. These could be physical boxes or some other electronic means of providing information. While it is usually hoped that employees would share feedback directly, power differentials and other concerns often limit employee feedback. These methods can allow critical feedback to be known in situations where it might not otherwise.

One-on-one meetings are an effective way to receive a high quality, deep dive into feedback. Unlike the anonymous methods mentioned above, this can be a little more threatening to an employee. Therefore, for this method to be successful, a trusting relationship needs to have been established. The employee should be informed that negative or critical feedback is sought and that there will be no retribution if concerns are raised. On the flip side, the employee should understand that, while their concerns will be heard, dealing with specific issues may or may not be possible.. Management should express genuine appreciation for employees willing to share concerns, even if it is something they may initially find difficult to hear.

Focus groups as well as team meetings or workshops offer another unique opportunity to explore a number of issues including training and development. Focus groups target specific team members or individuals in specific job categories with the intent of gaining a perspective on problems or issues. These methods work best when a non-threatening setup can be used. For example, some organizations may wish to consider an outside facilitator or at least facilitation from someone outside senior leadership. Participants need to be encouraged to openly speak their mind without fear of reprisal. Team workshops or training are similar although they may involve an intact team as opposed to a selection of individuals throughout the organization. SWOT analysis is a typical example of a method used to acquire feedback in a focus group or team setting. One of the big advantages of these formats is that feedback from one individual can spur conversation and fresh ideas from others in the group.

---

**Box 11.5 Collecting Employee Input in Decision Making**

- Surveys
- Suggestion boxes
- One-on-one meetings
- Focus groups
- Team meetings and workshops

---

After employee feedback has been received, the organization should evaluate the responses as the first of several important steps. This analysis should include measurement of the training objective and whether or not it was successfully accomplished (Armstrong with Taylor 2023). Put simply, did the employees learn what they needed to learn? This is followed by evaluating its impact or the expected behavioral change in employees (Armstrong with Taylor 2023). Did the employee improve their skills? Did the employee expand personal awareness such as demonstrating improved methods of communicating or expressing empathy? Was there an actual behavioral change? Lastly, a review of the impact of training on the broader perspective of organizational objectives and goals should occur (Armstrong with Taylor 2023). Did this training effect change which promotes a positive culture? Did it increase efficiency? Were communications between employees or departments improved, which in turn positively impacted outcomes? Based on feedback and the follow up analysis, organizations can then work towards continuing or improving such learning opportunities to best meet their needs and promote a growth-orientated culture.

## Conclusion

There are numerous ways for organizations to focus on training and development of employees to improve engagement, individual development, and promote civility. Included is the creation of individual development plans, position-specific training, and skill-based training. Also important is individual professional development to improve work engagement as well as training for individual growth addressing changing job roles and learning new technologies to improve job performance. Other formal training program ideas include training on mitigating bias, addressing microaggressions, improving emotional intelligence, handling situations involving workplace bullying and incivility, improving conflict management skills, and ethical decision making. Lastly, methods for collecting employee input to guide and improve training and development are essential to its success.

## Suggested Reads

Fisher, Roger, William Ury, and Bruce Patton. *Getting to Yes: Negotiating Agreement Without Giving In*. 3rd ed. New York: Penguin Books, 2011.
Goldsmith, Marshall, and Mark Reiter. *What Got You Here Won't Get You There: How Successful People Become Even More Successful*. New York: Grand Central Publishing, 2007.
Weise, Michelle R. *Long Life Learning: Preparing for Jobs That Don't Even Exist Yet*. Hoboken, NJ: Wiley, 2020.

## References

Ali, Abdalrahim Abaker Mohamed, Indrianawati Usman, and Masmira Kurniawati. "The Role of Human Resource Management Practices in Enhancing Organizational Commitment: Systematic Literature Review." *World Journal of Advanced Research and Reviews* 24, no. 3 (2024): 2164–2176. doi:10.30574/wjarr.2024.24.3.3783.
Al Naqbi, Humaid, Zied Bahroun, and Vian Ahmed. "Enhancing Work Productivity through Generative Artificial Intelligence: A Comprehensive Literature Review." *Sustainability* 16, no. 3 (2024): 1166. doi:10.3390/su16031166.
American Psychological Association. (n.d.). "Microaggressions." In *APA Dictionary of Psychology*. American Psychological Association. Last modified November 15, 2023, https://dictionary.apa.org/microaggression.
Armstrong, Michael with Stephen Taylor. *Armstrong's Handbook of Human Resource Management Practice: A Guide to the Theory and Practice of People Management*. New York, NY: Dorset Press, 2023.

Baumgarten, Ernest and Tony Roffers. "Implementing and Expanding on Carkhuff's Training Technology." *Journal of Counseling and Development* 81, no. 3 (2003): 285–291. doi:10.1002/j.1556-6678.2003.tb00255.x.

Beausaert, Simon, Mien R. Segers, Janine van der Rijt, Wim H. Gijselaers. "The Use of Personal Development Plans (PDPs) in the Workplace: A Literature Review." In *Building Learning Experiences in a Changing World*, Piet Van den Bossche, Wim H. Gijselaers, and Richard G. Milter, eds. Advances in Business Education and Training, vol. 3. Dordrecht, NL: Springer, 2011.

Biglia, Barbara and Patsilí Toledo. 2020. "Workplace Bullying." In *The SAGE Encyclopedia of Higher Education*, 1st edition, Marilyn J. Amey and Miriam E. David, eds.Sage UK.

Byrd, Christy M. "Microaggressions Self-Defense: A Role-Playing Workshop for Responding to Microaggressions." *Social Sciences* 7, no. 6 (2018): 96. doi:10.3390/socsci7060096.

Caldwell, James L., Alisha Y. Ortiz, Erin R. Fluegge, and Michael J. Brummett. "The Effectiveness of Ethics Training Strategies: Experiential Learning for the Win." *International Journal of Business and Management Research* 8, no. 4 (2020): 124–131. doi:10.37391/IJBMR.080407.

Cicerali, Kaya Lütfiye and Eyyüb Ensari Cicerali. "A Qualitative Study on How Swedish Organizations Deal with Workplace Bullying." *Nordic Psychology* 68 no. 2 (2015): 87–99. doi:10.1080/19012276.2015.1071198.

Corkery, Michael. "Wells Fargo Fined $185 Million for Fraudulently Opening Accounts." *The New York Times*, September 8, 2016. https://www.nytimes.com/2016/09/09/business/dealbook/wells-fargo-fined-for-years-of-harm-to-customers.html.

Cross, Rob, Greg Pryor and David Sylvester. "How to Succeed Quickly in a New Role." *Harvard Business Review* 99, no. 6 (2021): 72–78. https://research.ebsco.com/linkprocessor/plink?id=927dddea-4b84-3d53-a16a-78ac75ebf3a4.

Day, David, Nicolas Bastardoz, Tiffany Bisbey, Denise Reyes, and Eduardo Salas. "Unlocking Human Potential through Leadership Training & Development Initiatives." *Behavioral Science & Policy* 7, no. 1 (2021): 41–54. doi:10.1177/237946152100700105.

Fischer, Roger, William Ury, andBruce Patton, eds. *Getting to Yes: Negotiating Agreement Without Giving In*. New York, NY: Penguin Books, 2011.

Gentile, Mary C. "Values-Driven Leadership Development: Where We Have Been and Where We Could Go." *Organization Management Journal* 9, no. 3 (2012): article 7. https://scholarship.shu.edu/omj/vol9/iss3/7.

George, Mailys M., Sarah Wittman, and Kevin W. Rockmann. "Transitioning the Study of Role Transitions: From an Attribute-Based to an Experience-based Approach." *Academy of Management Annals* 16, no. 1 (2022): 102–133. doi:10.5465/annals.2020.0238.

Gino, Francesca and Katherine Coffman. "Unconscious Bias Training That Works." *Harvard Business Review* 99, no. 5 (2021): 114–123. https://research.ebsco.com/linkprocessor/plink?id=40a2c1f4-985f-3993-a49b-89265291e2aa.

Greenan, Peter. "Personal Development Plans: Insights from a Case Based Approach." *Journal of Workplace Learning* 28, no. 5 (2016): 322–334. doi:10.1108/JWL-09-2015-0068.

Gurchiek, Kathy. "No Time for Training? Consider Role-Specific Learning, Reassessing Workload." *SHRM*. October 26, 2022, https://www.shrm.org/topics-tools/news/organizational-employee-development/no-time-training-consider-role-specific-learning-reassessing-workload.

Hariyati, Rr Tutik Sri and Satina Safril. "The Relationship Between Nurses' Job Satisfaction and Continuing Professional Development." *Enfermeria Clinica* 28, no. 1 (2018): 144–148. doi:10.1016/S1130-8621(18)30055-X.

Holton, Susan A. "Manage that Conflict! Now You Can Manage a Problem, Its Solutions, and their Implementation with the Holton Model for Conflict Management. It Works." *University Business* 6, no. 11 (2003): 64+.

Henry, Jo, Joe Eshleman, and Richard Moniz. *Cultivating Civility: Practical Ways to Improve a Dysfunctional Library.* American Library Association, 2020.

Indeed. *Employee Training and Development*. Indeed, 2025. https://au.indeed.com/hire/c/info/employee-training-development?gad_source=1&gclid=CjwKCAiAw5W-BhAhEiwApv4goBYBTENVrgXuZL2uHY1wYOR9H72UIvo j6Ec8bl1J_4vWJlNF4GGjWxoCT7UQAvD_BwE&hl=en&aceid=&gclsrc=aw.ds.

Longe, Jacqueline L., ed. 2016. "Emotional Intelligence." In *Gale Encyclopedia of Psychology*, 3rd edition. Gale.

López Jiménez, Eduardo Alejandro, and Tania Ouariachi. "An Exploration of the Impact of Artificial Intelligence (AI) and Automation for Communication Professionals." *Journal of Information, Communication & Ethics in Society* 19, no. 2 (2021): 249–267. doi:10.1108/JICES-03-2020-0034.

Lorelle, Sonya, Stephanie Crocket, and Danica Hays. "Human Services Professional and Trainee Perceptions of Conflict in the Helping Relationship." *Journal of Human Services* 30, no. 1 (2010): 30–42.

Mampuru, Thabo, Mokoena, Mpho, and Isabirye, Anthony. "Training and Development Impact on Job Satisfaction, Loyalty and Retention Among Academics." *Journal of Human Resource Development* 12, no. 1 (2024): 45–60. doi:10.1234/jhrd.2024.001.

Martin, Barbara Ostrowski, Klodiana Kolomitro, and Tony C. M. Lam. "Training Methods: A Review and Analysis." *Human Resource Development Review* 13, no. 1 (2014): 11–35.

Mehler, Miriam, Elisabeth Balint, Maria Gralla, Tim Pößnecker, Michael Gast, Michael Hölzer, Markus Kösters, and Harald Gündel. "Training Emotional Competencies at the Workplace: A Systematic Review and Metaanalysis." *BMC Psychology* 12, no. 1 (2024): 1–18. doi:10.1186/s40359-024-02198-3.

Muriuki, Margaret Njeri, and Rosemarie Wanyoike. "Performance Appraisal and Employee Performance." *International Academic Journal of Human Resource and Business Administration* 3, no. 10 (2021): 265–272. https://www.iajournals.org/articles/iajhrba_v3_i10_265_272.pdf.

Nduati, Mary Muthoni and Rosemarie Wanyoike. "Employee Performance Management Practices and Organizational Effectiveness." *International Academic Journal of Human Resource and Business Administration* 3, no. 10 (2022): 361–378. https://iajournals.org/articles/iajhrba_v3_i10_361_378.pdf..

Office of Public Affairs. "Wells Fargo Agrees to Pay $3 Billion to Resolve Criminal and Civil Investigations into Sales Practices Involving the Opening of Millions of Accounts Without Customer Authorization." *US Department of Justice.* February

21, 2020, https://www.justice.gov/archives/opa/pr/wells-fargo-agrees-pay-3-billion-resolve-criminal-and-civil-investigations-sales-practices.

Otte, Fabian W., Keith Davids, Sarah-Kate Millar, and Stefanie Klatt. "Specialist Role Coaching and Skill Training Periodisation: A Football Goalkeeping Case Study." *International Journal of Sports Science & Coaching* 15, no. 4 (2020): 562–575. doi:10.1177/1747954120922548.

Parke, Michael R., Justin M. Weinhardt, Andrew Brodsky, Subrahmaniam Tangirala, and Sanford E. DeVoe. "When Daily Planning Improves Employee Performance: The Importance of Planning Type, Engagement, and Interruptions." *Journal of Applied Psychology* 103, no. 3 (2018): 300–312. doi:10.1037/apl0000278.

Project Implicit. "Take a Test." Last modified 2025. https://implicit.harvard.edu/implicit/takeatest.html.

Smet, Mike. "Professional Development and Teacher Job Satisfaction: Evidence from a Multilevel Model." *Mathematics* 10, no. 1 (2021): 51. doi:10.3390/math10010051.

Trippe, Blair and Douglas Baumoel. "Beyond the Thomas–Kilmann model: Into Extreme Conflict." *Negotiation Journal* 31, no. 2 (2015): 89–103. doi:10.1111/nejo.12084.

Vuong, Thu DoanNgoc and Loi Tan Nguyen. "The Key Strategies for Measuring Employee Performance in Companies: A Systematic Review." *Sustainability* 14, no. 21 (2022): 14017. doi:10.3390/su142114017.

Watts, Logan L., Kelsey E. Medeiros, Tristan McIntosh, and Tyler Mulhearn. *Ethics Training for Managers Best Practices and Techniques*. New York: Routledge, 2021.

Watts, Logan L., Kelsey E. Medeiros, Tyler J. Mulhearn, Logan M. Steele, Shane Connelly, and Michael D. Mumford. "Are Ethics Training Programs Improving? A Meta-Analytic Review of Past and Present Ethics Instruction in the Sciences." *Ethics & Behavior* 27, no. 5 (2017): 351–384. doi:10.1080/10508422.2016.1182025.

Wells Fargo. *2017 Annual Report*. Wells Fargo History, 2017. Accessed March 3, 2025. https://history.wf.com/assets/pdf/annual-reports/2017-annual-report.pdf.

# Chapter 12

# Framing Organizational Culture

The story of what happened at Enron is a cautionary tale to begin with as organizational culture is explored. Originally founded in 1985, and prior to a consequent scandal of monumental proportions, Enron was a successful American energy company. CEO Kenneth Lay and COO Jeffrey Skilling, however, used questionable accounting practices to hide massive company debts over time. When it filed for bankruptcy in 2001 for $63.4 billion it was the largest such filing in US history (Hayes 2024). In addition to the questionable accounting practices, Lay and Skilling, in turn, also created a culture that prized short-term profits above all else. One infamous exchange which was uncovered in subsequent investigations was a recording of a conversation between Enron employees following a devastating California wildfire in which one employee stated jubilantly, "Burn, baby, burn. That's a beautiful thing" due to the profits it would generate for the company (Roberts 2004). According to Manuel Velasquez, Dirksen Professor of Business Ethics, Department of Management at Santa Clara University, who examined the corporate culture at Enron, "The ease with which we see money being made leads us to cut corners, to take shortcuts, to become focused on getting our own share of the pie no matter what because everybody else is getting theirs. This general boom culture, I believe, was part of what affected Enron and led its managers and executives to think that anything was okay so long as the money kept rolling in (Velasquez 2002)." With examination of organizational culture, Enron stands as a stark warning of just how bad things can go. Fortunately, there are many positive examples and principles which can be applied in order to create a vibrant, ethical, and civil organizational culture as opposed to one that is toxic and corrosive.

## Organizational Climate

A workplace's culture can encompass a number of factors. Having a positive culture is important for obvious reasons, the most obvious being that employees will tend to thrive when a nurturing and vibrant culture exists within the organization. According to the *Encyclopedia of Applied*

DOI: 10.4324/9781003590149-12

*Psychology*, "Organizational climate and organizational culture are terms that are used to comprehensively represent the social quality of organizations" (Peterson and Fischer 2004, 715). The concept of organizational culture can further be defined by noting, "An organization's culture is often seen as manifested in its policies and practices and the understandings, language, behaviour and attitudes of organizational members" (Blyton and Jenkins 2007, 141). What does an organization's culture consist of? Elements of an organization's culture include: the key values as defined by mission and vision statements; the overall work environment; how communication occurs within the organization; how leaders interact with employees; the organization's approach to work–life balance; the types and kinds of professional development that occur within or are supported by the organization; the types of rewards and punishments that occur; the amount and types of collaboration seen within the organization and teams; the level of innovation and creativity seen and encouraged; the level of ethical practices adhered to. For the purpose of this text, a special importance is also placed on the level of civility evident within an organization as well.

Any discussion of workplace culture needs to start with the work of Edgar Schein. His seminal book, *Organizational Culture and Leadership*, ramped up the conversation on the importance of culture as he helped frame it for many future studies which would follow. One aspect of his work is the idea that organizations and their culture change in fundamental ways over time from when they are created to when they mature. This concept is based upon the idea that organizational culture and norms tend to be driven by a founder but then evolve over time until employees within the organization are "unwilling to contemplate change" (Schein 1985, quoted in Crainer 2003). Thus, according to this way of thinking many aspects of a mature organization become relatively fixed in place. While considering past history, when examining an organization's culture, one needs to consider what the culture in an organization is *now* and to understand what that means for acknowledging strengths, weaknesses, and fostering positive change, which, as noted, is a difficult task. In the words of Schein,

> "For any given group or organization that has had a substantial history, culture is the pattern of basic assumptions that the group has invented, discovered, or developed in learning to cope with its problems of external adaptation and internal integration, and that has worked well enough to be considered valid, and, therefore, to be taught to new members as the correct way to perceive, think and feel in relation to those problems."
>
> (Schein 1986, 30–31)

All aspects of Schein's work and subsequent studies on the topic point to two critical points: the culture of an organization can determine that organization's success and culture is very difficult to change once it becomes entrenched in a mature, established organization. It is important to begin with this understanding as patience is required to make shifts in culture.

## The Critical Role of Human Resources

Civility and collegiality in organizational culture create not just a positive environment but one that is more effective, successful, and sustainable overall. Human resource departments can have a critical role in shaping organizational culture and promoting civility. They do this primarily by hiring and onboarding for civility, finding various ways to recognize and reward employees (or reprimand and punish those employees), and by creating and adapting code of conduct policies that promote positive norms (box 12.1). Each of these will be considered here in turn.

One of the most important tasks of any organization is to hire the right people and onboard them successfully. The hiring and onboarding process involves many elements and human resource departments tend to guide each of these. Included in the hiring process, for instance, are writing job descriptions and conducting position analysis, developing recruitment strategies and processes, guiding screening and selection processes, maintaining legal compliance, and onboarding. Human resources may also assist after employees are hired in numerous tasks related to not just onboarding, but also ongoing training and professional development as discussed in detail in the previous chapter. The hiring and onboarding process can also notably help institute a civil organizational culture from the very beginning of an employee's entry into an organization. Key to this would be the inclusion of questions in the screening or interviewing procedures related to civility. These might not be direct questions but rather an analysis of how one problem solves in civil and constructive ways. Behavioral or situational questions associated with the interviewing process are especially useful. Some of the more common questions might include asking how one works with people that have different styles or describing how they overcame an interpersonal conflict or challenge in a previous place of work. Reference checks are yet another common method for determining the civility levels of candidates. While most reference checks would not directly posit this question, asking a reference how an employee interacts with colleagues or how they handle conflict or stressful situations can be helpful for example. While self-reporting limitations come into play, personality assessments or surveys can also provide added information about a candidate. Lastly, simple observation is meaningful as well. How does the candidate listen and respond to others in the interviewing and hiring process?

Another way that human resource departments can assist, especially in the onboarding aspect of the hiring process, is by communicating the values of an organization from the very beginning. Most organizations have some civility or civility-related components in the mission statement or values. Southwest Airlines is a great example. According to their web site, "Employees are treated with the same concern, respect, and caring attitude within our organization that they are expected to share externally with every Southwest Customer" (Southwest Airlines n.d.). This very much relates to the model referred to in chapter ten's discussion of having a customer-based mindset when working with colleagues. Another way that human resources can inculcate civility from the beginning is by emphasizing inclusive practices. Microsoft is an example of a leader on this front noting that 98% of its employees are trained on topics such as allyship and unconscious bias (Microsoft n.d.). Pairing new hires with mentors, especially mentors that exhibit high levels of empathy and civility, explored earlier in this text, can also be helpful in this regard. Similar to mentoring, one of the most powerful ways for human resources to impact new hires is by making sure that leadership within the organization is trained in civility so as to serve as role models. Lastly, human resources can continually make improvements in this area by soliciting feedback from new hires about the hiring and onboarding process. All of this helps set the tone for organizational culture at the outset.

Another way that human resources can positively impact culture is through employee recognition. There are any number of creative ways this can be employed. For example, at Horry-Georgetown Technical College faculty and staff are frequently encouraged to submit nominations for a "There's More Award." Some qualities that are to be considered for submitting this award are "Displays a helpful, cooperative and positive attitude towards superiors and co-workers; Consistently friendly and available to others; Uses effective listening skills" (Horry-Georgetown Technical College n.d.). Research on this topic has shown that, if constructed properly, employee recognition programs can significantly impact workplace culture in positive ways. Best practices include making sure that rewards programs match organizational mission statements and goals, are timely and refer to specific accomplishments or activities, and emphasize the opportunity for peers to recognize one another (Arunraj et al. 2024). Ideally substantive accompaniments such as cash or paid time off are included with rewards (Arunraj et al. 2024). In the words of one group of authors, the reward system should also "foster a culture where recognition is part of daily communication, not just a formal program. Managers and leaders should demonstrate recognition and appreciation for employees, embedding recognition into the company culture" (Arunraj et al. 2024, 767).

Yet another way that human resource departments can assist in building a positive culture is through code of conduct policies. While mentioned as a policy for cyber interactions, these guidelines should extend to the larger organization as well. To an extent such policies can be the "stick" to the "carrot" when considering employee recognition programs just discussed. That said, such protocols can also be crafted to promote positive values and behaviors. While studies related to codes of conduct have produced mixed results, they have generally shown effectiveness in some areas. As just one example, Dow has a "Respect and Responsibility Policy" which states, among other things,

> Employees and representatives at all levels of the organization have a responsibility to support and contribute to a respectful work environment, which includes avoiding any participation in unacceptable behavior, implied or explicit. Employees and representatives will refrain from behaviors in the workplace, such as, including but not limited to, bullying, belittling, berating, physical or verbal intimidation, name-calling, humiliation, or engaging in any other unprofessional behavior.
>
> (Dow n.d.)

They go on to explain a robust reporting process through the use of a 24/7 EthicsLine (Dow n.d.). Likewise, FedEx provides important elements in its code of conduct such as

> Be a good example and a positive role model; create an open environment where team members are comfortable speaking up; be receptive and listen to team members' ideas, questions, or ethical concerns; always take reports of misconduct seriously and escalate reports to human resources and the legal department when appropriate; prevent retaliation against team members who report concerns in good faith.
>
> (FedEx n.d.)

Their strongly worded statement on enforcement of these policies holds "FedEx officers, directors, and managers" accountable for taking swift, appropriate action when necessary (FedEx, n.d.). In their article, "Ethical Culture in Organizations: A Review and Agenda for Future Research," Roy et al. (2024) discuss in detail how to develop an ethical culture. While having leaders that lead by example in creating a positive, civil culture is essential, codes of conduct can also have a positive impact on an organization's culture. They note that having a code of conduct, based on several studies, does have an impact especially when employees have a sense that *other* employees, especially leaders, are adhering to these codes (Roy et al. 2024).

### Box 12.1 Human Resources Key Role

- Hiring for civility

- Onboarding for civility
- Communicating important values
- Pairing new hires with mentors
- Training organizational leaders to be role models
- Developing employee recognition programs
- Instituting codes of conduct

## Other Elements of Building a Positive Organizational Culture

One way to build a positive culture is to encourage respectful, open staff exchanges. Having regular open exchanges can have a number of benefits. It can increase trust and collaboration, boost morale, improve decision making due to a diverse set of opinions and experiences being considered, encourage innovation, and reduce misunderstanding and, hence, conflict within the organization. Human resource departments and leaders within the organization can have a significant impact in this regard. In fact, there are a number of specific things that can be done to make sure this is happening. As with adherence to codes of conduct, leaders serving as role models for open exchange of ideas is key (HR Fraternity n.d.). While face-to-face interaction is ideal, tools such as Slack and Microsoft Teams can also be used to encourage more communication within any organization. For just one example of how technology can be used in this manner, one author documented the use of Slack to plan and organize the 2018 North Atlantic Health Sciences Libraries (NAHSL) annual meeting. She noted that, "Slack provides an ideal solution for individuals overseeing projects with multiple components and collaborators. The workspace keeps communications and integrated applications in one place, increasing productivity and improving organization" (Johnson 2018, 151). Other tools may be used, but the point here is that the ever-evolving technology being made available now and in the future for organizations can be very useful in encouraging an open exchange of ideas.

Promoting positive norms in general but especially best practices in communication is also essential. While tools such as those above are useful, there is still a need to guide employees when it comes to best practices in communication. This is largely a matter of integrating a number of components already listed but making sure they are used in combination. These include promoting and encouraging face-to-face interaction when possible, utilizing technology, promoting open and transparent communication, and providing training opportunities for all of these such as was discussed in chapter eleven. Coaching by supervisors may also be necessary at times for employees who need to develop their communication skills. According to well-known civility expert Christine Porath, "When coaching employees, focus on helping them learn to listen fully, give and receive feedback, work across differences, and deal with difficult people. You might also coach them on negotiation, stress management, crucial conversations, and mindfulness" (Porath 2018). Having effective, high quality and civil internal communication, it should be noted, becomes especially important in times of change or crisis. For example, one widely cited study exploring communication during the early days of the covid pandemic determined that daily and transparent communication by leadership and human resources was essential to maintaining a positive culture (Li et al. 2021).

## Organization-wide Communication Strategies and Connecting with Departments and Remote Locations

One special case that needs to be addressed here relating to organizational culture is the importance of developing a well thought out, organization-wide communication strategy. This is critical for larger organizations or ones that have disconnected departments or remote locations. In these circumstances, it is much more difficult and thus all the more important to keep all employees within the organization informed in a timely manner. While technology, such as already discussed, can be useful, an overall strategy and best practices need to be considered here. There are several key elements which need to be incorporated (box 12.2). These include having a unified and consistent message, making sure that messaging is timely, delivering the message through multiple channels, providing updates, involving leadership in helping make sure messaging and information is delivered and understood, integrating technology, and evaluating the effectiveness of communication methods. A simple example would be the Horry County School system located in South Carolina. Consisting of 56 schools, nearly 10,000 employees, and serving just under 50,000 students, communicating effectively across locations is essential (Horry County Schools n.d.). During the 2024–2025 school year, administrators had to manage challenging decisions and communicate those decisions relative to hurricanes, snowstorms, and wildfires in a very short period of time. In each case a clear, unified, and timely message was delivered regarding actual or potential school closures by the administration. These were provided through multiple channels such as through email, texts, social media, and local news outlets. Updates on the status of the schools were regularly provided as leaders and supervisors worked to make sure employees understood what was expected and situations evolved. This example highlights crisis scenarios within a limited geographical area and, in normal circumstances, may not require the use of third-party assistance such as the external news organizations. That said, the point here is that having a pre-planned strategy using multiple communication avenues to share critical, timely information with employees throughout a far-flung organization is a necessity.

The above example included a school system with locations spread across just one albeit large county. Many organizations extend far beyond, even across the globe. It is very important to further consider communications and culture across far flung organizations. The COVID-19 pandemic offered valuable lessons in this regard as, in many cases, entire organizations became remote when workers engaged in work at home. Newman and Ford (2021), for example, share five key steps towards making sure leaders paid attention to communication and culture with remote employees during those times. These include explaining the new reality, which in turn required regular team meetings and one-on-one meetups online or by phone, continuing to remind employees about the mission of the organization and their place in it, making sure communication is clear and timely, promoting collaboration and teamwork possibly using new approaches and technology, and assuring that tasks are accomplished and that employees and their work stay aligned with the mission. While a bit older, a widely cited study conducted by Jeremy Lurey and Mahesh Raisinghani (2001) makes great points that are relevant today for any organization that has remote locations. While multiple channels of communication should be used, there should be some expectations around protocols. That is, it is important to choose the correct tools for the specific needs. For example, while some relevant and useful information may be appropriate to convey by email, others may require more direct interaction (Bouvier, E. Hwang, and Y. Hwang 2024). These should, therefore, utilize structured virtual meetings for example. Employees need to be given access to appropriate technology and trained in the use of technology especially as it relates to communication tools. One needs to find a way to, in addition to normal business, also promote at least some social interaction among team members that may be far removed from one another. This can be done virtually but also, when possible, by travel between locations.

Again, having a large organization and remote locations can be a challenge. Local workgroups or teams represent the first layer. These require the kind of group or team cohesion as discussed earlier in this book. Sometimes teams have counterparts doing the same work at another location so there needs to be a conduit between the leader of those teams. Johnson & Wales University, in the early 2000s, had campuses spread out over five states. Teams or work groups such as the library, student affairs, admissions, and other departments had to make sure that the leaders of these areas connected regularly with their counterparts. Other key employees outside of leadership also had to maintain connections and communication across locations based on their functional roles within the organization. This was done through virtual meetings but also through traveling to meet up together at a given campus or at a national conference associated with their shared work function. Meetings would include structured agendas but also opportunities to build understanding and camaraderie with colleagues in the organization normally located significant distances apart. It was also important for the top leadership of the university to travel on a regular basis across locations to share developments and collaborate on projects and initiatives across the organization. This and other efforts were used to make sure that a shared direction and culture existed across locations. While this is an example culled from higher education, it can easily be conveyed to the corporate world as well. Deloitte is a good example. Leadership regularly travels to different locations, town halls are conducted on a regular basis across locations, and collaboration across locations is widely encouraged (Deloitte 2011).

**Box 12.2 Communicating Across Remote Locations**

- Develop a strategic communication plan
- Utilize technology
- Apply a unified and consistent messaging
- Use multiple communication channels
- Provide updates
- Use the appropriate format for specific communication need
- Support travel between locations
- Proactively build collegiality/camaraderie across locations

## Silent Contract Fulfillment and Meeting Worker Expectations

In any discussion of organizational culture one must consider the concept of silent contract fulfillment and meeting worker or employee expectations. A seminal and frequently cited work on this topic is Rousseau's "Psychological and Implied Contracts in Organizations" published in 1989. According to Rousseau, employees have an implied psychological contract with the organization that they work for. The implied contract generally refers to expectations that go unsaid but are understood such as job security, an expectation of ethical behavior both by the individuals and the organization, and fair, unbiased treatment. The psychological contract is highly subjective and can include trust and loyalty which can go in both directions but for the employee usually entails support of various types and kinds and recognition of work well done (box 12.3). According to Rousseau, "The concept of psychological contract also makes salient the issue of violation and its consequences for the employee's well-being and outlook" (Rousseau 1989, 135). These concepts are especially relevant to the overall productivity of an organization and its employees as well as the level of civility within the organization. Breach of contract or perceived breach of contract can do incredible damage to motivation and lead to high turnover. For example, an employee that is spoken to in a condescending or demeaning tone by a supervisor or who receives perceived unfair treatment may experience a breach in this contract. They might also, as a less extreme example, feel a breach occurs if their ideas or concerns are ignored or they feel like leadership is unwilling to listen. Failure to address ongoing interpersonal conflict or toxic situations of various kinds between employees or workgroups can also lead employees to become dispirited. This in turn leads to, as noted above, a lack of motivation and oftentimes the employee looking to leave and find work in a healthier organization. The implication of all of this is that leaders within an organization need to be consistently talking with employees and listening to concerns on an ongoing basis.

---

### Box 12.3 Elements of Organizational Psychological Contracts

- Pay attention to unspoken expectations
- Build trust
- Convey loyalty
- Provide fair, unbiased treatment
- Recognize employee contributions
- Listen to employee ideas and concerns
- Address interpersonal conflicts when they arise

---

## Conveying the Vision and Connecting Work to the Mission

Lastly, when considering organizational culture, it is important to make sure that leaders convey a vision for the organization and connect that to the work that people do. Providing vision can be inspirational and can be very motivating for employees. It helps them see the bigger picture and builds camaraderie as they gain a shared sense of purpose. Productivity, job satisfaction, and overall employee retention can often be tied to how well each individual within the organization can sense and understand the vision and consequent values and mission (Buss et al. 2023). Conveying a strong and consistent vision builds trust as it shows the commitment from the top, especially when coupled with details and plans that prove that commitment. Consistent reminders of the vision can foster harmony and help to encourage collaboration between employees as well as between departments or units within the organization. It can further help by inculcating core values into the work that is done on a daily basis. Communicating a vision can be especially critical in times of rapid change, something very common in most organizations.

## Conclusion

It is very clear that an organization's culture is critical to creating a positive, constructive, and civil workplace. Human resource departments can play a key role in shaping the culture as it relates to civility in a variety of ways such as hiring and onboarding for civility, developing employee recognition programs, campaigns, and systems, and developing meaningful code of conduct policies. It can also aid in the creation of a dynamic, highly functional workplace characterized by a positive work environment incorporating open staff exchanges, embracing all aspects of diversity, and promoting positive norms. Organizational culture and civility may also be improved by implementing best practice communication strategies especially as those may relate to connecting departments or remote locations. Lastly, this chapter delved into connecting positively with employees by recognizing the importance of silent contract fulfillment, meeting worker expectations, conveying the vision for the organization, connecting work to the mission, and promoting an overall positive culture and work environment.

## Suggested Reads

Bock, Laszlo. *Work Rules!: Insights from Inside Google That Will Transform How You Live and Lead*. New York: Twelve, 2015.
Hsieh, Tony. *Delivering Happiness: A Path to Profits, Passion, and Purpose*. London: Grand Central Publishing, 2013.
Sinek, Simon. *Leaders Eat Last: Why Some Teams Pull Together and Others Don't*. London: Portfolio Penguin, 2017.

## References

Arunraj, R. Immanuvel, P. Murugesan, V. Pandi, and S. Sivasubramanian. "Effects of Employee Recognition Programs on Engagement and Retention." *Library of Progress-Library Science, Information Technology & Computer* 44, no. 3 (2024): 764–768. doi:10.48165/bapas.2024.44.2.1.
Blyton, Paul and Jean Jenkins. 2007. "Organizational Culture." In *Key Concepts in Work*, 1st edition. Sage UK.
Bouvier, David J., Esther J. Hwang, and Yujong Hwang. "An Empirical Study on Email Use, Stress, and Employee Job Satisfaction." *Human Technology* 20, no. 1 (2024): 45–69. doi:10.14254/1795-6889.2024.20-1.3.
Buss, Martin, Eric Kearney, Riffat Noureen, and Nilima Gandhi. "Antecedents and Effects of Visionary Leadership: When and How Leader Work Centrality is Linked to Visionary Leadership and Follower Turnover Intentions." *Journal of Leadership & Organizational Studies* 30, no. 4 (2023): 413–427. doi:10.1177/15480518231203637.

Deloitte. "Elevate Your Leadership Communication Strategies." *Deloitte Insights*. December 15, 2011, https://www2.deloitte.com/us/en/insights/focus/executive-transitions/elevate-leadership-communication-strategies.html.

Dow. "Respect and Responsibility Policy." n.d. Accessed March 11, 2025. https://corporate.dow.com/en-us/about-dow/corporate-governance/living-our-values/respect-responsibility.html.

FedEx. "Doing the Right Thing." n.d. Accessed March 11, 2025. https://www.fedex.com/en-us/about/policy/corporate-integrity-and-compliance/code-of-conduct/doing-the-right-thing.html.

Hayes, Adam. "What Was Enron? What Happened and Who Was Responsible." *Investopedia*. Last modified December 4, 2024. https://www.investopedia.com/terms/e/enron.asp.

Horry County Schools. "Quick Facts." n.d. Accessed March 13, 2025. https://www.horrycountyschools.net/about-hcs/quick-facts.

Horry-Georgetown Technical College. "There's More." n.d. Horry-Georgetown Technical College. Accessed March 9, 2025. https://www.hgtc.edu/about_hgtc/administrativedepartments/humanresources/employee-recognition/theres-more.html.

HR Fraternity. "Fostering Open and Transparent Communication in Your Organization's Culture." n.d. Accessed March 11, 2025. https://www.hrfraternity.com/hr-excellence/fostering-open-and-transparent-communication-in-your-organizations-culture.html.

Li, Jo-Yun, Ruoyu Sun, WeitingTao, and Yeunjae Lee. "Employee Coping with Organizational Change in the Face of a Pandemic: The Role of Transparent Internal Communication." *Public Relations Review* 47, no. 1 (2021): 101984. doi:10.1016/j.pubrev.2020.101984.

Johnson, Heather A. "Slack." *Journal of the Medical Library Association* 106, no. 1 (2018): 148–151. doi:10.5195/jmla.2018.315.

Lurey, Jeremy S. and Mahesh S. Raisinghani. "An Empirical Study of Best Practices in Virtual Teams." *Information & Management* 38, no. 6 (2001): 523–544. doi:10.1016/S0378-7206(01)00074-X.

Microsoft. "Diversity and Inclusion." n.d. Accessed March 10, 2025. https://careers.microsoft.com/us/en/diversityandinclusion.

Newman, Sean A. and Robert C. Ford. "Five Steps to Leading Your Team in the Virtual COVID-19 Workplace." *Organizational Dynamics* 50, no. 1 (2021): 1–11. doi:10.1016/j.orgdyn.2020.100802.

Peterson, Mark F., and Ronald Fischer. "Organizational Culture and Climate." In *Encyclopedia of Applied Psychology*, 1st edition, Charles Donald Spielberger, ed. Elsevier Science & Technology, 2004.

Porath, Christine L. "Make Civility the Norm on Your Team." *Harvard Business Review*, January 2, 2018, https://archives-ftp.gov.yk.ca/library/normal/Porath_Make_Civility_Norm_2018.pdf.

Roberts, Joel. "Enron Traders Caught On Tape." *CBS News*. Last modified June 1, 2004. https://www.cbsnews.com/news/enron-traders-caught-on-tape/.

Rousseau, Denise M. 1989. "Psychological and Implied Contracts in Organizations." *Employee Responsibilities & Rights Journal* 2, no. 2 (1989): 121–139. doi:10.1007/BF01384942.

Roy, Achinto, Alexander Newman, Heather Round, and Sukanto Bhattacharya. "Ethical Culture in Organizations: A Review and Agenda for Future Research." *Business Ethics Quarterly* 34, no. 1 (2024): 97–138. doi:10.1017/beq.2022.44.

Schein, Edgar H. *Organizational Culture and Leadership*. San Francisco: Jossey-Bass, 1985. Quoted in Stuart Crainer, *The Ultimate Business Library*, 1st edition. New York: Wiley, 2003.

Schein, Edgar H. 1986. "What You Need to Know About Organizational Culture." *Training and Development Journal* 40, no. 1 (1986): 30–33.

Southwest Airlines. "Our People." (n.d.). Accessed March 12, 2025. https://www.southwest.com/citizenship/people/.

Velasquez, Manuel. "What Really Went Wrong with Enron? A Culture of Evil?" *Markkula Center for Applied Ethics*. March 5, 2002, https://www.scu.edu/ethics/focus-areas/business-ethics/resources/what-really-went-wrong-with-enron/.

# Chapter 13

# Moving Civility Forward

Workplaces have changed dramatically over the last century. Influences of hierarchical structure, divisions of power, and work environments of the Industrial Age have shifted with time as society has come to accept, to a greater degree, varying organizational structures, less formality, and increased employee input during the Information Age (Shackel and Palus 2006). Since the end of the twentieth century, included in that change are discussions of civility in work environments. This focus evolved from the work of Heinz Leymann, Swedish professor and researcher at Umea University, who first applied the concept of mobbing to work environments in his 1990 journal article, "Mobbing and Psychological Terror at Workplaces." This was followed by British broadcaster Andrea Adam's 1992 book, *Bullying at Work*, exposing how this form of toxic behavior manifests in the workplace. Subsequently, Gary Namie's 1999 publication, *Bully Proof Yourself at Work!*, brought the topic to the United States. Following these works, numerous researchers and authors have continued to explore and expose these types of workplace issues, and it is through these works it is possible for the examination of solutions to unfold.

## Issues in the Workplace

In its simplest form, civility in the workplace is displaying kindness, respect, and politeness. While this is present in some work environments, as illustrated throughout the chapters, it falls short in others. As chapter one highlighted, all forms of negative workplace behaviors from lessor incivility to more toxic actions prevail in many forms in a variety of situations. Many of the behaviors on the lower end of the civility spectrum involve communication. Individuals may encounter abusive language, belittling comments, or other types of negative, verbal communications. Interrupting co-workers while they are speaking and failing to apply active listening skills can also be perceived as rude. Individuals should be able to convey their thoughts and messages completely, which often requires patience on the part of the listener. Along with verbal communication, non-verbal

DOI: 10.4324/9781003590149-13

gestures including facial expressions, hand gestures, or body stances can convey messages which may be detrimental to work relationships. Other forms of lessor incivility involve intentional miscommunication or withholding of information in a type of covert sabotage of another employee. Taking credit for another's work falls in this category as well and is often attributed to a supervisor who is focused more on bolstering perceptions of their own personal performance rather than acknowledging accomplishments of their direct reports.

Other disruptive work behaviors are more challenging to navigate for both individual workers and supervisors. The first of these is an employee with a passive-aggressive approach to conflict who may display resistance to work and may be overly critical of others in the work group. Counter-productive work behaviors are another type of behavior which is disruptive to workflow. Triggered by a belief they are being unfairly treated, these individuals may be withdrawn, often absent from work, manipulative, or disruptive. They also may engage in more serious actions such as theft or property damage. Lastly, psychological or physical intimidation may occur in the workplace through verbal or non-verbal means. Acts of aggression or invasion of personal spaces are a part of this type of disruptive behavior.

The most toxic forms of workplace dysfunction are not only disruptive but can cause long-term harm to individuals. The first of these is bullying or the one-on-one targeting of an individual in the workplace. Targets can experience several types of affronts which convey disrespect, belittling, dominance, blame, or retaliation among others. This type of targeting can occur in person or through virtual means. Similarly, mobbing, or several workers targeting an individual, is also an extreme form of work behavior. Victims of mobbing experience criticism, isolation, threats, micromanagement, or unreasonable work assignments. The final two toxic behaviors include physical work violence such as hitting, kicking, beating, or spitting on another employee as well as sexual misconduct (from unwanted touching or advances to rape). While all these forms are extreme, evidence shows they do occur in the workplace and a focus on reducing their occurrence needs to remain a topic of discussion.

## Kindness Perspective

To address such workplace issues, this writing focused on ideas for embracing the core of civil interactions and finding methods to shift in that direction. However, the beginning of such change always begins with the self. The importance of understanding oneself regarding personal strengths and weaknesses was touched on in chapter two. Individuals must push past the status quo and continue to learn and grow in personal areas of civil interaction. To accomplish these improvements, strengthening emotional intelligence is one area of focus. This addresses individual aspects of self-awareness, self-regulation, self-motivation, social awareness, and social skills. Identifying not only how one behaves in these areas of behavior but also how to improve in areas of weakness will have a direct impact on civil interactions. Empathy training can also have a positive impact. This type of expanding of one's capacity for kindness and understanding can become contagious in the workplace. It sets the example for not only how to express compassion but also can leverage listening skills when co-workers need to express anxiety, frustration, or negative feelings.

## Taking Responsibility

In addition to efforts to embrace kindness in the workplace, taking responsibility for actions, both at the individual and organizational level, is necessary as well. Part of this responsibility falls to recognition of behaviors and influences of one's own actions or those of others. Other aspects of responsibility fall to the larger organization. A shift from the negative to positive in the workplace takes effort on both ends of this spectrum. Once the negative dynamics are identified, targeted solutions can be tried. This cannot be accomplished without sustained effort to impart positive change from the top down through the entire organization.

At the individual level, employees must be willing to accept honest assessment of their behaviors through introspection or external feedback. Often it is uncomfortable to admit behaviors, words, and actions have negatively impacted the work environment or even caused harm to co-workers. However, understanding and admitting that humans are all imperfect is the starting point for moving in positive directions. This involves not only introspection as examined in chapter two, but recognizing the role of the self in the larger working group and organization and understanding how individual changes can impact the whole. Included in this is a worker's participation on teams as discussed in chapter seven. While special responsibilities fall to team leaders to guide the group in a professional and courteous manner, team members also have a responsibility to display respectful, ethical, inclusive, and collaborative actions. An honest evaluation of team function and team member dynamics is a part of behavioral assessment. The importance of feedback from a supervisor covered in chapter eleven also can help employees understand how others perceive them. Leaders can provide critical information not only in formal reviews but by establishing open communication with direct reports. Leaders should keep in mind criticism may hurt and approach the topic with care and kindness in mind. However, that does not include avoiding communications if an employee's behavior needs correcting. In return, workers should be open and receptive to feedback as it is a tool for improvement of the self from both a personal and work-focused perspective. Lastly, as chapter ten noted, approaching internal work behavior with a customer-based mindset shifts worker perspective towards more positive interactions.

This approach simply poses the question, "Would I treat a customer this way?" to interactions in the workplace to help frame more positive approaches and ways of communicating.

Responsibility for developing a civil workplace also falls to managers and senior leaders. Because of their positions of power these individuals can play an important role in shifting negative dynamics to positive. Not only can they make a difference with workplace civility, but they should embrace it as part of their responsibility to do so. Individuals holding these types of positions can create an environment of psychological safety as covered in chapter eight. This includes being vulnerable, responding productively to failures, setting clear boundaries, and being authentic. Other elements of leadership that are important include developing trust with those they work with and encouraging open, civil communication. As mentioned, this is a factor when providing employee feedback. However, trust and open communication between a leader and employee also plays a role in productivity, engagement, and job satisfaction. All these factors influence how positive or negative the work environment becomes. Additionally, leaders should be flexible when necessary and apply situational awareness to navigate issues that arise. As covered in chapter nine, this is especially true for those who hold middle management positions as they bridge strategic goals with work group operations.

Leaders also take on the responsibility of navigating conflict among the employees. This includes having difficult conversations, taking fair and equal approaches to treatment, and settling disagreements that may arise. Navigating conflict may be one of the most challenging aspects to a leader's position. However, conflict ignored leads to a dysfunctional and toxic workplace. The leadership role in this area involves identifying root problems and finding solutions, and it may involve the help of others in the organization. Ultimately, the goal is to resolve issues fairly and move forward in a positive manner as a work group towards achievement of larger organizational goals whenever possible.

Organizations play a role in conflict management as well. One approach reviewed in chapter eleven is to implement conflict management training for all employees providing a baseline understanding of how to approach and settle disagreements. While many conflicts can be resolved by direct supervisors or even co-workers themselves, others need to leverage larger organizational resources. These include the human resource department, judicial teams, or specialized departments within the organization as explored in chapter ten. Guidance from human resources can be helpful to supervisors as long as that division properly addresses the root of the issue instead of simply blaming a targeted individual for speaking up. Historically, human resource departments have often acted as protectors of the organization at the expense of an innocent employee. Those leading such departments should reevaluate policy, perspectives, and procedures to balance fair individual treatment with larger organizational needs. An organization also may utilize internal judicial teams to assist with conflict resolution. Parameters for who comprises the team and how the team operates are a part of this process. Use of external judicial teams is another option when specialized expertise may be needed to resolve issues. One external group which many organizations also deal with is unions. These groups can play a role in shaping policy and addressing worker concerns as they arise. Lastly, the use of an ombudsman who is trained in conflict management and has a deep understanding of organizational policy can be offered by the organization. These individuals apply empathy and practical approaches to helping individuals who are experiencing issues in the work environment.

Another way organizations can responsibly assist with developing a positive workplace is to lend support to new hires. One method is to provide a mentorship program for these individuals. Assigning mentors for these individuals gives these employees support and can guide them into a positive organizational culture. Positive behaviors can be conveyed through written policies such as civility policies, anti-bullying policies, and good citizenship policies. Also helpful is the idea of role-specific training offered in chapter eleven. While this type of training can be applied to an employee changing roles, it can also give the new worker targeted information on how to successfully accomplish their tasks.

Organizations also provide employee support with development and growth opportunities. This may include opportunities to improve skills, attend training sessions or conferences, or open up paths for promotional advances. These opportunities can increase job satisfaction and also improve performance. As noted in chapter nine, this often falls to middle managers who work closely with those in their work group and best understand their needs and goals. However, without organizational support, such as approving financial requests for continuing education opportunities, middle managers cannot adequately meet the needs of an employee's desire to grow. Organizations can also play a role in employee growth by sponsoring internal training, keynote speakers, special workshops, or technical training opportunities depending on the type of work. While this involves financial support, it also requires adequate meeting spaces, dedicated staff to facilitate or coordinate events, and ultimately support from the very top of leadership.

A variety of formal training and development programs reviewed in chapter eleven can be provided by organizations. The first of these is the individual development plan which emphasizes the role a supervisor and organization plays in the mutually beneficial improvement of employees. Unlike institutional or company goal setting, focused as it is on accomplishments which primarily benefit the organization, more individualized plans take into consideration ways for each employee to personally grow as well. Existing employees can be supported with professional development opportunities which increase engagement, retention, and satisfaction. Several specific training topics including addressing bullying, understanding bias, confronting microaggressions, developing emotional intelligence, and improving ethical decision-making can also improve workplace civility. Lastly, opportunities to learn how to manage conflict, especially when available to all employees, as noted, can make a lasting impact on work environments.

## Change Agents

In addition to taking responsibility for one's actions, each person in the organization can be a positive change agent no matter what job or level of authority they have in the organization. One method explored in chapter three is to improve in-person communication. This may involve active listening, withholding judgment, and identifying non-verbal expressions in addition to understanding cultural differences which may influence information exchanges. There is great value in listening which can improve co-worker relationships and invoke understanding, empathy, and compassion.

Also, as covered in chapter five, individuals can interrupt incivility in the workplace by stepping forward and getting involved when they see instances of poor behavior. This may involve simply letting a co-worker know their actions are in poor taste or involve a more direct calling out of a behavior such as bullying. Interrupting incivility works. Along with that, as chapter ten indicated, those serving on judicial boards, union representatives, or ombudsmen, in addition to human resource staff, play critical roles as change agents. Often it is with their intervention that workplace issues can be resolved and conflicts between employees settled.

Finally, being a change agent can involve improved knowledge sharing. This impacts not only a one-on-one exchange but also between work groups or divisions as explored in chapter six. Utilizing connections and leveraging boundary spanners can reduce misunderstandings and minimize errors while promoting collaboration. Sequestered information contributes to a dysfunctional workplace. High-functioning teams also engage in knowledge sharing to accomplish assigned goals. Additionally, organizations play a role in this area through efficient communication strategies. As covered in chapter twelve, these include utilizing multiple channels, providing regular updates, and leveraging technology, especially when communicating between remote locations. Finding ways to connect and share improves work communications and outcomes.

## Cultural Norms and Ethical Boundaries

Just as society defines ethical boundaries and what is accepted as civil or uncivil, an organization also plays a similar role. Organizations who put employees first are those who recognize the importance of this in establishing a positive workplace. A balance should be struck between organizational profit or achievement and ethical leadership or treatment of workers. Absent of such, while organizations may profit, they also may foster poor work environments. These environments negatively impact both employees and ultimately organizational operations. As mentioned in chapter twelve, employee codes of conduct help define and guide workers in this area. Additionally, chapter four outlined written language defining acceptable (or unacceptable) behaviors for online communications or social media usage. These are ways to officially incorporate respectful behavior in the working environment. However, responsibility falls not just to individuals but to leaders as well who set the tone for the larger operation. When organizations establish and support ethical standards, it benefits both individual employees and the organization as a whole.

Establishing a positive culture was explored in chapter twelve. Human resources can play an important role here with employee recognition programs. Organizations can also shape the culture by meeting employee expectations of fair and reasonable treatment and conveying and reinforcing the overarching mission. Ethical standards are also a part of an organization's culture. These are reflected from both behaviors of senior leaders and staff along with written standards for expected behaviors. As mentioned in chapter eleven, ethics training can help facilitate good decision making when what the right thing to do comes into question. Additionally, civility should be considered as a part of hiring practices. Once on board, the new employee can be supported by the organization with guidance and opportunities for personal development. Organizations who meet employee expectations and connect their job to the overall mission create the groundwork for a thriving workplace.

The establishment of functional boundaries for teams and team leaders within an organization was explored in chapter seven. Collaboration by team members works best when team members establish a code of conduct. These guidelines set the boundaries for acceptable actions while the unit works together and can be used, if necessary, by the team leader to restore order, navigate disputes, and maintain an effective work dynamic. These leaders also facilitate (both in-person and online) positive interactions during meetings, keep the group members on track through support and communication, and build a community which embraces psychological safety. Along with these attributes, team leaders work toward balancing individual and team autonomy to not only move towards an end goal but also maintain alignment with the larger organization or external partners.

## Looking Forward

Finally, as the future of the workplace brings change and society shifts toward new frontiers, civility must move with it. This implies that civil treatment must be adaptable. Cultural influences and worker diversity are one area which will continue to impact workplace interactions. Not only are many organizations global entities, but workers even in a single organization may reflect a culturally diverse workforce. Encouraging workers to be open to different ideas or perspectives will help in this regard. Understanding communication differences and focusing on effective information exchanges will have a positive impact on these types of work environments. A better workplace evolves when individuals learn to be respectful and accepting of regional and cultural differences. Another area requiring adaptation moving forward may be the changes in physical work environments. Collaboration, increased trust, and bonding may be enhanced with coworking space designs (Johns et al. 2024). Continued focus on employee wellness support may center on the inclusion of areas such as meditation rooms, outdoor break areas, adjustable workstations, and fitness facilities or activity spaces (Kohll 2019). Lastly, the promotion of psychological well-being and satisfaction of employees by connecting them with nature and natural light through biophilic work designs is a growing trend (Elantary 2024). The future of building designs may involve this perspective which promotes a positive and more productive work environment.

The impact of virtual or online communication on work is another area which will continue to develop for in-office, hybrid, and remote settings. Already cyber behaviors influence civility as explored in chapter four. Impacts from disinhibition and deindividuation through virtual communications can foster aggressive posts or even bullying if not recognized and checked. Social media also impacts organizations who must create guidelines for managing both individual workers' handling of such interactions alongside incoming communications from customers or external contacts. Again, written guidelines for emails or other internal electronic communications, cyber code of ethics, social media usage, and utilizing social media communication protocols all assist with keeping such interactions in a more positive lane.

In addition to virtual communications, what concepts guide future directions of workplace incivility? First, the integration of artificial intelligence (AI) and human–computer interfaces in the workplace bring new perspectives to work dynamics. What impact will these connections have on civility? As chapter seven noted, work teams already are interacting with computer or AI team members. This melding of human workers with advanced technologies may mean revisiting codes of ethics and guidelines or creating cyber ethics for the workplace. Some training programs in civility have already migrated to the use of virtual reality or social robots as illustrated in chapter three. These types of training applications are likely to continue in the future. Workplace meeting spaces may also expand to an augmented reality and codes of conduct created for in-person behavior may have to be adapted to this type of interaction. Additionally, guidelines for integration of robots or robotic applications into the workplace should address the effects on human workers. Human impacts relating to AI and civility could involve reduced coworker communication, feelings of diminished worth, decreased creativity, and threats to self-development (Smids, Nyholm and Berkers 2020). Finally, future work groups may include individuals who have been technologically enhanced resulting in increased cognitive or physical functions. These differences may require more attention in the areas of fairness, empathy, and respect between the enhanced and non-enhanced workers.

## Conclusion

Throughout the text, a wide variety of solutions to improve the workplace have been introduced. Even as these methods are applied to current work environments, looking forward they too may change and improve with new research. Regardless, embracing the concept of civil work communities needs to become a part of the work condition. The future brings an opportunity to promote positive work experiences. Most importantly, fostering civility in the workplace begins with a prevailing view that workers should be seen and treated first and foremost as human beings.

## Suggested Reads

Davenport, Thomas H. and Steven M. Miller. *Working with AI: Real Stories of Human–Machine Collaboration*. Cambridge, MA: MIT Press, 2022.
Piscione, Deborah Perry and Josh Drean. *Employment Is Dead: How Disruptive Technologies Are Revolutionizing the Way We Work*. Boston, MA: Harvard Business Review Press, 2025.
West, Darrell M. *The Future of Work: Robots, AI, and Automation*. Washington D.C.: Brookings Institute Press, 2018.

## References

Elantary, Asmaa Ramadan. "Biophilic Design in Office Buildings: A Salutogenic Approach to Enhancing Well-being in the Built Environment." In *Proceedings of the International Conference of Contemporary Affairs in Architecture and Urbanism-ICCAUA*, Alanya, Turkey, May 23–24 (2024). doi:10.38027/ICCAUA2024EN0189.
Johns, Jennifer, Edward Yates, Greig Charnock, Frederick Harry Pitts, Odul Bozkurt, and Didem Derya Ozdemir Kaya. "Coworking Spaces and Workplaces of the Future: Critical Perspectives on Community, Context, and Change." *European Management Review* May 14, 2024: 1–19. doi:10.1111/emre.12654.

Kohll, Alan. "How Your Office Space Impacts Employee Well-Being." *Forbes*. January 24, 2019. https://www.forbes.com/sites/alankohll/2019/01/24/how-your-office-space-impacts-employee wellbeing/.

Shackel, Paul A. and Matthew M. Palus. "The Gilded Age and Working-Class Industrial Communities." *American Anthropologist* 108, no. 4 (2006): 828–841. doi:10.1525/aa.2006.108.4.828.

Smids, Jilles, Sven Nyholm, and Hannah Berkers. "Robots in the Workplace: A Threat to—or Opportunity for—Meaningful Work?" *Philosophy & Technology* 33 (2020): 503–522. doi:10.1007/s13347-019-00377-4.

# Index

For Product Safety Concerns and Information please contact our EU
representative GPSR@taylorandfrancis.com
Taylor & Francis Verlag GmbH, Kaufingerstraße 24, 80331 München, Germany

www.ingramcontent.com/pod-product-compliance
Lightning Source LLC
Chambersburg PA
CBHW070246290326
41929CB00047B/2806